IN BRAZIL

FRAN BRYSON

SCRIBE

Melbourne • London

Scribe Publications
18–20 Edward St, Brunswick, Victoria 3056, Australia
2 John St, Clerkenwell, London, WC1N 2ES, United Kingdom

First published by Scribe 2016

Cover image: Capoeira on the beach, iStock_000021130388

Typeset in Adobe Garamond Pro by the publishers
Printed and bound in Australia by Griffin Press

CIP data records for this title are available from the National Library of Australia and the British Library

9781925321142 (Australian edition)
9781925228373 (UK edition)
9781925307405 (e-book)

scribepublications.com.au
scribepublications.co.uk

For my parents,
with love and gratitude

Into my arms, O Lord
Into my arms

Nick Cave

Contents

The Southeast

Back to the North and the Northeast

IN BRAZIL

Prologue

'At certain periods it becomes the dearest ambition of a man to keep a faithful record of his performances in a book; and he dashes at this work with an enthusiasm that imposes on him the notion that keeping a journal is the veriest pastime in the world, and the pleasantest.'
Mark Twain

On the nights that the wolf does appear, he always waits for dark.

The Pousada Santuário de Caraça was originally a monastery. I found it on one of my early trips to Brazil. It is a fine example of the blending of the religious and secular, so typically Brazilian. In my life in Australia, monasteries were — as was religion itself — cloistered away. Religion was mysterious, elusive, a bit like the wolf.

The sanctuary offered by the church today is still good for the soul: guests can go bushwalking and witness the occasional appearance of the maned wolves, which sometimes take their supper on the church steps. Each night I join the other guests, most of them members of Brazil's fast-growing bourgeoisie, sitting on garden chairs around the terrace edge as we chat, sipping rough claret and hoping for an encounter with the wild.

The old church spire soaring over the trees is visible from almost any point on the property. Some of the stone buildings go back two hundred and fifty years — not a lot of time by Brazilian standards, but long enough to tell some of the country's plethora of stories. In 1968, fire gutted the four-storey sandstone library, and hundreds of books were lost. A dozen columns remain, and wall damage has been repaired with smoked glass. The modern is braided with the old.

The monks' quarters offer visitors basic accommodation, with hot water and electric lighting. The rooms are spotless, and the wooden floors have been worn by years of trailing robes. Typical Brazilian fare is offered as part of the package: chicken and pork; beans and rice; potatoes mashed, or chopped into soggy fries. Lunch is dinner reheated. Each morning, I clumsily rap the edge of a butter knife against the shells to spill my breakfast eggs straight onto the ancient wood-stoked grill.

Mass is offered several times a week by Father Marcos. He's a sporty-looking twenty-eight-year-old who schmoozes like a presidential candidate. A gaggle of guests attend him like courtiers. I am introduced to each group proudly as an *estrangeira*, as if I am the priest's first foreign guest. And perhaps I am. Father Marcos is the one hundred and eightieth padre at Caraça, although he's probably the first to wear jeans. His brief (which he admits one night after he thinks I have drunk too much red wine) is to make money for the church.

Each evening, Father Marcos brings a tray of bones onto the church terrace, and we gather in hope that the wolves will come. Scraping the tray along the tiles with his foot, his call echoes across the steppe. In concert with the vegetation across these hills, the wolves are delicate, not bulky, and often elusive. The fact that they have not become extinct in Brazil is due more to good luck than good management. My sudden desire to see one comes with a pang of surprise.

But we wait, and we refill our glasses, and as the hour grows later a curious hollow forms inside me as the possibility that the wolf may not arrive becomes a probability. We are unable, Padre Marcos says with a laugh, to offer refunds if the show is cancelled. My hand grips the wine glass with more force than necessary. The idea of the wolf is so tantalising. Seeing such a creature seems, for some reason I can't quite fathom, necessary. Suddenly, it is a life goal I hadn't realised I had.

Then from the darkness there's a movement. It snags my attention. The Brazilians raise their cameras, and I feel like shouting, 'Stop — don't frighten it away!'

But I don't. I am the stranger here.

A snout appears over the lowest step. '*Guara*,' the priest greets him (it looks to be a him). Will he come up or disappear back into the shadows? He glides up — one step, two; stops. Taking the last three steps as one, he lands on the tiles in front of the church, bright eyes hooded and alert. '*Guara*,' the priest says again. It is the *índio* word for 'red'. But his colour is lost in the staccato burst of camera flashes.

The wolf gazes upon the priest with something approaching disdain. His muscles are taut, ready to bear him away at a moment's notice. Sitting still, I find myself praying that the Brazilians will not scare him away. A dozen or more swirl around him, taking photos; a few look ready to spring towards him. But, to my relief, he seems as used to the barrage of flashes as a modern-day prince.

He steps with guarded care but shows no fear. Four graceful paces, and his snout hovers over the battered metal tray. Choosing a bone as long as his foreleg, he lifts it with expert, gentle jaws. He is beautiful. With front legs jointed low, he moves like a dancer.

For a time, the wolf lets temptation override caution, and the sound of crunching bone bounces off the old stone walls like rifle cracks. The wolf's jaw junctions close to his skull, providing leverage. I can feel the power in his bite.

Eventually, he looks up and examines his audience with such open curiosity, I feel a link with him, a strange kinship as well as a sense of awe. The other guests are so busy with their cameras they don't seem to notice his majesty or feel privileged by his arrival. Until that morning I had never heard of the maned wolf, but now I feel as if I have been waiting an age for him to materialise on this terrace.

The next night we gathered beside the church again, but the wolf declined to offer an encore.

I have never been a diary writer, but I wish I'd kept one now. Of course there were travel journals, recording the daily experiences. And notebooks: there are boxes of notebooks, full of little things noticed on the bus, at a festival or museum, or from a café table. But if I'd kept a diary, I might have written in the sort of personal shorthand one can use in private: '*Wolf: solitary, curious, alluring. A private messenger perhaps?*'

And that's the kind of thing that kept happening to me in Brazil. I'd be there, trying to live in the moment, and something would happen to me that felt entirely different from what was happening to those around me. And entirely different from what I was expecting. A simple trip to the mountains to do some hiking provided a unique, even transformative, moment that made me look at the world afresh. A good many Brazilians would tell me it was a sign from the heavens. So what began as a light-hearted look at a wonderful country made me stop and consider life, to make new — if sometimes odd — connections between things. Brazil opened up another world for me: a world for which the wolf became, in a way, a metaphor.

In Brazil is a means as much as a story. For you, the reader, it's a means of getting to know Brazil as much as it was for me, in writing about it. Before travelling in Brazil, my knowledge bank included little more than a few school-learned facts about the country: the Amazon River is the biggest by volume of water in the world; the Amazon Rainforest is the largest in the world, contributing around twenty per cent of our oxygen, and is being logged at some alarming rate each year. You know the sort of thing. I hadn't really clocked that Brazilians spoke Portuguese rather than Spanish, or that the mega-city São Paulo has the world's largest number of helicopter commutes each day. It's how the richest of the city's workers beat the choking traffic. Some are reputed to never set foot on the ground.

Now my head is filled with many facts — some might say useless ones. Did you know that in the Amazon jungle Henry Ford owned a rubber plantation about the size of Lebanon that he called Fordlandia? Now it's a ghost town. The country has more species of monkey than anywhere else. There are more people of African descent in Brazil than in any country in the world except for Nigeria. This is due to the fact that more than one hundred million Brazilians are descended from slaves taken from Africa. (There were some millions more slaves taken to Brazil than to the United States.) And the rate of logging in the Amazon Rainforest is truly astounding: every sixty seconds of this new millennium has seen us lose the equivalent size of fifty football grounds. That's a total area of ten times the size of the United Kingdom — with only a third being re-forested — since the year 2000!

Why choose Brazil? It's a question I'm asked a lot. The answer is that its people are so fascinating. It's a country diverse and vibrant. Part of the attraction is that it's relatively unknown to travellers from elsewhere. Brazil's foreign tourism industry is growing by about ten per cent per year, but it still receives considerably fewer international tourists compared with other countries with large populations. Brazil welcomes only six million foreigners a year, compared with sixty-two million in the United States and twenty-three million in Mexico. So that means you don't feel as if you're surrounded by your own people — that you are really experiencing something 'foreign', another way of life.

Though it's vast, Brazil is relatively easy to get around. It has more airports than any nation other than the United States. And you can get anywhere by bus — except in the Amazon, where you can get most places you'll want to go by boat. Because the rapidly growing middle class travel, infrastructure is good for travellers.

Brazil is for all manner of travel. If you are 'on tour', you will find more than enough sights to marvel at and photograph. There is a surfeit of beaches, hot springs, and resorts for those who wish, as the saying goes, to 'get away from it all'. If you believe TripAdvisor, Brazil has the world's best beach (at Baía do Sancho, on the remote island of Fernando de Noronha). The service is fabulous on most Brazilian beaches, where everything comes to you: from oysters shucked in front of your sun lounge to freshly shaken cocktails; from newly tatted lace to the world's skimpiest bikini. And if you are the kind of traveller, as I am, who wants to see how other people live, you can spend months and months, as I did, constantly visited by surprise and wonder.

Wonder is the lifeblood of travel writing. In his book *As I Was Saying*, Australian author and broadcaster Robert Dessaix tries to remember the last time he felt wonder: 'the sensation of being whisked out of time and space as I normally experience them, to be bathed in a sort of startling, epiphanic delight in something I don't understand and don't want to, not completely.' This wonder I have felt, and often, in Brazil.

When we think about travel, we tend to think first about places, to think spatially, geographically. It's easy to forget that people are often — usually, perhaps — more interesting than places. We can forget that people populate places; they bring them to life. The Brazilians — *brasileiros* and *brasileiras* — I encountered surprised and fascinated me at least as often as the landscape, the history, the sights.

For me (though not for Brazilians), Brazil is the land of the unexpected, the perfect antidote for routine. You might have heard that the buses don't run on time. In fact, often they do; it just takes a while to work out where they might go. In my country, 'shopping' can be a verb or a noun but not a destination. First visiting Rio de Janeiro, I was prepared for the beaches that curl lazily around the city, but not to witness oil rigs being towed across Guanabara Bay. This startling sight you can see from the top of that tourist icon, Sugarloaf Mountain. In Brazil, *favelas*, or slums, often cling precariously to the cliffs and mountains above cities, giving the poorest people the best views — although I suspect the locals don't have a lot of leisure time to enjoy them. In Brazil, there's something unexpected around every corner.

Everything is bigger there. Not content with one god, Brazilians turn to a veritable raft of colourful deities for inspiration, courage, love, health, and happiness. Religious processions can be two million strong and offer rhythms that would make Bob Marley jealous. Brazilians bring a level of commitment to the things they do that puts the rest of the world — or at least the world I live in — to shame, whether it's worship, football culture, resistance, or celebration.

You will notice the episodic nature of *In Brazil*. The order of chapters bears little resemblance to how they occurred in real life because I made many trips over some seven years, criss-crossing the country, following curiosity rather than any structured route, often led by a calendar of events. Take, for example, Carnaval: the most important five days of the year for many Brazilians. Attending Carnaval in different years and in different places was necessary (and fun) because writing about Brazil without mentioning Carnaval would be like writing without verbs.

For locals, Carnaval offers many of the same boons as travel. It allows Brazilians a break from regular life. Daily roles and responsibilities can be suspended. It's been pointed out that exotic travel, especially, affords a 'moral "time out" … a fantasy world where all the moral rules — of decorum, taste, narrative, plausibility, and cause-and-effect — [can] legitimately be suspended'. Carnaval is like that too.

Both travel and Carnaval afford the space — and the privilege — to take on new roles. For Carnaval, folk dress up for their roles: the Brazilian Portuguese word for 'costume' is *fantasia*. With travel, the costume tends to be metaphorical. Folk who study travel narratives have identified a whole gamut of roles that can be donned like new coats. We can be the Spiritual Quester, substituting travel for pilgrimage. The Inveterate Wanderer and the Collector of Experience are also tempting. Like Bruce Chatwin, the traveller can be the Aesthete and the Gatherer of Other People's Stories, the Eccentric or the Nomad. There's the Anthropological Participant-Observer (though it's a coat with a cut that just doesn't seem to suit me). There's the Pseudo-Scientist and the Adventuring Hero, roles less commonly played these days, where few journeys require a machete or the opportunity for the naming of species.

Until recently, Brazilians have not been widely known as international travellers, unlike Australians. Last year, Australians — who number merely twenty-two million people — made some 8.4 million trips out of the country. But we're put to shame by Britain, whose sixty-five million residents made nearly fifty-five million trips overseas — they do have a distinct advantage in that they have a tunnel that leads 'overseas', whereas Australians are restricted to air or sea transport. The number of trips overseas is equal to 84 per cent of their population (although some will have made more than one trip). By comparison, citizens of the United States hardly travel internationally at all: sixty-eight million trips suggest that a maximum of 22 per cent of the population travelled overseas in 2014, and that includes business trips or to visit family. Until recently, Brazilians weren't much for exotic travel; instead, Carnaval is what gets many of them through the often difficult everyday.

In addition to its episodic nature, you may notice, too, that nearly half of what made it into this book takes place in the country's Northeast region. That's no accident, really. Although I'm yet to find an uninteresting part of Brazil, the people who most captured my interest lived, as often as not, in the Northeast.

The first few times I ventured into Brazil were during a 'gap year', when I took an epic journey around South America — all thirteen countries on the continent — with my partner, Peter. We were a decade or so older than most of the backpackers we met on our meandering course. The three regions in Brazil we visited were all close to borders that we slipped over from somewhere else (Colombia, Paraguay, Bolivia), to see some convenient sight while we were vaguely on the way to somewhere else.

After we returned home to Flinders Island, references to Brazil kept cropping up. It was as if the country — or one of its deities — was demanding I pay more attention. Brazil's presidents were mentioned on television in contexts other than military *coups d'état*. The nation's growing role on the world stage was reported in the media. Brazil was to host the FIFA World Cup and, two years later, the Olympics. The nation's economy, I was reminded seemingly constantly, was soon expected to give Brazil another fifth place in the world, a trophy to place beside those of 'fifth-biggest population' and 'fifth-largest landmass'. Brazil is a member of the BRIC economic block, with other big countries Russia, India, and China, and has become one of the world's main oil producers, the largest exporter of coffee, a leading producer of hydroelectric power, the biggest grower of soybeans ... Suddenly it seemed the world was obsessed with Brazil. It was contagious.

I began to notice the similarities between my country — Australia — and Brazil. Both are big places. Both have the great majority of their populations on the coast. That beckoned questions: what are the differences when one country has nearly ten times the population of the other in roughly the same landmass? They were colonised by European powers, Brazil nearly three hundred years before Australia. The regions had healthy, happy indigenous populations before that, and neither do now. These were the questions and observations — some of them seemed rather lofty — that began to come at me more and more relentlessly, like mosquitoes in the Amazon, the more I thought about and travelled in Brazil. Of course, many of these questions were also pertinent to a range of other countries, such as the United States. So I became curious about the interests and concerns of Brazilians and how similar they might be to those of Australians and people in other 'Western' nations.

I told Peter that I'd have to go back. He wasn't as keen as me, being rather more taken with the Spanish-speaking countries. Brazil had already provided me with more surprise than one could reasonably expect, given that the total time we'd spent there was a little more than a month. That required following up.

In 2009, I dragged Peter back for another few months. We travelled the length of the country while I tried to work out what it was that had captivated me and how to write about it. After the first draft of what would become *In Brazil*, I made further trips, shorter trips — a month or two at a time. Twice friends joined me, and for the final month Peter did again, although I travelled alone too. Sometimes, in deference to brevity and focus, I haven't included my companions' presence in a chapter. And sometimes, for reasons of politeness or the failures of memory, I have changed the names of those I met.

So this is my Brazil: at once boisterous and mysterious, elusive and confounding, a total chameleon. She could even be the wolf I felt so fortunate to see.

My very first foray into Brazil went something like this: we were on a day trip from Argentina. We'd been told that you didn't need a visa for such a short visit, which we hoped was right because Peter had been mugged, just three days after we arrived in South America, and his passport stolen. He was travelling on a temporary one we were pretty sure didn't comply with Brazilian entry requirements. We'd come across the border to see the famous Iguaçu Waterfalls and to watch Brazil play Australia on the big screen during the 2006 FIFA World Cup. This was a novelty in itself; we weren't accustomed to being able to go to another country for a day. It takes the best part of a day's plane ride or a sea cruise just to leave Australia.

A guy on the bus gave us directions to a restaurant at which we could watch the game — of course we soon learned that every restaurant, bar, coffee shop, taxi stand, kiosk, and bus station was a potential venue for watching it. The entire country shut down for the match.

A huge marquee had been erected next to the restaurant, in which we grabbed the last table, and Peter headed to the bar to find out how to order a couple of beers. Suddenly five hundred voices around me began chanting the Hino Nacional Brasileiro. They made it sound more like a clubroom victory song than an ode to country. The Australian anthem started up next. We burrowed into our seats.

But once the game started, it didn't take long for a few Brazilians to realise Peter and I weren't barracking for their side. Australia was managing to hold Brazil goalless, and we were trying not to grin.

The Brazilians tapped and wriggled; they itched with concern. When the ball went within cooee of the net, I ducked as the people around me exploded into the air with the force of dynamite in a mineshaft. When the ball eluded the goal, each body deflated — man, woman, and child — collapsing hard into their seats. The curious, exhilarating, exhausting rhythm continued (I felt bruised just watching them) until on the giant screens Adriano scored for Brazil four minutes into the second half. The Brazilians sagged with relief before raising the roof again when Fred — really, Fred? Not something exotic like Paulo or Pedro, Thiago or Vinícius, but Fred? — tapped the second Brazilian goal expertly into the net with mere seconds of the game to go. Brazil 2, Australia 0. Not, I admit, unexpected.

After the final whistle, a woman of about twenty who had been sitting at the next table approached ours. Did she want to gloat? I had noticed her during the first half of the match, buying Cokes for three dusty street urchins who had crept into the marquee to watch. Her hand was outstretched. 'I am sorry,' she said in heavily accented English. She clearly wasn't, but I was grateful for the friendly commiseration.

The waitress was handing me our change in the almost empty marquee when its walls dropped to the ground — literally — and we were deluged by sound. My ears were assaulted by piercing noise from long plastic horns that people of all ages were blowing relentlessly. The sound of a children's birthday party rattles my bones; this was much louder. When breath ran short, they merely waved the horns in the air victoriously.

The road was jammed with people, the gridlock providing ample opportunity for drivers to contribute to the din by planting their elbows on their horns. We were the only un-jubilant people in sight. A television crew must have noticed: a microphone materialised in my face. '*Australiana?*' But even had I the Portuguese, I wouldn't have been heard.

Now, a good part of my life has been spent on a small island in the middle of Bass Strait — that's the stretch of water between Tasmania and the Australian mainland. It's where Peter and I live permanently now.

The island has a population so small the Australian Bureau of Statistics probably thinks it's a waste of their budget to count us. Most Australians don't even know where Flinders Island is. When you live there, you are used to tranquillity. It's a place to love for its beaches and its beauty, but mostly for its peace and quiet. Overwhelmed by the pandemonium, I felt like I was Steppenwolf, in Hermann Hesse's novel, and had found myself in the Magic Theatre that was 'for mad people only'. It was as if the entire population of Brazil — then a shade under two hundred million — was storming triumphantly onto the main street of Foz do Iguaçu and celebrating Brazil's victory. Loudly.

It wasn't just the noise that was challenging; these people celebrated with their whole beings, with a commitment in a way that was entirely new to me. I was yet to learn that Brazilians do nothing by halves. Someone had painted the carapace of a VW Beetle in blue and yellow and green, the colours of the Brazilian flag. It was parked on the street and people flowed around it, like rapids around a boulder in a riverbed, throwing streamers, waving flags. Some wore patriotically decorated hats; others striped their faces in a tradition I discovered was not limited to English soccer fans.

A car inched past, its open boot filled with speakers, and the *doof doof* of the music felt like a punch to my chest.

Then a man appeared — he had an air of hobo about him. He stepped from the park carrying a flagpole twice his size and walked to the centre of the road. We stopped to watch. He planted the pole on the asphalt like a mast on a ship. Amid the noise, in the centre of the tornado-like bedlam, he began a silent demonstration of his own satisfaction — he danced languorously around it as if he had his own private maypole. There it was, the unexpected, the juxtaposition: the calm in the eye of the storm.

The North and the Northeast

Chapter One

The Sound of Commitment

BELÉM, PARÁ

'Only Siberia and the Sahara can rival Brazilian vastness, and they have deplorable climates.' John Updike

The Brazilian North is nearly a continent away from the Brazilian South in a way you just don't see on a map. The faces in the South tend to be more European. In the North, you can see the entire history of the three major races of Brazil writ large on its inhabitants. While the South has highways, in the North you are lucky to find something that can pass for a road. The South took careful notes during the Industrial Revolution: its giant populations are organised into cities. The North feels like a frontier — a sprawling, insidious region seemingly unable to be conquered. If you live in the North — whether in the interior, with its baking arid backlands, or in the torpidity of the cloying jungle — you keep your machete sharp. You have the toughness the North requires, and a certain kind of lunacy that goes with permanent perspiration.

Leabharlanna Fhine Gall

Most of the reading I've done over the years supports this view of the Brazilian North. After his presidency, Theodore Roosevelt joined a couple of naturalists floating down rivers no white man had floated down before. They were hunting jaguars.

Travel writer Peter Fleming ventured into the Brazilian wilderness, too. He was looking for lost explorers — more particularly, for members of the expedition led by Colonel Percy Fawcett, thought to have been eaten by cannibals.

Peter and I had only been in Northern Brazil a week or so, most of that on a boat down the Amazon River, before we arrived in Belém. It was some months since that Australia–Brazil World Cup soccer game. Since then, we had bussed across Argentina, collected Peter's new passport in Santiago, and wended our way slowly along the Andes Mountains through Northern Chile, Western Bolivia, and Southern Peru to those amazing ruins called Machu Piccu. We'd been — and this was pretty much all we knew — vaguely heading for Pucallpa, a Peruvian town on the Ucayali River. While the starting point for the Amazon River is contested, we put our money on the Ucayali, as the longest tributary that flows into the Amazon. From there, we had travelled the entire length of the river by boat from Peru to Belém.

In the six months we'd been travelling, the whole universe seemed to have slowed and our priorities rearranged. The world, to my not-inconsiderable relief, had not ended when I closed down my Melbourne-based literary agency to go travelling. After twenty years of whirlwind activity, I needed to have a rest, to have time to think, to find a new direction. Modern city life moves at a pace that underrates the value of thinking. There wasn't a tipping point, just lots of little things that eventually overbalanced the scales or broke the camel's back, choose your own cliché. A big part of my decision was because literary fiction, the type of writing I most liked to work with, doesn't sell in the numbers it deserves to, and the unhelpful voice in my head kept suggesting that the modest sales of many of my clients' literary fiction projects was because

I, as an agent, was doing something wrong. A hubristic notion, perhaps. For my own part, a deep tiredness, an emptiness even, had opened up in me. I could barely speak. It was as if words were fuel and my tank had run dry. There had also been a constant urge to travel — the travel bug, as they call it, had bitten deep years before. Peter, too, had wanted to travel. His work was easier, at least in a practical sense, to leave: he'd been working as a wool presser in the shearing sheds in the Outback, and then as a concreter, when he moved in with me in the city. His work was casual, from place to place, from contract to contract. When I made such a radical life change, my family and friends were caught between horror and envy.

I had learnt a little Spanish in those six months we'd been on the road, no easy task for a thirty-something third-generation white Australian who went to school during the days when government education policy ignored the teaching of grammar. But I'd had an easier time than Peter, who hadn't had even a few words in another tongue before.

My university degrees hadn't helped as much as I expected them to. But I had realised that you had to learn *how* to learn another language before you could, in fact, learn one. And I began to see why translators might have the difficulties and proclivities they do. Translation isn't a simple matter of swapping words one for another.

So by the time we got to Belém, I'd been conjugating, compounding, and confusing Spanish verbs for some time, expecting that would help with Brazilian Portuguese. After all, the languages *look* similar, don't you think? They mostly use the same alphabet and root verbs. But, of course, Brazil soon turned that notion on its head.

Our choosing to travel to Belém by boat wasn't just for the adventure. Much of the Amazon region simply isn't accessible by vehicle, even some of its cities. We bought passage on and crossed the gangplanks of four boats in order to travel the more than four and a half thousand kilometres from Pucallpa in Peru to the point close to where the Amazon floods into the Atlantic in Brazil. It was a journey that took some weeks and included more than one unscheduled stop on a sandbank. I'd found it peaceful — apart from one boat called a *rápido,* which, translated, means thirteen hours of teeth-chattering hell as it whumps on every single tiny wave.

The guidebooks don't tell you that the Amazon River is corrugated.

The Amazon is wide and brown, relentless really. It also hides a subtext: a subterranean river — even bigger, slower, and more relentless, and hundreds of times as wide — flows beneath it.

You see very little wildlife from the river. Much of it has been sold, and we saw some of what was left on its way to market: a trussed turtle lay under our first boat's communal dining table. Disembarking the *rápido* — before I'd even stopped rattling — I was offered a scarlet and green macaw. On another boat, a teenage girl dropped a small cardboard box and a cloud of Love Birds fell out and then skittered over the deck like mercury. With little to see, we'd played cards until we slept with spades staining our eyelids.

By the time we got to Belém, I was looking forward to a little relief from beans and rice but was not expecting much change of pace. But the purpose of travel — for me anyway — is the unexpected, which serves a purpose: it punctuates life.

Belém is a steamy city at the mouth of the river, close to the point where it spills into the Atlantic. As a river city, it's usually a languid place. Most days, the main action is on the brown channels writhing with wakes as they're crossed by canoes, ferries, floating shops, barges, speedboats, and the odd raft. There's a vibrant food market, from which you can watch the river craft while you nibble on a stuffed and fried crab carapace, one elbow resting on a kiosk counter.

Our boat was met by a number of taxis at the floating wharf, and we hopped in one. After ten minutes or so the driver stopped on a side street, but I knew that our hotel was on an *avenida.* '*Está lá!*' he announced, punching the air with a fist. Despite being unable to decipher the driver's rapidly bitten syllables, his message was obvious: this was as far as he'd take us. We peeled ourselves out of the cab much more slowly than he'd have liked. Making a fast five-point turn, he sped away.

Packs shouldered, we headed in the direction indicated, only to find a wooden beam barricading the street. Peter rolled under it before I could even protest. I hesitated; despite having been a rebellious teenager, I tended, these days, to be more conservative, to stick to rules. Rules and signs can be especially useful, I find, if you don't speak the language. It was clear to me what the barricade meant.

'Just roll under it,' Peter said and waved a hand over his shoulder. 'There's our hotel.' So I knelt and rolled onto my back, just like Peter had. Except that I got stuck halfway. There I was, caught like a beetle on its back. Suddenly there were two men in military uniforms peering down at me. I didn't need to speak their language to see they were trying not to laugh.

In South America, military presence is much more obvious, more ordinary, than in countries such as Australia or Britain. Members of the military help enforce borders, fight smuggling, maintain public order, and terminate governments. Military coups on the continent are notorious. In Brazil, regular police, run by each of the twenty-six states, are called military police who, if required, can be pressed into national service, as an arm of the Forças Armadas do Brazil. The reverse is also true. Military personnel are often called upon to keep the peace, and it looked like they regarded me as disturbing it.

I suddenly realised that there had been another beginning point for my interest in Brazil, a Chatwin-esque moment which I can pinpoint when Brazil as a country appeared on my mental map. I'd travelled a fair bit, more than most of my friends. But for me Brazil had been just been part of the mysterious lump on a map that is South America until one of the writers I represented as a literary agent came to me with a book for young adults. It was called *The Candelária Massacre*.

How on earth had I forgotten this until now?

Bruce Chatwin — a favourite writer, one of my heroes — begins *In Patagonia* with his childhood fascination with a piece of skin belonging to some unidentified prehistoric creature that had been found by his grandmother's cousin Charley Milward in Patagonia. In this way, Chatwin became aware of Patagonia: 'a country in South America, at the far end of the world'. (It's not, of course, a country but a region.) James McQueen was my Charley Milward; he was responsible for Brazil becoming more real to me. But my beginning had much more brutal overtones. The novel that my client handed me was based on a true story: the horrific murder of eight homeless children as they slept on the steps of the Candelária Church in Rio de Janeiro in 1993. They were murdered by Brazilian military police.

McQueen was a skilled novelist, so in addition to the snippets of information floating around my head about Brazil over the years — Carnival, samba, coffee — I had this vivid scene of Brazilian military police shooting sleeping children. And here were two such men looking down at me, trying not to laugh.

Using one arm each, they hauled me to my feet by my pack-straps.

While wondering why they were dressed in camouflage here in the city streets, I suddenly became aware of the noise. It was coming from somewhere to my right. It seemed both blunt and multi-layered, swollen — not like any noise I'd heard before. Kaleidoscopic, even. Sure, noise is not uncommon in Brazil, but this was something different. It was moving, *coming towards me*. My brain seemed to race and cloud at the same time. Tsunami? (Surely too far from the ocean.) It sounded human, but not. My scalp started to crawl.

Peter — often quicker on the uptake than me — was already gesturing alternately at his pack and at the hotel across the road. That's when I saw the long line of khaki uniforms, shoulder to shoulder, between us and the road. Between us and our hotel.

Stuttering in poor Spanish, Peter tried to convey that we really, really needed to get across the road and into our hotel. *Ahora*. Luckily the word is nearly the same in Portuguese as Spanish: now. The taller of the military men shot a question at the shorter man, who flicked a hand in expeditious reply at our packs and then in the direction of our hotel. Suddenly the taller one turned and fired off something incomprehensible towards the military blockade, which parted like the Red Sea.

With an admirable efficiency of movement, the two men flanked us. One took my elbow, and, since my gaze was firmly focused on the hotel, I can only imagine the other took Peter's. They marched us across the wide no-man's-land that was the city's main avenue. An identical line of military parted for us on the other side. When we reached the hotel, each man grasped a door handle and whisked open the twin glass doors with what might have been a flourish, and deposited us into the lobby like jetsam.

It was almost silent.

Elevator music drifted from a couple of boxy speakers on each side of a vinyl lounge.

It felt like the moment that Dorothy was aiming for in *The Wizard of Oz*, when she could fall down into the darkness and safety of the hurricane shelter under her house and let the wooden doors fall closed above her. Instead, she got swept to another world by the wind.

Shaking my head a little to clear it, I rested my pack against a faded armrest and walked to the counter. '*O que* ...' It seemed I was trying to channel Portuguese from somewhere. 'What —'

But the saints were smiling on us that day: the hotelier spoke some English. We had arrived in Belém in time for the *procissão*, the highlight of the Festa do Círio de Nazaré. 'The biggest *festa Católica* in the world, *entendeu?*' he said proudly and pointed upwards. 'You see — best view in Belém!'

Brazilians often call theirs the biggest, be it statue, supermarket, theatre, or church, but a quick check of my guidebook confirmed that this event was indeed big: a couple of million Catholics were about to walk past our hotel.

Although my parents are not religious, I have always been interested in the concept of religion, if not the practice. To the incredulity of my classmates, I sometimes used to sneak into the religious instruction classes my parents ensured I was excused from at primary school. Though I'd never read the Bible, I was fascinated by the pomp and ceremony of Christmas Mass when I could find someone to take me. After toying with the idea of studying religion at university, I didn't, nervous about my lack of knowledge and experience. (Although that also became an unexpected problem in studying literature.) So, before Brazil, my exposure to religion had been minimal at best.

In Australia, worship tends towards the private. Services take place in designated and enclosed spaces: church, synagogue, mosque, temple. Prayer outside those places happens in the home — occasionally in the community hall, perhaps — but only on rare occasions does it happen in public, on the street, as it does in some countries. Only two exceptions come to mind: when the Pope said Mass at the Melbourne Cricket Ground, one of the largest sports stadiums in the world, people came from all over to participate; and when Sydney hosted Catholic World Youth Day, there was a huge crowd, boosted by 250,000 foreigners. For the most part, private and sombre is how I would describe Australian devotion. Christmas has been secularised; Easter, as well. In Australia you can virtually go through life unaware of religion.

So for me, religion was an interest, but it largely played along in the background, a track I never listened closely to. Some of my friends, I've been vaguely aware, prepare for Passover. In Melbourne, I need to book a taxi early if I want it around noon because a good many of Melbourne's taxi drivers follow Islam, and noon is one of their prayer times. When I have guests, I try to remember which of them eat beef. At the general store, next door to my home on Flinders Island, the Anglicans and the Catholics have morning tea each week after church. (It's usually a combined service due to lack of numbers and the fact that the parishioners have to pay to fly in the reverend or priest.) So this massive throng assembling for a religious event was amazing for me.

The hotelier was rightly proud of the view from his rooftop. It was a right royal view. A *monarchic* view. The perfect place to watch one of the world's great spectacles.

By the time we dropped our bags in our room and got to the roof, the leading edge of the procession had passed, but the road still heaved with people. I was not alone in my excitement: small children darted around me, running from balcony to balcony. The littlest kids pogo-jumped to see over the railing.

White is the uniform for many Brazilian events, Catholic and otherwise. But looking down to the *avenida* I could see specks of red, blue, and green. It was like looking down on a confetti-strewn, white-watered sea.

When you take part in the annual procession of Círio de Nazaré, you are part of two devout lines. Possibly the world's longest queues, they are a human version of double white lines. It took nearly ten hours to pass.

I was glad for my place above the spectacle. In the procession, I would be jammed up against the clammy back of the youngish person in front of me — the stamina required appeared to limit the age range. I would be clutching one of two very long ropes, thick as a muscled arm, and be shuffling — indeed, groaning — up the Avenida Presidente Vargas pulling on the ropes, face screwed up with the very effort of staying upright. Like the people below were. Instead, I had my bird's-eye view.

Most striking was the sound. The noise swirled around me so acutely it could almost be tasted. It was dull and full one moment, acrid the next. From below came grunts and groans, shouts and yelps, all underscored by a bare-footed shuffle. Low murmurs competed with high cries. The sounds piled upon one another, individual and blended at once, forming an artwork, a mosaic of sound that could have been titled 'Cacophony'.

This was not the sparsely populated, wild Amazon of Claude Lévi-Strauss, Redmond O'Hanlon, or Evelyn Waugh that I have read about. I turned to Peter to ask what was going on. Although brought up Catholic, he shook his head; clearly he had no idea either.

In Australia, our biggest gatherings are on ANZAC Day, to commemorate those fallen in war. The number of participants has grown a lot in recent years, but not even their solemn commitment could compare to the numbers or the effort that the people below me were putting into their devotion. I began to suspect that it took more energy than I had to be a Brazilian.

White-capped teams of volunteers carried folded canvas stretchers, holding them aloft, clear of the crowd. Some distributed bottles of water, a cure for the cloying effects of the humidity that did nothing to dampen the fervour. A woman in a white headscarf sank from view. Waving hands summoned a stretcher, and a moment later the woman appeared on it, catatonic. My eyes followed the stretcher as it floated above the crowd, moving on a conveyor belt of hands. The corner of my eye caught someone new slipping onto the rope.

This procession, I discovered later online, dates from around the time Australia was 'discovered' by the British, more than two hundred years ago.

If I had been born around here, the story behind the procession would be as familiar as my own childhood tales. It goes like this: a poor *caboclo* (as men of mixed *índio* and Portuguese decent were known) called Plácido José de Souza came across a statue of the Virgin Mary on a bank of the Murutucú creek. The Jesuits had been spreading the word of their Christian God across Brazil for a couple of centuries by that time. The man took the statue and placed it on the altar in his hut. When he rose the next morning, the statue had vanished. Finding the statue in her original position by the creek, the farmer bought her home, and again she returned to her place by the creek. The man built a waterside altar for her, the Nossa Senhora, and worshipped at it each day. Word spread of the miracle, and the local people joined him at the altar in prayer.

Then the governor caught word of the miracle and decided the town chapel was a more appropriate home for Our Lady, ordering her transported thence. The statue, however, differed in opinion, and returned to her home by the creek. Then, as now, Brazilian men like to think they rule the roost, and the governor had her returned to the chapel. To and fro, Nossa Senhora went — I imagine she was growing quite cross — until the governor relented and built a beautiful basilica around her. The Basílica

Santuário de Nazaré now stands on the bank of the Murutucú creek, and every year for more than two hundred years, a procession of worshippers has pulled a cart through the city carrying the Nossa Senhora de Nazaré.

Fireworks cracked like rifle shots from the roof of the post office opposite me. Acrid smoke drifted with the ticker tape that surfed the breeze. It took me a while to realise that those on the rope formed teams, were one another's support crews: they held one another up, passed bottles of water, and swapped places on the line, supportive and competitive at once.

The sound was different from the noise of an Australian crowd. I tried to work out why. When we gather in support, the sound moves in and out, it rises and falls, dependent on the game-play. When we gather in protest, the sounds are strident in rhythm or clipped in anger. At a public event you might hear expressions of wonder, respectful silence, murmurs of agreement, or the patter of applause. From the pilgrims below rose a spectrum of sound. Among it all, I heard effort and excitement mixed with prayer. Each person seemed to have both a unique and a collective experience.

Suddenly Peter grabbed my arm and pointed to a man wheeling a barrow of opaque limbs. Plastic arms reached eerily over the metal lip. Adult-sized legs lay in a mournful pile next to pair of child-sized heads and a neatly balanced breast. Body parts? They looked like pieces of plastic doll: what were they doing at a religious procession? Then I spotted, walking on the near edge of the procession, a man carrying a metre-long ferryboat above his head, clear of the crowd. Behind him another man wielded a replica of a house. Toys? One bloke toted a small apartment building. These people and more, burdened with replicas, joined the crowd that moved slowly down the road with all the determination and inevitability of a glacier.

Then, as if that glacier had calved, a portion of the crowd surged towards the corner below us. Moving to the other side of the building to overlook the side street, I peered down on the broad bottoms of a dozen women bending from the bed of a truck. They passed out tiny bread rolls to waving hands. More women stood on the ground, distributing small bottles of water scooped from huge baskets — even I could recognise the elements for Mass.

As if in confirmation, a voice began to intone from further up the *avenida*. The clergyman's words were in Portuguese, broadcast through speakers that hung from trees, but the cadences of Mass were — are — universal. A mass Mass. It would not be out of place in Vatican Square or Lourdes, perhaps, but this was the Amazon Basin.

Eventually the procession settled into a stately gait, as purple-robed bishops and white-frocked priests passed by, flanked by the two ropes, which were tied to a carriage. On the flower-drenched float rested a gaudy gold-and-glass cabinet. Inside was the pale, epiphanic image of the Virgin of Nazareth holding her child. Behind the church leaders, a row of dump trucks was inching forward with their loads: men in orange uniforms who leaned on long-handled brooms. Women in green scrubs began appearing from side streets. With my bad back, I didn't envy them their task as they bent and straightened, filling their baskets with the plastic bottles that covered the road like a long-awaited frost. Soon this swarm of Brazil's efficient low-wage workers would remove all traces of the massive event, leaving only my amazement and something I would take a while to identify: my interest in how people make sense of the world.

~

Rather than through religion, I make sense of the world through books. This is not to suggest for a moment that the two things are mutually exclusive. One of my favourite literature teachers at university was the wonderful poet and Jesuit priest Peter Steele S.J. (may he rest in more peace than we students ever offered him). He combined both religion and books, as many do.

Another way to make sense of the world is through travel. Bruce Chatwin wrote, 'Travel does not merely broaden the mind. It makes the mind.' Books, of course, make the mind as well. What we read helps to form our beliefs. Many a time in Brazil I noticed people on buses or in bistros — the toilet attendant waiting for a new patron — reading prayer books. They don't do that nearly so much (in public, at any rate) in Australia.

We are, I believe, more likely to be what we read than, as the popular saying suggests, what we eat. You can tell a lot about a person from what's on their bookshelf and from what people have read to them as a child. Among the range of stories my father read to my brother and me were Indigenous Australian stories. So, despite my contact with formal religion having been more or less limited to shifting the Gideon from one hotel drawer to another to make room for my socks, because my father read to us, I was aware from a young age that people make sense of the world in different ways.

My father was a marvellous reader. Is still such a marvellous reader; I can't bring myself to read to my nieces today for fear of not living up to his standard. Even before he left the law to become a writer, he read to my brother and me and to himself. He read to us in his deep, assured voice about Goorialla, the Rainbow Serpent, who made the rivers and taught the people how to dance. One day a great rain came, and two brothers who couldn't find shelter were swallowed by the Rainbow Serpent, who then fled, fearing the wrath of the villagers.

When the people finally tracked him down, the Rainbow Serpent was asleep on the top of a mountain. They sliced him open to find that the boys had transformed into rainbow lorikeets, which promptly flew away. The serpent awakened and, discovering his loss, tore the landscape apart with his fury. The people fled from his rage, changing themselves into the animals, insects, birds, and plant life that inhabit Australia today. And to this day, on seeing a shooting star, I like to think that it is the eye of Goorialla watching us, echoing the illustrations remembered from my childhood. These days *The Rainbow Serpent* is on YouTube, narrated superbly by Australia's most distinguished Indigenous actor, David Gulpilil; but, I contend, my father's reading will always be the most magical.

Regardless of the 'truth' of one story or another, meaning is socially constructed. It cannot exist in a vacuum. Books and stories, travel, lore, and beliefs all aim at making sense — making meaning — of the world. (Although the ultimate way of seeking to make sense of the world is to write about it, as I recently discovered.)

Chapter Two

Rebellion in the Rainforest

UNIÃO DOS PALMARES, ALAGOAS

'The past is present in the Northeast.' Peter Robb

Claudio, my language teacher, beamed at me when I asked him how to get to the site of the *quilombo* at União dos Palmares. 'You know about Zumbi and the slaves?' he asked in surprise. Brazilians often seem surprised that foreigners might know something about their history. 'I've never been there — maybe I come with you,' he said. As the *e* at the end of a word is pronounced in Portuguese, Claudio actually said 'comee'; if he was less ingenuous I'd have suspected him of manufacturing this trait. It was heartening, struggling as I was to learn his language.

Reading about the pre- and early European history of Brazil, I didn't need to be Einstein to understand why I was experiencing more than a little *déjà vu*. It is remarkably similar to the pre- and early European history of Australia. In both countries, the native populations were decimated by the colonisers. But I will get back to that beginning later. For now, let us be content with a short history refresher.

The beginning of the Portuguese history of Brazil and its Catholic history are one; they coincide precisely.

Brazil was 'discovered' at a time when Europeans divided the world into only two categories: Christian and non-Christian. (In fact, it could be said that it's getting more like that again today.) Throughout the Middle Ages, the Portuguese, like the Spanish, had been at war with the Moors who had flowed across the Strait of Gibraltar, preaching Islam and planting rice. It took some five hundred years of bloody battle to send the Moors back.

I had a vague recollection of being taught this in European Studies at high school by Mr Hamer, a portly man who wore — unusually for an Australian state school — an academic gown. He stalked a well-worn path, right to left, left to right, in front of the blackboard with all the gravitas of a pendulum.

After wresting the Iberian Peninsula from the infidels' grip, the Portuguese and the Spanish turned to exploring the world. When the Spanish began to 'discover' the Americas, King Ferdinand and Queen Isabella petitioned the Pope to assign the 'new' territories to Spain. Pope Alexander VI — a Spaniard — drew a line one hundred leagues west of the Cape Verde Islands, which were already held by Portugal. He proclaimed, in essence, that everyone east of the line would speak Spanish, and all in the west would speak Portuguese. This treaty (it sounds suspiciously like a decree) was known as the Treaty of Tordesillas.

Dom João II appealed when he became King of Portugal, complaining, presumably, of the Pope's Spanish bias. The new Pope, Julius II, revised the treaty, and the line was moved a further hundred and seventy leagues west. So in 1500, when Captain Pedro Álvares Cabral arrived after his fleet was blown off-course on its way to India, he claimed Brazil for Portugal.

The institution of slavery, like the Church that thoroughly approved of the practice, also played a major role in Brazil. It was the Jesuits who were nominated by Portugal's king, Dom João III, in the mid-1500s to lead the religious settlement of Portugal's New World territory. In the guise of saving the native peoples from the gangs of slave hunters who wanted to mine the 'red gold' in their veins, the Jesuits used *índio* labour to build missions from the Amazon River in the North to the Iguaçu in the South.

It's a time in history I find confronting, and it's not dissimilar to what happened in Australia when it was settled by the British. Manuel da Nóbrega, the priest who said the first Mass held in the then-capital Salvador, called the native people 'dogs who kill and eat one another'. But the original Brazilians — my politically correct term, not theirs — proved unfit for the hard work of building a new colony, and there were not enough of them: estimates range from only two to five million.

Turns out that it didn't really matter: some decades before, cheap and plentiful labour had been sourced by a Portuguese prince who became known as 'Henry the Navigator'. His legacy — slavery — is evident in Brazil today. And his story is both fascinating and repelling.

Henry was one of those people who was born to be interesting. His *nacimento*, cast by the royal astrologer upon his birth, found that Mars was in the 'House of Secrets and Ambitions', which, combined with the influence of the position of Saturn, would cause the prince to make 'great and noble conquests' and reveal 'secrets previously hidden from men'.

As a son of Portuguese king João I and his wife, Philippa of Lancaster, Henrique was weaned on the chivalry of his English ancestors. His motto — chosen in the Anglo-Norman tradition — was 'hunger to perform worthy deeds'. On her deathbed, his famously pious mother charged her sons to find fame fighting the infidel. Henry was only twenty-one when he was proclaimed commander-in-chief of the Portuguese armed forces and began his crusade to turn the world to Christendom.

The prince's ambition for exploration and domination was driven, in part, by a burning desire to bypass the Moors and acquire the spices and other riches making their way from the Far East to Europe via North Africa. The fact that the trade was controlled by heretics incensed him, and he directed his forces to take the Canary Islands, the Madeiras, and the Azores. He claimed the Cape Verde Islands before his ambition was curbed by the Pope's treaties. I have wondered just how angry that would have made him — they were, after all, mere lines on a map.

When one of his ships rounded the West African cape known by sailors the world over as 'the cape of no return', Henry was credited — although not a sailor himself — with having sailed further south than any European before him. It was the agile caravel, the type of ship that Pedro Álvares Cabral would sail when he 'discovered' Brazil, that enabled the feat. The caravel was a squat craft, with a deck at the rear, raised as a skirt might be, before its wooden swooping hull crested to a wave. Caravels could sail between Lisbon and the Cape Verde Islands in just twelve days.

The Pope appointed Henry military commander of the Order of Christ, the notorious martial order whose origins lay in the Templars. Henry had the Order's bold red square cross sewn onto the triangular white sails of his ships so it was the first thing the heathens saw. I imagine most of them later wished it was also the last thing they saw.

On his ships' bows, Henry had painted eyes to encourage the notion that — so good was Portuguese navigation — his ships could see. It was 1444 when Henry's fleet transported the first full cargo of slaves. The townspeople lined the port in Brazil for its landing.

Perhaps it went like this:

A man in a frock coat wipes his brow as the ships' sails appear on the horizon. They grow larger, and he lifts his son to his shoulder and points to the bound and fettered people on the deck, where some of the men, women, and children weathered the journey; there was no room left for them below. His wife stands next to him, swishing her skirts in the heat. Never has she seen such a spectacle! They watch as the ships drop anchor and the city's officials are rowed out to count the cargo, to tally their worth.

The man murmurs into the ear of his son, explaining how the sum is calculated for the Crown to receive the twenty per cent tax they called the Royal Fifth. (Documents written on the day show that Prince Henry, from atop his horse, chose forty-six of the best slaves in satisfaction of the tax. He nominated two young specimens to be donated to the Church.

The idea was for them to teach priests their native tongue, to better spread the Word of God.)

Then the crowd begins to thin. My imaginary man feels the stirrings of a welcome breeze. He watches as the slaves are unloaded. He witnesses sons torn from fathers, brothers from sisters, husbands from wives.

He watches as the cargo is 'formed into five equal lots' for auction. You might imagine that the stench of unwashed humans worries him, but he's accustomed it — the *índios* of Brazil had not yet taught the Portuguese to bathe daily.

But now the man's son, growing bored, wriggles down from his father's shoulder. A woman with shiningly dark skin is being beaten for clinging to her tiny daughter, and it seems to the man as good a moment as any to turn for home.

The histories record that Portuguese townspeople did indeed gather at the wharves to witness the unloading of that first cargo of slaves. I wonder if they realised they were witnessing the birth of such an ugly institution: the Atlantic slave trade. It would see ten million or more removed from Africa.

More than half of them would be taken to work in Brazil.

I was glad that Peter wasn't with me when Claudio summarily dismissed my suggestion that we go by bus — buses go everywhere in Brazil, and they're clean, cheap, convenient, and comfortable, unlike in Australia. A few days later, Claudio told me there were no guides for the site, but he had hired José Maria to drive us and four other students in my language course to the memorial commemorating Zumbi and his famous band of runaway slaves, who made their brave stand against government forces.

I was surprised there were no guides for such a culturally important site. There seem to be guides available everywhere in Brazil. The language school had engaged one the weekend before, just to take us to the beach.

(So relentlessly had the young man blasted his whistle to round us up, I nearly jammed it down his throat.) Not being one who likes being told what to do, I decided there were some advantages to having no guide.

And it was interesting that Claudio hadn't made this journey before. Australians tend to be obsessed with personal journeys into our history. We walk the Kokoda Track. We stand vigil at Gallipoli. We pay homage at Uluru, which for a time was called Ayers Rock. Claudio's tight black ringlets advertised his links to Afro-Brazilian history, but he hadn't been to one of the hallowed sites, even though it wasn't — by my standards, anyway — very far away.

Soon after the Portuguese arrived, Dom João III drew lines on his map from the east coast inland to divide Brazil into fifteen 'captaincies'. These he granted to favoured members of his court. The 'captains', of course, needed forts to defend their holdings. They needed labour to build the forts, and they needed labour to tend crops, so they began to import human capital directly across the Atlantic from Africa.

And almost from the moment that the first cargo of slaves was brought to Brazil, a determined few began to escape.

The escapees gathered in hidden communities called *quilombos*. I like to think of *quilombos* as symbols of hope for the slave population. The *quilombo* at Palmares is the most famous of them all. Brazilian children learn about its people's courage and tenacity in fending off the government forces sent to destroy them. If I wanted to understand Brazil, I would need to know more about the *quilombos*, and about Zumbi, one of modern Brazil's most famous heroes and who soon became one of mine — except, perhaps, for the bit when he poisoned his uncle, but we'll get to that shortly.

When we arrived in Unãio dos Palmares, a rural centre in northern Alagoas, we could find no indication in which direction the Parque Memorial Quilombo dos Palmares might be.

We did pass a muscle-bound statue of Zumbi. He looked poised and alert, one leg forward, one back in a spear-throwing stance. It reminded me of depictions of Australian Aborigines in the early days of Australia's colonial past: Zumbi as 'the noble savage'.

Brazil and Australia have similarities when it comes to race and slavery — perhaps not as many as Brazil and the United States, but they're there nonetheless. Not only did both empires capture the indigenous peoples, who were unsuited to hard labour and treated appallingly, but also in both cases an alternative source of labour was found: African slaves were brought to Brazil; English convicts, and later South Sea Islanders, were taken to Australia.

José Maria stopped the car to ask for directions to the site from two girls in the uniform of northeastern Brazil: tight denim shorts, Havaianas or thongs — as Australians call flip flops — and singlets with plenty of bling. They giggled and looked at each other, waving their sparkly fingernails vaguely straight on.

Further along the street, Claudio asked for directions from a middle-aged man on a stoop, who unfurled an ambiguous hand that José Maria took for a U-turn.

On the third try, a woman advised Claudio bossily, a cluster of nods was exchanged, and we were on our way. 'Brazilians,' I commented wryly, 'never admit if they don't know when they're asked for directions. It even happens when a Brazilian asks in perfect Portuguese.'

'*Com certeza!*' José Maria agreed, after Claudio had laughingly translated for him.

The road up the Serra da Barriga — the name means 'stomach hill' — was so steep that José Maria's tyres slipped on the dirt. When we eventually arrived at the *quilombo*, it was to find it surrounded by a fortification of tall sticks of bamboo with sharpened tips. Was it, I wondered, a faithful reconstruction?

Brazilians know a thing or two about fortifications: across the country you see jagged glass shards or sharp metal prongs cemented to the tops of walls and fences. It strictly demarcates house from street. The order of the house — for those who have houses — is protected from the unruliness of the street. It's not just about security; fences and facades delineate between private and public in a most emphatic manner. It is pervasive and puts me on edge.

Fences in Australia are gentler, more trusting — often absent entirely. My home on Flinders Island is unfenced. Inviting nature in, I guess. And emphasising our freedom and safety. The only Brazil-like barrier in my town is the confronting razor wire erected recently at the wharf to conform to new Australian maritime laws. These were designed to protect against refugees and terrorists, neither of which we are likely to see on Flinders Island well beyond my lifetime.

I'd read that the *quilombo* was a network of a dozen or so villages in the 1600s. The fugitive men and women cleared the land, taking care not to expose their refuge nestled in the bosom of the forest. They planted beans and corn and squash, handy and hardy plants that also grow in my own garden.

Since they had become expert on the plantations of their masters, they also planted sugarcane. Brazilian sugarcane fed 'Europe's sweet tooth', and still grows today in the fields. Over the course of decades, in the below valley and surrounding hills, the rebels built houses, mills, and forges; they made baskets and bowls and clothes. They built churches in which to worship — many had been turned to Catholicism by their masters — and altars dedicated to the Orixás, the ancestral deities of Africa.

Near one such altar, some lithe young men were playing a game of *futebol* on a grassy terrace. A faded sign advised me in both English and Portuguese that the slaves used the terrace as a herb garden: 'Plants and roots were used for cures, baths, and offerings in the cultures of many African and Amerindian peoples,' I read.

The then-dense Atlantic Rainforest provided prolifically. Palms, guava, and papaya — all the fruits that appeared each morning on my hotel breakfast buffet — grew wild. The fugitives traded with local farmers. The thick forest also, of course, provided protection: military police spent years hacking their way through 'the most inhospitable and hunger-ridden wilderness in the world', trying to recover the landowners' 'property'.

Into this forest the *quilombo*'s most famous son, Zumbi, was born. He was captured as a child and taken to live with a priest on the Alagoan coast. Zumbi was fifteen when he escaped and returned to his people, where his uncle, Ganga Zumba, was king.

The community grew, and Zumbi became leader of his *mocambo*, or village, and joined his uncle's war cabinet. Wave after wave of militia was sent by the government in response to the plantation owners' demands to halt the depletion of their labour reserves.

Between 1654 and 1678, more than twenty military expeditions were sent against the *quilombo*. I love that: the slaves held out for *twenty-four* years. I wish I could report otherwise — like any good Australian, I'm a fan of a triumph-of-the-underdog story — but eventually the government forces won. (Although the shape they were in when they did mustn't have been good: they had to get through the fields that the slaves had mined with spikes and skewers, the double stockade that ringed the base of the hill, and the moat that was filled with sharpened sticks.) King Ganga Zumba, tired of war, had sent an envoy clad in animal skins to the state governor to accept an offer of peace. An agreement was signed that called for the villagers to move from the *quilombo* to a nearby valley and surrender all future runaway slaves. Zumbi, who had become his uncle's war leader, was one who objected to the agreement. He suspected — rightly, it transpired — the government of duplicity, and hatched a plan to poison his king.

The reconstructed village fired my imagination: lean dark men drawing their bowstrings taut at one end of the grassy plaza, eye to arrow, carefully sighting a target. Finely muscled and now king, Zumbi shouts a command — in perfectly polished Portuguese, if I were to believe the films about him: 'Fire!'

A few grass-covered huts make up the village now. They all have electric lighting. I was disappointed to see the restaurant closed; I could have done with a cool drink. Perhaps a can of Guaraná, the national fizzy drink that's a natural pick-me-up. But the restaurant looked like it hadn't been open for some time.

At the mill-house, where the rebels ground their *farinha* — manioc flour that's roasted to make a topping that Brazilians are so fond of adding to their food — was a huge mill wheel. A park officer perched on the edge of the big flat oven gestured for me to sign the register that lay open beside him. Every gallery, every museum, palace, and memorial across Brazil has one of these registration books, and although I know it's not rational, I really resent having to sign them. I feel as though I'm being tracked. But there's no avoiding it, ever. In Brazil, the keepers of the register take their jobs very seriously.

For the final siege, the authorities employed *bandeirantes* to supplement their regular military forces, determined to crush the rebels once and for all. The band of mercenaries they hired was the most famous in Brazil. A flexible lot, they made their fortunes 'slaving, prospecting, raiding, and exploring'. The government force of three thousand was joined by the twelve hundred–strong band: eighty-four whites commanded a 'flesh-eating' native force.

From a place called Toculo's Lookout, you can look across the pretty patchwork valley to the Mundaú River. A sign told me that it was from this point that Zumbi commanded the resistance's last stand and that cannons were used for the first time. The sign didn't say that the battle raged for twenty-two days and that hundreds of men, women, and children were killed, and hundreds more captured. The sign didn't say if they were eaten, either, and I wondered who Toculo was.

When Claudio had told me there were no guides, I wondered whether my teacher couldn't be bothered to find one or whether Claudio had wanted to take on the role himself. Both, perhaps. I liked Claudio and had spent the last few weeks being taught Portuguese by him, enough time with him to know he was more party-boy than scholar.

Forgive me for sounding churlish, but I'd been wanting to go to the *quilombo* for some time. I'd even travelled to the wrong town — also called Palmares and in the same region — once with Peter. We had a comic time wandering around trying to ask people where the *quilombo* was. 'Zumbi?' we'd enquire. No one knew what on earth we were talking about. I didn't realise it was the wrong town until we were at home on Flinders Island again. So this time I was determined to get all I could out of it, and in lieu of a guide I had turned to the internet.

It hadn't surprised me that there was a fair bit of information available online: Zumbi is nowadays one of Brazil's national heroes. In São Paulo there is a university named after him; a school in the southern state of Paraná has proudly taken his name. My plane had landed at Maceió's Zumbi dos Palmares International Airport, and on the way to the memorial we had driven past the Zumbi dos Palmares guesthouse and the Zumbi dos Palmares driving school. The day of his death, 20th November, is a national holiday, when white-clad followers of the Orixás gather to set offerings on the smooth surface of the memorial's lake.

All of this is by way of explaining why, when one of the pale-skinned, soccer-sweaty players from the herb garden ran up to me and asked, in English, if I wanted a guide, I stammered out a confused 'no thanks'. Our group had been at the site for a while by then. The signs dotted around were unexpectedly informative — despite being in desperate need of replacement — and my notebook was full. Always one for getting ahead of myself, in my mind we were already at lunch.

When I rejoined the group, Claudio proudly introduced the young man to me as his 'colleague and guide'. I was surprised. My classmates looked at me curiously. Clearly, they had expected me to be delighted.

I trailed the group and the young man self-consciously over to the mill-house. I hadn't caught his name. It might have been Márcio. He pointed to the oven and explained that this was where the rebels cooked the *farinha* flour. He said we must sign the book; Claudio told him we already had.

We were led to the herb garden where Márcio had been playing *futebol*. In an authoritative voice, he said, 'Plants and roots were used for cures, baths, and offerings in the cultures of many African and Amerindian peoples. Understand?' Talk about *déjà vu*.

Márcio led us to Toculo's Lookout. He pointed to the Mundaú River. He told us that they used cannons here for the first time. I asked who Toculo was. Márcio ignored the question and turned back towards the path. Plainly, he didn't know the answer.

Lagging behind, annoyed, I wondered where this resentfulness came from. Perhaps it was the weight of roles, having judgements or assumptions made about me — one of the things, when travelling, it is easier to avoid. I was unsure how this young man had labelled me: a student, dumb, ignorant, an easy mark? It wasn't about the money he would be expecting, although I didn't want to pay for this. It was about showing respect for people. I felt disrespected being fed such twaddle.

The trees were whispering their stories. We were away from lots-of-people sounds. It felt like a million miles from anywhere, not a common experience in Brazil. Down at the lake, I could hear Márcio, who'd taken his cue from the sign that explained the huge Gameleira tree was a member of the *ficus* family. The Orixá of the white Gameleira tree — of all white Gameleria trees — is Irôko. She is one of the deities brought to Brazil by the slaves. I fancied I could sense her presence trying to soothe my irritation from among the shiny leaves.

With a start, I wondered whether the label was, in fact, 'uninterested'. Perhaps the tourists — especially the *estrangeiros* — that Márcio had come across simply didn't care if he was merely repeating the words on the signs. After all, my classmates didn't seem to mind. And Claudio had been astonished when I first asked him about the memorial, which suggested his other students weren't as interested in Brazilian history as me. Perhaps it was the same in Márcio's experience. For me, this memorial was a bit like going to Gallipoli, or the Alamo in Texas, or perhaps even Uluru. It was a symbol, almost sacred. Its importance isn't only about war but national identity. The story of the *quilombo* and the rebel slaves is a crucial chapter in Brazil's national story. How could one not be interested?

So I forced myself to smile at Márcio, handed him a note, and went to find José Maria before the little voice in my head could remind me that sometimes I took myself way too seriously.

~

It took some time for Zumbi dos Palmares to become a national hero. And it wasn't until 2003 that a public holiday to commemorate his death — celebrated as Black Consciousness Day — was decreed.

Public holidays can provide insight into national characters. Those in Australia include the Queen's Birthday, which doesn't fall on Elizabeth Regina's actual birthday, but that doesn't matter because no one takes any notice what the holiday is for anyway. We're too busy drinking beer and watching football. Another holiday that is imported from Britain is Boxing Day: although originally dedicated to the worthy activity of giving unwanted Christmas presents to the poor, it now offers Australians a day dedicated to drink and sport (cricket and yacht-racing). Melbourne Cup Day — officially only a state holiday but increasingly celebrated nationally — is a day for drink and gambling. And the popularity of Anzac Day is growing probably because it provides — after we spare a thought for those who have fought in wars on our behalf — a day for drink; sport; *and*, for some, gambling. On Australia Day, known by some as Invasion Day, there is no sport because it's usually too bloody hot. But there's still sausages (sometimes even prawns) barbecued in the backyard or down the beach, with a lot of cold beer in the esky, as Australians call their coolers or ice-boxes. Yet aside from Carnaval, Brazil's national days are more sombre. Brazil commemorates their national saint on Our Lady of Aparecida Day, workers on Labour Day, and — newly but not yet pervasively — the aforementioned Black Consciousness Day. The republican rebel Tiradentes is commemorated on the anniversary of his being executed by the imperial government. On both Republic Day and Independence Day, folk flood onto the streets to wave flags and watch parades of the armed forces in their crisp dress uniforms, although often this is followed by *churrasco*, as Brazilians call their barbecue. Australians celebrate and Brazilians observe Christmas and Easter. And although our current Christian-dominated government might find the notion of allocating public holidays to Corpus Christi, All Souls, and All Saints Days attractive — these, too, are observed in Brazil — the Christian God knows that Australians would likely dedicate them to drinking and sport.

The date of 13th May, the day that the Golden Law abolished slavery in Brazil, isn't celebrated as a holiday. Instead, activists use the day to highlight ongoing inequality between racial groups. The abolition of slavery was popular with the people, but was pretty much forced on those in power by those countries around the world who had enacted such laws already. That was more or less every country except King Leopold's Congo. And the abolition of slavery wasn't all that empowering. Had I been a slave freed by the law of 1888, I'd most likely have found myself homeless and out of work; the landowners showed a preference for encouraging immigration to supply their labour needs rather than employing their former slaves. And the freedom on offer was a limited freedom. There would have been things forbidden to me by law, such as worship of my chosen deities (unless that was the Christian God) or the play of capoeira, the graceful, acrobatic combination of martial art, dance, and game. In these ways and more, post-abolition Afro-Brazilians were still denied their cultural heritage. I guess it's understandable they prefer to celebrate the day of Zumbi's last courageous stand.

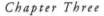

Chapter Three

The Sisterhood
of Good Death

CACHOEIRA, BAHIA

*'She recalled the mangled saints' statues tied to people's roofs
in punishment for their poor service. Reverence was always
conditional.'* Frances de Pontes Peebles

From the edge of the crowd, I watched as the procession of black women
came out of the red house in billows of white, like smoke pouring from a
burning building.

They held long white candlesticks. Their heads were wrapped in white
scarves and their skirts fell to their knees in virginal waves. Pressing closer
to the wall, I tried to give them more room to haul their creaking bones
up the step that separated the small plaza from the chapel.

Proudly bearing the ornately carved 'Staff of the Nossa Senhora', the
Provedora led her Sisters to the small stone chapel. With the crowd of
well-wishers, I squeezed inside to witness the Sisters mourn, as they do
each year, the passing of Our Lady of Good Death. Some of the women
were so dark that their blood seemed undiluted by time, and despite the

immigration policies designed to 'whiten' Brazil that were in place in the late nineteenth and early twentieth centuries.

In Australia, it is not considered politically correct to talk about someone's skin colour. That doesn't mean there's no racism. In the United States, you are either black or you are white. But in Brazil, talking about skin colour is a part of everyday life, and the range of skin colours recognised is impressive.

These days, the census is limited to five categories of race and colour, but in 1976, the Brazilian Institute of Geography and Statistics asked Brazilians themselves to describe their colour. In the census, Brazilians came up with one hundred and thirty-four different one-word or hyphenated descriptions of their own colour. The list included black, dusky, toasted, florid, cinnamon, reddish, lily, and coffee-with-milk. My personal favourites are 'no doubt about it' and '*burro* running away'. The latter, with its reference to a donkey, a *burro*, apparently indicates a dubious ancestry.

On Copacabana Beach, a sign displays different levels of recommended sun protection for '*mulatos e negros*', '*morenos escuros*', '*morenos claros*', and '*ruivos e loiros*', as the different skin-colour groupings are called. A Brazilian artist is working on a project to match her models' skins to the Pantone paint company's colour chart.

Three years earlier, I'd been captivated by the words 'Irmandade da Boa Morte' ('the Sisterhood of Good Death'), but frustrated by its closed doors. The words curled around a large wooden disk, like a guild's motto, above a tall arched doorway. This time I had returned to the town of Cachoeira for the Festival of Good Death.

The concept of a 'good' death befuddled me. In the West (interesting, isn't it, how a few rich countries managed to hijack an entire compass point), we regard death as bad. It is frightening, even for — and this is especially curious — many of those with faith. In the great binary world we live in, death is in opposition to life, like good or bad, light or dark. Death is a door through which we do not want to walk. Death is a shadow. Poets can make death beautiful, yet there-but-for-the-grace go the rest of us. So I had hopped on a bus to Cachoeira, which is about two hours inland from the original capital Salvador, to find out what this notion of a good death was.

Inside the chapel, the Sisters' voices swelled with hymn, their skins attesting their slave heritage. This first Mass of the three-day festival mourns the passing of the Sisters' saint, Our Lady of Good Death. On a litter rested the statue of the saint. The image — I would call it a statue but Brazilians would call it, her, an *imagem* — lay face up, in a cocoon of satin and tulle. Pale and brunette, she was surrounded by white-clad, slate-skinned Sisters. The Provedora kept one plump hand firmly wrapped around the staff, while with the other she fussed with the folds of the white shroud that draped over the litter.

Before travelling in Brazil, I hadn't grasped the importance of the saints in Catholicism. But they play a greater role in everyday life in Brazil than elsewhere. The saints are front and centre; their help is sought constantly. The Vatican doesn't seem so keen on this shifting of focus away from God and from guilt, but I find it refreshing.

The famous Brazilian sociologist Gilberto Freyre also found it a phenomenon worth commenting on. From the moment a Brazilian is born, he noted, 'Saint Joseph rocked the baby's cradle; Saint Anne lulled it to sleep at its nurse's breast; Saint Benedict protected it from being stung by great poisonous ants.' And of the saints, Our Lady, the Nossa Senhora who goes by many titles — including Our Lady of Good Death — is the most lauded in Brazil.

Images of a saint can be worth a lot of money. A recent Italian film told the story of a town whose saint was stolen. The thieves planned to sell it and get rich, but the entire town mobilised, like an army, and first trapped then executed the thieves.

Portugal had — has — a long tradition of brotherhoods and sisterhoods that were firmly ensconced in the bosom of the Church. Each was devoted to a particular saint and to a form of charitable work. African slaves were also encouraged to form fraternities. One of their common and publicly stated missions was to raise funds to provide decent Christian burials for their members, families, and friends. For the slaves, the organisations served clandestine purposes as well: secretly, these black fraternities would act as credit unions, some of them raising funds to emancipate their fellow slaves.

Historically, black fraternities also provided cover for the practise of forbidden African traditions and rituals, such as the potentially deadly dance-game capoeira and the religious ceremonies of Candomblé, which involve the worship of African deities, called Orixás. Until recently, both the dance-game and celebration and worship of African deities were illegal, which must have been really difficult, especially for those in Northeastern Brazil, where such worship is quite pervasive. Even now, some of the Sisters aren't comfortable discussing their connection with the Orixás, even if they are the leaders of their own *terreiros* (as temples are called in Candomblé).

The Sisters' grief this year mourned more than their saint. Just ten days before, their leader had walked the passageway to heaven. Dona Estelita was one hundred and five when she died, and had been a Sister for nearly fifty years. I'd heard with some dismay before I arrived that the celebratory, profane part of the *festa* had been cancelled. The party would have filled Cachoeira's cobbled streets with beer cans and samba dancing for two days after the religious observances were concluded. I've always been a particular fan of the word 'profane', with its connotations of naughtiness; an appropriate antidote for guilt.

The new Juíza Perpétua (it means Perpetual Judge — what was I saying about judgement and guilt?) was Dona Filhinha. 'She has one hundred and seven years,' one of the Sisters told me, so it could be some time before samba washes through the town streets once again.

In English, we refer to age as if it were a state of being or, perhaps, a quality. We 'are' a given age, as we 'are' short, tall, or pretty. In English, age seems solid, incontrovertible. In the Portuguese language, as with Spanish, age is referred to as something one 'has'. In Portuguese, age is imbued with preciousness, as if one holds it carefully in one's hands, something

46

that might be dropped or spilled. When one has one hundred and seven years, one would, I imagine, not want to spill a drop.

The Provedora, who was still fussing with the folds of the image's shroud, is the second in charge of the Sisterhood of Good Death. She is the 'provider', responsible for the festival, and the keeper of the *bastão*, the staff that holds the ritualistic power, the 'force of the Sisterhood'. I watched as, in the chapel next to her, the Sisterhood's treasurer smoothed the statue's white veil.

Brazilians are big on hierarchy and complex liturgy. My eyes began to burn as the priest swung his incense burner in great billowy arcs. Usually I try to leave a service before the incense, but I was jammed in. Only by looking at the screens of digital cameras held high could I even see the ritual. Singing once again, the Sisters formed up around their saint's litter. They turned towards us and waited for the crowd of snap-happy tourists to clear a path. When they didn't, four white-suited litter-bearers started forward, making their way down the aisle as if dredging a channel in a silt-filled river.

A man in a cream jungle suit stepped up onto one of the wooden pews, eyes trained on his camcorder. One of the Sisters swatted him as she passed, with a chubby, toffee-coloured hand. Then I was sucked outside by a tide of onlookers, who were unconcerned with the mere protocol of letting the Sisters leave first. I hauled myself behind a column as the mob turned, realising they had nothing to photograph: they had left the Sisters in their wake.

From the plaza, the Nossa Senhora was borne away to lead a pilgrimage around the town, accompanied by those Sisters able enough. Most of the tourists disappeared into the night to find their buses for the two-hour journey back to Salvador. The *festa* is popular with African Americans on personal pilgrimages; they come to get in touch with their roots. Earlier in the evening, I'd watched through the open shutters of the red house that is the Sisterhood's headquarters as they had flocked around the Sisters like paparazzi. I admired the women's patience: all I could hear was a chorus of North American accents with an annoying refrain of 'I want'.

'I want a picture with her,' cried a woman in white pedal-pushers, pointing to an especially aged Sister and handing her camera to her friend.

'I want to know, does she live upstairs?' someone in a snowy sundress asked of her tour guide, whose certification hung like a noose around her neck.

'Look, honey!' called a man to his wife. 'I want to show you this.' He was pointing to a wall of Sisters' portraits. 'Do you think they make these in postcards?'

Maybe I'm being ornery: African Americans have been good to the Sisters. They helped buy the buildings that house the Sisterhood's headquarters, and the museum and church below. Their donations also helped fund the fight against the Church after Padre Hélio, Cacheoira's priest, confiscated the Sisters' liturgical items in 1989. He was, locals told the newspapers, jealous of the Sisters' growing fame. He refused to release the sacred articles for that year's festival. An outraged lawyer, funded by a raft of equally outraged African Americans, took the Church to court. For ten years, the priest refused to let the Sisters hold their opening Mass in the Capela D'Ajuda; for ten years, he refused to say Mass for them at all. Talk about ornery.

There has always been tension between the black and white in the Brazilian Church. For the most part, black Catholics were denied access to white fraternities. It is thought that Padre Hélio wouldn't have taken a set against the Sisterhood if the Sisters were white. When the first court found for the Sisters, the Church appealed. When the appeal also found for the Sisters, Padre Hélio had no option but to return their treasured pieces. Whether they allow him to say their Masses today because they are generous or because they don't have a choice, I don't know; it's not a topic anyone likes to discuss. To me, his actions seem disrespectful — unforgivable even.

Gilberto Freyre, the sociologist, became famous for his theory that Brazil was a 'racial democracy'. He said that because of inter-marriage between whites, *índios*, and African slaves, Brazil didn't have the racial divisions and violence that could be seen, for instance, in the United States. Freyre — who is commemorated by a museum in the city of Recife — believed miscegenation would result in a superior 'meta-race' of Brazilians. But, as most scholars now acknowledge, his theories promoted the lightening of Brazil's skin. His theories also ignore the fact that Brazil's least prosperous states, those in the Northeast, have vastly higher populations of black descendants that those in the South, and that the *favelas* are mostly black and *mulatto*. And, like the fraternities of today, the favelas tend to be self-segregated.

As with celebrations the world over, food is fundamental to Brazilian festivals. The first night of the Festa da Boa Morte features white-coloured food. White food is associated with the Candomblé god Oxalá, and the Sisters throw their doors open to all who wish to join the meal.

When I finally gained entrance to the red house, I found the banquet for the Sisters laid out on a long table. As I queued to be served from the kitchen, my mouth was watering: there were plates of fish-and-potato pie, bowls of bread and salads, fried fish, and fried *mandioca*, the root vegetable that is ubiquitous in Brazil. There was enough rice to feed a small nation, though there was none of the *dendê* oil that lights up many an Afro-Brazilian dish like a sunset. The Sisters said two prayers and tucked in. Their ability to ignore the unrelenting chirrup of cameras was amazing. I noticed that the sisters were served according to age — there's always a hierarchy in Brazil. It didn't matter that I'd be one of the last served. Hierarchy linked to age, I can deal with.

In Cachoeira, you can stay in a converted convent. The rooms are comfortable, though simple, as you would expect of a convent. The building's wings surround a stone plaza, where a pool has been put in to help guests combat the heat. But when I stayed, the pool was empty, since technically — if not practically — it was winter.

After a huge breakfast (breakfasts are prized in Brazil; one hotel in Foz do Iguaçu advertises that it offers 170 items on its breakfast buffet, and it is no idle boast), I left the convent and arrived at the Sisters' house sweating. The door was open, and I skirted a television crew filming an interview with some of the more energetic Sisters. Lining the walls, and once again costumed in white, several other Sisters were holding court. Each clutched the looping handles of a soft red bag. A plump, bespectacled Sister waved, motioning me into the seat next to hers, which looked as if carved from ice. She continued to nod at a woman who spoke to her in English loudly and gestured often. The Sister — who I am sure didn't understand a word — nodded and smiled and opened her bag, into which the woman dutifully dropped a note. Unable to resist the snow-soft look of the Sister's skirt, I furtively brushed my hand against it, to find it firm with starch.

The Sisters' 'look' is synonymous with the state of Bahia. The state's tourism authorities have commandeered this image: white or brightly coloured bulbous skirts, white lacy blouses that contrast starkly with dark skin, heads swathed in top-knotted scarves. They use it to promote Bahia as a tourist destination. You see women similarly attired in Candomblé ceremonies, selling the local delicacy, *acarajé*, on street corners, and wandering the streets of Salvador's historic centre offering to pose for your camera. The use of the image by state authorities is a source of ongoing controversy, but judging by the number of government and media representatives in town, it appeared the Sisterhood of Good Death weren't among the most strenuous objectors.

Only twenty-two of us remain, the Sister told me, stroking her red bag. The rural dialect she used was a kind of shorthand that, for a few minutes, had me convinced she wasn't speaking Portuguese at all. In the past, there have been up to two hundred members, she continued. To join, one must be over forty and a widow. Or never married, she added. This last was an afterthought, as almost everybody marries in Brazil. It's quite a handy organisation, I thought, knowing from experience that there was little use for a lone woman in this country.

The second day of the *festa*, she continued, would begin in the evening with a funeral Mass for Nossa Santinha, 'our Little Saint' — she used the diminutive. Tomorrow she ascends, so she has her good death, and we celebrate, but our leader has died and the celebrations will not be as usual. '*Entendeu?*' Brazilians have so little faith in foreigners' ability to understand Portuguese they constantly ask if you understand. She smiled broadly and her red bag gaped open. I dropped some *reais* into it and dutifully took a photo of her before she turned to her next well-wisher.

I wandered off to the market that often blocks a half-dozen of a Brazilian town's streets. There were rows and rows of DVDs on folding tables, with more hanging from poles. Packages of tarpaulins were arranged in stacks between hammers and files and sharp-toothed saws. Bouquets of aromatic herbs hung above piles of the bright-orange mounds of tiny dried shrimps that flavour so many Bahian dishes. Frying pans dangled from hooks above more DVDs in plastic sheaths, blow-up swimming pools, and bed sheets. Unfurling roll after roll of dress fabric onto the pavement, a customer tilted her head, squinting at patterns too floral for my taste. Under a tree, a gaunt-looking horse waited, every so often flicking his tail at a persistent fly.

Back at the Sisters' church, the crowds were gathering again. Being a Brazilian event, there was a roped-off area, reserving the best view for some privileged few. I watched people glide past the gatekeeper, greeting him perfunctorily. Apart from the fact that they were better dressed than we tourists in our shirts and shorts, I couldn't tell what made them special. It was as if they had invisible credentials hanging around their necks. Most of them were light-skinned.

I approached the entry to see the stage better, and the dark-suited man moved to block me. My hackles rose. In Australia, we're used to the idea of discrimination at, say, a ticketed event, where the more expensive seats are the better seats. Apart from that, Australians are obsessed with egalitarianism; we assume we have the right to equality (although refugees are generally excluded from that favour). Often in Brazil I've had to recalibrate my outrage meter when faced with seemingly un-egalitarian behaviour. I have to remind myself that Australia's veneer of equality — like that across the 'West' — is just that, a veneer. And, to be honest, I'm more accustomed to being inside the arena of privilege than outside it.

The first time I noticed privilege working in Brazil, I'd been sitting on a bottom-numbing bench in the federal police office for three hours, where I had been told to wait for computers to be fixed so I could have my visa extended. A couple, dressed in the height of Milan fashion, waltzed in. They shook hands with the suddenly smiling officer. He suggested they get a coffee, relax, just leave their paperwork with him, and as soon as the computers were fixed, it would be ready. I hadn't noticed money changing hands, but maybe it did. Such favours don't always require money in Brazil, though. Other rewards, such as family ties and social position, work well too. Privilege and shortcuts are common practice for some in Brazil. The practice has a name that comes from the words for 'to find a way': *jeitinho*. Perhaps in Australia we have it too, but better disguised. Or does familiarity makes me blind to it? 'One is unable to notice something because it is always before one's eyes,' as Wittgenstein said.

For the feast on day three of the Festival of Good Death, the Sisters fed us Brazil's national dish, *feijoada*. The kitchen staff had cooked up huge vats of the aromatic and artery-clogging stew of pork and rice and beans. Like most Brazilian food, they topped it with a mugful of crunchy *farinha*. I was at the back of the queue, and the crowd had begun to thin when I took my plate outside to sit on the bluestone plaza steps. My mind was awash with thoughts about hierarchies and privilege and the dispute between Padre Hélio and the Sisterhood — it was dubbed a 'Holy War' by the press. I was dabbing a tissue ineffectively at some beans that had slopped onto my white blouse when my attention was snagged by a familiar, even universal, scene. Out of the door of the red house tumbled a gaggle of teenage girls in tight shorts and tank tops rife with bling. As so often happens at home, a swaggering crew of teenage boys in sagging jeans were being sucked along in their wake.

~

A 'good death', I learnt, is more about the burial and the soul getting to heaven than the death itself. Manner of burial, of course, is a near-universal human concern. Personally, I'd like to be cremated — after my useful bits are recycled — with my ashes scattered over Franklin Sound, where the sea nestles (or rages) among the islands that I love to see every day at home.

The stories my father read taught me early that burial, or the treatment of bones, is especially important to Australia's Indigenous peoples. Although I shouldn't generalise when it comes to the beliefs of Indigenous Australians, I think this pertains to most groups' beliefs: Aboriginal remains must be returned to their Country, and stay there, or the spirit will not be able to rest. But for the best part of two centuries, bones were stolen in the name of science and exported to museums around the world. It wasn't statues or other precious artefacts, although I find that abhorrent too; these were people's ancestors.

In his essay 'Because It's Your Country', Martin Thomas describes documentary footage filmed by a National Geographic expedition in Arnhem Land, in Australia's far north, in the 1940s. The footage shows a scene that was common, though the recording of it was not: an anthropologist stealing bones that had been interred in a cave in the individual's ancestral country. Obviously knowing that his actions were objectionable, the white man waited until his Indigenous guides were sleeping before going to the burial place and stealing the bones, hiding them in an ammunition crate. What an astonishing lack of respect for the very culture they were studying. My outrage meter was brimming, reading the essay.

Everywhere my mind was turning lately seemed to emphasise the utter disregard some humans have for others. Henry the Navigator thought he had some right — religious duty and/or fiscal need — to enslave as many of the often trusting people of Africa as his minions could lay their hands on. Even being a member of the same church, it would seem, does not provide you immunity from being preyed upon by other, more powerful people putting their 'right' before yours. Padre Hélio, in taking things sacred to the Sisters, displayed what for me was another consummate example of profound disrespect. Colonialism, perhaps, in miniature.

Chapter Four

Goddess of the Sea

SALVADOR, BAHIA

'He believed in spirits, and in fate.' John Updike

In Brazil, heroines are harder to find than heroes. Gender equality doesn't run very deep or straight — at least public gender equality. The major roles in the national story — those lauded, memorialised, and celebrated — tend, fairly pervasively, to have been filled by men. Female role models, women famous for something other than appearing in films and *telenovelas* or on catwalks, are not conspicuous. Brazil's first female president (who came before Australia's first female prime minister), Dilma Rousseff, despite seeming to me like a suitable candidate for a heroine, doesn't seem to be so regarded by most Brazilians — at least not anymore. She was nominated as successor to the previous, super-popular president, nicknamed '*Lula*', or 'Squid', who reached the maximum number of terms he could run. ('Squid': I love it. Australia is a nation of nicknamers, but no politician called Squid would see a first term, let alone two.) Rousseff won her second term, though it was a much harder-fought election than her first. After a popular start, she has been lumped into the category tarred 'politicians', with her male cohorts, rather than remaining 'female revolutionary', as she started out. It certainly looks as though she's stopped trying to raise the numbers of women in government: the percentage of female ministers in her latest cabinet has fallen from twenty-eight per cent to fifteen per cent. She has only filled sixteen per cent of posts to the judiciary with women.

A quick email poll of my Brazilian friends named heroines such as Princess Isabel, who signed the Golden Law that abolished slavery in 1888. The great Brazilian poet Cecília Meireles and the freedom fighter Anita Garibaldi were also nominated. Chica da Silva, the slave-turned-diamond-mogul, certainly qualifies as a Brazilian heroine — we all love a rags-to-riches story. Infamous television personality and now media magnate Xuxa has also inspired several generations of *brasileiras*. Gisele Bündchen, a model and entrepreneur who is number fifty-six on the *Forbes* 'most powerful celebrities' list, is admired for her fame and fortune. Foreigners might suggest Carmen Miranda, who rose to international fame as an actress and comedian; there is a tiny and ill-funded museum in Rio de Janeiro dedicated to Miranda, who was born in Portugal.

Two female figures who have leading roles in the national story and attract a lot of attention in Brazil are the national patron saint, Nossa Senhora Aparecida, and the Orixá Yemanjá, goddess of the sea and patroness of the state of Bahia. The influence of these two figures on Brazilians varies, partly according to whether one lives in the North or the South.

Fireworks had been announcing the imminent start of the Festa da Yemanjá for some time before I hauled myself out of bed. It was five in the morning, still dark. Good thing I'd left Peter at home, he not being one for waking at five for a goddess. I'd been looking forward to this day since I first heard about it the previous year. 'The day for the sea goddess is big for the *terreiros*,' a hotel receptionist told me. He was undergoing his initiation as a *filho de santo*, as male 'children of the gods' are called. Candomblé is a mediumistic religion where the gods come to visit, possessing or 'riding' their medium-conduits — their children. So I'd made a mental note to be in Salvador for the festival one year and here I was, dragging myself onto the streets of Rio Vermelho in the dark.

Salvador is to Candomblé as Rome is to Catholicism. Not, you'll understand, a precise comparison, but you get the general idea. There are 1,155 *terreiros*, as Candomblé temples are called, mapped in the city. At risk of stating the obvious, that's a lot of temples.

Candomblé is firmly rooted in African culture. Some of the ancient gods snuck aboard — or otherwise accompanied — Henry the Navigator's caravels as they were loaded with their human cargo. These stowaways (or chaperones), unnoticed by the Portuguese crewmen, are shared by a number of similarly rooted syncretic religions, such as Santería, Umbanda, and Voodoun.

In some religions deities were never human, but the African Orixás did once walk the earth. Because they were human, the gods are not always good; they can be capricious. Each Orixá is responsible for at least one realm or pursuit: woods, rivers, hunting, war, metal, the sky. There's an Orixá for every element of the universe. Yemanjá's realm is the sea. If religion is a way of explaining, of making sense of the world, those that have multiple deities, each with their own area of responsibility, make the most sense to me.

Yemanjá, Iemanjá, Yemoja. Her name varies according to language, region, and religion. Yemanjá was once the Queen of Saki, a Yoruba town in what today is Nigeria. The younger wife of Oxalá, greatest of all Orixás, she gave birth to most of the other Orixás, and so she is also goddess of motherhood. She protects mothers, children, and fishermen, as well as — somewhat inexplicably to me — business enterprises. Yemanjá is warm, maternal, cool, and collected, and — perhaps more than any of her children — stable. Yet like all Orixás, she has human characteristics:

idiosyncrasies and desires that demand to be fed. Gifts of food and trinkets are offered to encourage her benevolence and care.

Yemanjá is worshipped in many of the Afro-Brazilian religions, including in Candomblé, which is the prevailing African religion in Salvador. The central tenet of these religions is that the gods can appear right there in front of you; the pantheon of gods regularly call to, and manifest in, their followers. Yemanjá is not omniscient or always present; when she appears, she calls upon one (or more) of her 'children' to serve, and after the 'child' responds by performing suitable offerings and prayers, Yemanjá borrows that body to get about in. For someone brought up on a bland diet of atheism with an underscore of Christianity, and with an interest in how people explain and make sense of the world, it was bound to excite.

The streets of Rio Vermelho — this suburb of Salvador is named 'red river' because of the *índio* blood spilled here — were already lined with vendors. Some were still shoving cans into white foam boxes, while others waited patiently for the appearance of the coffee cart, or the Kombi van from which they'd buy ice. A few lucky souls were still asleep in their cars.

A gentle wave of white-clad bodies was trickling from side-street tributaries, and surging in one direction to join the main channel of worshippers. We were all heading for the same point: where the Casa de Yemanjá overlooks the sea.

Candomblé lore is rich and specific: each Orixá has a strict set of favourites and foibles, likes and dislikes. Yemanjá's colours are blue and white; her metal is silver; her candle, white; her animal, the fish. In Rio de Janeiro, she is patroness of New Year's Eve, and offerings are made to her on the surface of Guanabara Bay. In Bahia, her day is 2nd February.

Of the extensive range of religions on offer in Brazil, if I chose one to follow it would be Candomblé. I find the colour and movement, the stories and characters, quite mesmerising. Of the pantheon of gods who manifest in the bodies of initiates at ceremonies, and in priests and priestesses who predict and heal, if I were a follower of Candomblé I would want Yemanjá to be the deity who 'takes my head'. When they manifest in earthly form, the Orixás carry props, and Yemanjá's are suitable for the adventuress I like to style myself: on the earth she wears a sword and a bracelet. She, too, likes coconut pudding and papaya. My time in Brazil having cured me of wearing all black, I have reverted to my childhood favourite: blue. That blue would be Yemanjá's colour makes sense, since she is goddess of the sea. Living on an island, I'm surrounded by sea. Peter, ever flexible work-wise, now dives into its depths for a living, harvesting abalone from the seabeds. If she were my goddess, she might keep him safe.

That Yemanjá's favourite drink is champagne would surely seal my fate.

But it doesn't work that way. The initiation period is long, the study intense, and who will take your head is determined by divination, by the throwing of the cowrie shells. The cowrie shells are thrown by a priest or priestess as they are possessed by their god. Thus, who your gods are is determined by gods themselves.

Brazilian religious events favour white apparel. So, not wanting to stand out more than absolutely necessary, I had dressed in a white muslin blouse and denim shorts. I chose these particular shorts because they had only a small scattering of bling on the pockets, instead of all over them. Like most around me, there were Havaianas on my feet. I'd not been a fan of Brazil's national footwear — despite their popularity in Australia — until I grew to know Brazil. They're great in a tropical climate.

Heading for the beach, where the festivities would take place, a woman in her thirties quickly overtook me. Her hair was plaited into cornrows and her arms were wrapped around a basket of blue and white flowers. A mother dodged around me, one hand holding her daughter's wrist, a blue-and-white iced cake in the other.

Instead of being able to see sand when I turned a corner, the beach was covered by a human mosaic of blue and white. Colour-coordinated gazebo tents had been erected sometime between when I was there the previous evening and the leading edge of dawn.

In front of some of the tents, *rodas* (circles of people) had formed. Each circle surrounded a dancer, a 'horse', as you are called when an Orixá has your head. A tinny drum beat a tight staccato: *duh-da, duh-da, duh-da-da*. The Orixá — I wasn't familiar enough with the gods to recognise which it was — danced in the circle, upper body swaying up and down, like a horse prancing. The audience held their palms aloft to better catch the *axé*, the power or energy that makes up the world and emanates from the gods. The singers surrounding the god sang in what could have been Yoruba, adding to the energy that was shaking off the darkness.

In the strengthening light, I could see that umbrellas and gazebos speckled the beach. Beside each was an altar, and inside were styrofoam ice boxes, baskets of flowers, and one or more drums. It seemed like every second gazebo sheltered a drummer leading a *roda*. White-clad worshippers spilled out of those tents, clapping and singing ancient songs, adding to the manic, joyful cacophony. Every so often, my ears could pick out the high clank of a cowbell. The whole scene was a language that everyone on the beach understood but me. In the depths of my soul, there it was again: wonder.

Rio Vermelho's beach curves like a sleek fish's tail and is cradled by the road. A queue of people, perhaps one hundred metres long, now inched toward the Casa de Yemanjá. Most were holding flowers. The line was flanked by vendors, and it would triple in length later in the day. People also lined up at flower stands, choosing long-stemmed gladioli, multi-coloured roses, or yellow carnations. But the offerings were not restricted to flowers. In the sun-wrinkled arms of one grandmother was a woven basket; on Flinders Island, such bounty would be prized as a raffle hamper. On a bed of white satin, she had arranged brushes and combs; beads and cosmetics; several small, smiling dolls; lip-gloss; a mirror; and small cakes of soap. It was a fine offering for her often-vain goddess.

Having visited the goddess' small shrine the evening before, it was evident to me that it was not going to hold all of the offerings. I wondered where they were being put.

There was plenty to amuse those waiting in line. Despite the early hour, a party of bare-chested lads — they're called *moços* — danced expertly to rap next to a ghetto-blaster, beer cans in hand. Not looking inclined to join the queue with a bunch of flowers, they could have been celebrating the goddess in their own way, but in Brazil any excuse is a good excuse for a party.

As I got closer to the shrine, the Casa, it became apparent that the line snaked past it. A battered Kombi pulled into a roped-off area, and a Candomblé troop tumbled out. Leaving a couple of fresh-faced men to lift out two huge baskets of blooms, a young woman walked around to open the passenger side for her Mãe de Santo — the 'mother of the saints'. The head of the *terreiro* was a thin old woman. Women in Brazil seem to move from pre-child-bearing slimness through plump middle years and wind up thin with age. The Mãe held a silver cowbell in one bony hand that she rattled maniacally, clearing a path. Another initiate announced the arrival of the members of his *terreiro*, sending two rockets skyward from a hand-held launcher. The group pushed past the queue with calm authority and were swallowed up by the crowd.

The seawall provided a good view of the bay: it was bobbing with all manner of vessels, from stubby fishing boats to state-of-the-art watercraft. A rotund man, perhaps in his late thirties, was dressed as a Son of Gandhi, the famous Salvadorian Carnaval group. Loops of beads cascaded down his chest, each bead a dollop of sapphire or salt. I watched him pass his basket of pale carnations to the boat boy and, one hand holding his shirts out of the water, turn and plonk his bottom over the gunwale, inching himself backwards and onto the bench. The boy handed him the basket, which he settled on his paunch and was rowed from the shore.

The sun suddenly crested the roof of the Catholic Church next door to the Casa, and I had to grope for my sunglasses. They would mark me out further as a stranger, but I probably wasn't fooling anyone anyway; the camera was a giveaway, let alone the notebook.

Over the plaza, between the church and the kiosks from which local fishermen sold their wares, a broad roof had been thatched with palm fronds. Under the thatch stood a statue of Yemanjá. She had dark tresses tumbling down her back and an evening dress of silvery scales that caught the sunlight and sparkled like a mirror-ball. If you don't want to hire a rowboat to take you and your offering out to sea, you can leave it in the cordoned-off area next to the statue. It is a waiting room for baskets and blooms. From there, attendants will transfer them to the beach and onto boats. On the other side of the barrier I could see carnations and chrysanthemums. Roses in red, white, and yellow, some with the artificial tinge of blue. Gladioli, lilies, daisies, and cornflowers; statices for remembrance, and sweet-smelling lisianthuses. And if the fragrance from the flowers isn't enough, the attendants stop by periodically and spray their charges, wielding perfume dispensers like pump-action shotguns. Yemanjá must like her odours strong.

Not everyone is as enamoured of the Afro-Brazilian religions as I am. Until 1985, the practice of Candomblé was forbidden by law. Even in 2014, a Brazilian judge ruled that the Afro-Brazilian religions were not religions because they have no central text, and lack 'a hierarchical structure and a God to be worshipped'. Candomblé has also suffered attacks from other religions, most especially the fast-growing Evangelicalism, some adherents of which have violated Candomblé *terreiros*, destroyed sacred items, and abused Afro-Brazilian religious leaders on blogs and on YouTube.

Over the centuries, Candomblé has become heavily influenced by Catholicism. Because they were forbidden from worshipping their Orixás, followers of the African deities camouflaged their devotions by matching each deity with a Catholic saint. Yemanjá is linked to Our Lady of Immaculate Conception.

And like Candomblé itself, the goddess is hard to pin down. She appears in a number of guises. Inside the Casa, a mural of Yemanjá depicts her with hair like a blue-and-gold peacock's feathers, swimming with a golden-scaled tail. On the altar in the corner, she is all elegance in shimmering silver. You can buy life-size statues of her in the African market in Salvador in a long, flowing white gown or wearing blue. From a street vendor, I had bought a silver statue the size of a small sardine in perhaps her most common pose: arms are open like Rio's Christ, right leg slightly forward, left hip jutting out sexily. That was new for me — I'd never thought of a god's potential to be sexy.

But surely Yemanjá is most compelling in her flamboyant ceremonial dress. When she mounts her 'horses' and dances in the *rodas* or *terreiros* she dresses in bulbous skirts, usually blue. The skirts accentuate her 'sexually potent buttocks', according to anthropologists. Indeed, big bums are prized in Brazil, I have noted with relief and admiration. When she dresses for a ceremony, Yemanjá's backside is enhanced by at least two heavily starched petticoats. A fringe of crystal beads generally falls from her silvery crown to veil her face. Knobbly metal symbols hang from a chain at her waist. Holding a sword and a round metal fan with a mirror in the centre, she shakes bracelets, armlets, and bangles in an eerie, captivating dance.

Outside the Casa, two scaffolding towers provided platforms for the cameras that televise the *festa* live throughout Brazil. In the shade of the platforms, three *curandeiros*, or healers, had set up tables. One was a man in white muslin with blue beads and a cap that looked like one of my grandmother's lace doilies. He brushed me lightly with a blessing, running a wet branch of leaves up and down my body and then sprinkling my skull with cleansing popcorn. Was that little bit of specialness I felt my imagination, or was the air indeed imbued with magic?

Beyond the Casa is a low rocky point. To get to it, I had to weave my way through an obstacle course that was a haphazardly erected food court. A short man had placed a flower basket on a plastic seat as if it were an honoured guest. In the basket he had arranged a long fried fish and three cans of beer around a small statue of Yemanjá. No problems with idol worship here. He had wrapped the gift in cellophane. There was a beer in his hand and an aromatic plate of *rabada* in front of him. Although tempted by the suggestion of oxtail stew for breakfast, I continued past.

The sea was licking at the edges of the pockmarked rocks as a child might savour an ice-cream. On the furthest point stood a tall woman, sheathed in a cream dress that would not be out of place next to a groom at the altar. As she threw roses into the water, in long, languorous arcs, I felt a sense of calm envelope me. She could have been the goddess herself. One by one, they swept through the air to float, red, yellow, and white, on the mercury-tinged surface.

Returning to the throng, I found the mood had changed. It took me a few minutes to realise what was missing: the allure and authority of the Candomblé. The queue was longer and younger, still moving at a glacial pace. More were now clad in shorts and shirts than robes or skirts. They clutched single flowers rather than baskets. Yemanjá's children, those whose heads she possessed, were gone. They had 'fed' her, honoured her on her special day. They had, they hoped, appeased her with their offerings so that she would provide them with help during the year to come. They'd done this at dawn, as is the traditional time to honour her, and then disappeared. They had, it seemed, retreated to their *terreiros* and left the day to the more fickle, and to the noisy, beer-sodden street party that inevitably followed.

~

The travel writer and novelist Graham Greene found travel wearisome — something that I, especially when coming across events as entrancing as the Festa de Yemanjá, find hard to grasp. I might be tempted to make a tart retort, but you wouldn't do that to Graham Greene, would you?

Why do you like to travel so much? The question is evident on the faces of friends as I leave home again; most are too polite to actually ask. As if it might be mistaken for criticism.

Trying to answer them without sounding pompous and ponderous is difficult. Trying to add coherence into the mix starts doing something strange to my metaphors. Is travel for me like drugs for a junkie? Perhaps:

I don't know what that feels like. A sense of restlessness builds up in me, but it's more like an absence that slowly intensifies. A nagging feeling: like missing a loved one, perhaps. Like the persistent heaviness of your head the morning after a glass-too-many of red wine, but it gets worse, not better, with time. It is an overwhelming desire to see new terrain, to see how others live and what they do to make sense of this world.

Which presents another conundrum, like that complex problem in maths that never seems to get to a point of resolution. Because home is a great place to be, too. Flinders Island is a tourist destination, and my community is there. It has been part of life since my parents bought a farm there — here — when I was five years old. I have walked nearly all of its one hundred and twenty (mostly) white sandy beaches. The red lichen that is such a feature of its rocks runs through my veins. Even the ugly grey blocks of which most of the public buildings are constructed awake the dreary fondness you might apply to an old maiden aunt.

But over the weeks or months, restlessness builds up. The island's familiarity and community's closeness is both comforting and something of a curse. For some reason that I can't quite fathom, stasis and sameness feel like slow death. So I'm not like Graham Greene — more like Bruce Chatwin (although that too feels presumptuous), who had 'a compulsion to wander and a compulsion to return'. Certainly it's not a problem on the same scale as, say, not knowing where your child's next meal is coming from, but it's more disturbing than a few grains of sand in your shoe.

Travelling, I'm not the first to observe, allows you to reinvent yourself. For the people living their everyday lives around me — in this case, Brazilians — the roles I play and the labels they give me are different from those at home, and often irrelevant — to them? to me? — entirely. (Is it strange to seek to be irrelevant? We seem to spend so much time trying to be otherwise.) Michael Crichton wrote, 'Stripped of your ordinary surroundings, your friends, your daily routines, your refrigerator full of your food, your closet full of your clothes — with all this taken away, you are forced into direct experience.' The 'me' as daughter, agent, sister, aunt, stepmother, colleague, committee member, or friend can be left at home. Those have the ring of familiarity but can also feel like a prison uniform. The traveller can be less specific and more anonymous: passer-by, guest, foreigner, passenger, client, mark, stranger. Under the guise of anonymity (or irrelevancy), I've found it easier to come to know what is important to me and to better see what is important to others — as time and again I have seen that gods, goddesses, and saints are of vital importance to a great many people in ways that they are not in my regular life.

Taking my cue from the goddess' children, and tired from my early rising, I returned to my hotel room and watched the last of the festival broadcast live on television. I was reminded that images, as in statues, are central to worship for many of Brazil's religions. The screen showed the image, with her tail of silvery scales, being carried through the streets of Salvador accompanied by thousands of white-clad figures. Then the sound was drowned out by the sudden thrum of a bass guitar as it exploded from one of the hotel's party rooms somewhere above me. The subsequent pounding of drums rattled my window as the sacred gave way to the profane.

Chapter Five

War on a New Jerusalem

CANUDOS, BAHIA

*'Brazil has an incredible capacity to survive disasters
created by the State.'* Roberto DaMatta

By anyone's standards, but particularly Brazilians', the backlands, *os sertões*, are empty. They can be mesmerising and they can be bleak. As Frances de Pontes Peebles, a Brazilian-born, Miami-raised novelist, mused in her novel *The Seamstress,* Brazilians 'rarely said countryside or interior. They preferred backlands, a word that made Emília think of the musty recesses of a hard-to-reach drawer or cabinet. A dark space filled with forgotten things, opened only in moments of need or nostalgia and then quickly shut.'

In *A Death in Brazil,* Peter Robb tells of another Brazilian injustice. It happened in a place called Canudos, and I wanted to go there, into the backlands, to see where it happened. The Brazilian government has more or less erased all traces of the town, and the massacre of its people.

You get there by taking a bus from Salvador to a market town called Feira de Santana, where you wave off the other *estrangeiros* — mostly

67

backpackers, who are heading east to Lençóis, where they will hike, kayak, abseil, and party. A few might be interested in the diamond-mining history of the region or in seeing Bahia's most impressive rock art.

The bus, shuddering through a vast and changing landscape, can take time because, as Peter Fleming so succinctly put it, 'Delay in Brazil is a climate.' As you travel, watch the lush fields of fat-leafed bananas and tall, shiny sugarcane give way to dry orange dirt barely able to sustain saltbush and cacti. Occasionally you will see evidence of some brave backlander's attempt to tame his environment: a crop of sugarcane turned brittle and brown, a fence-line of emaciated sunflowers. Somewhere out there, beyond the horizon, is Canudos.

When Peter handed our luggage receipts to the conductor, asking him to retrieve our bags from the under-bus compartment, the man was stunned. 'You're sure?' he asked. '*Aqui? Em* Canudos?' Peter couldn't quite believe we were getting off there either. He does seem to spend a lot of time humouring me. His humour wasn't so great after a power failure blacked the streets as we searched for the town's sole hotel.

In Brazil — even in Canudos — they serve fresh juice with breakfast. The next morning, the hotel owner set ours down with a flourish. After announcing that he knew why we were here, he jabbed his stubby finger at his mobile phone and told us that a guide would be round with a taxi to collect us in half an hour. 'Before it gets too hot,' he said. '*Entendeu?*' I was getting used to people asking if I understood, as well as to the rural Portuguese people used in these parts. Then he swiped a pockmarked lump from a shelf and laughed as it crashed to the floor. 'Cannonball,' he said, handing the leaden lump to me, still amused. 'Found it myself. *No sertão*. From the war.' Although he was casual, I felt a twinge of awe, standing there, holding history. And it was heavy.

After you get over its exoticism, the word *sertão* invokes notions of dryness, wildness, and, for many Brazilians, stupidity. A parched word, and a fascinating one. *Os sertões* evokes the curious mix of romanticism and danger that the words 'the Outback' and 'the bush' do in Australia.

Sertanejos were regarded — and still are today, if people are honest — as backward. Life was — is — hard in *os sertões*, and at the time the soon-to-be-murdered settlers were building their New Jerusalem at Canudos, life expectancy was just twenty-seven years. The *sertanejo* 'is ugly, awkward and stooped', wrote Euclides da Cunha in his famous account of the War of Canudos that occurred at the end of the nineteenth century. His was a typical view from the South. Backlanders had a 'downtrodden mien' and a 'dour look'. He obviously never met our hotelier, who was exuberance personified.

Antônio Vicente Mendes Maciel was a preacher who became a messianic and millenarian leader. He was a Brazilian who attracted so many followers and inspired such devotion that he was regarded as a threat to the stability of the newly Republican government. It was a threat so major that the government sent waves of troops to quash it.

Antônio was born into the *os sertões* in 1830. He was, by all accounts, a studious child, but nothing hinted that he would grow to polarise a nation. That life was unforgiving in the backlands was a lesson he learnt early. His grandfather and uncle were beaten to death, another chapter in a long-running blood feud with a wealthier land-owning family. Revenge was swift: the shooting of a groom as he wed; his blood stained the bridal gown. The families retaliated until there was no one left in the male line but Antônio and his father. The latter became a penniless drunk.

Antônio himself had several failed careers, and after his wife ran off with a soldier, he began to wander the *sertão*. An oft-fasting and barefoot penitent, he started to preach. It was a time when priests preferred to live on the coast — life being cushioned there — and so it was not uncommon to find lay preachers in the backlands. But Antônio Conselheiro ('the Counsellor', as he came to be called) didn't limit his ministrations to preaching: he fixed bridges and rebuilt chapels, weeded cemeteries and dispensed advice.

Brazilians have an easy relationship with time. The battered taxi arrived only half an hour late and took us to a hill that overlooked

New Canudos. I have found that Brazilian guides often employ drivers with cars: guides themselves seldom own cars, and it provides work for their friends. The four of us stood dwarfed by a crudely crafted statue in a dark robe. The figure's fist was clenched around a staff, and a large golden cross hung from his neck. I suspected it was a romantic rather than an accurate depiction.

The statue faced away from the new town, his attention directed towards the past. There was no hint of what Peruvian writer Mario Vargas Llosa, in *The War of the End of the World*, a novel based on the events at Canudos, called 'his icy, obsessive eyes'. When I faced the same direction, all I could see was water. The government submerged the old Canudos in making the Cocorobó Dam. Were they trying to erase the memory of Antônio Conselheiro? To smooth the wrinkles from the national psyche?

I asked Jamison, our guide. '*Não sei*,' he responded. Was Jamison being evasive or did he really not know? I was too polite to push.

But now a little more history: in 1808, with Napoléon Bonaparte's army marching for Lisbon, the Portuguese royal family and its thousands-strong court sought refuge in Brazil. Their arrival gave Brazil the dubious honour of being the only colony worldwide ever to be the seat of its monarch. The royal arrival saw money lavished upon their new home. Universities, schools, and hospitals were built. Brazil's first bank was established, as well as the Botanical Garden in Rio de Janeiro — still a sensational garden — and an opera house.

Rio de Janeiro had taken over from Salvador as capital some forty years before the Bragança family settled there; they were waiting for Britain to deal with the threat from Napoléon. When the king, João VI, returned to Portugal, he left his son, Pedro I, as regent and took the royal coffers with him. He probably wasn't expecting Pedro I to declare 'independence or death!', as he did, to become emperor of an independent Brazil in 1821. It was a sudden end to more than three hundred years of Portuguese rule.

It was around the time when much of South America was trying to throw off the yolk of Spain. The rule of Portuguese monarchy might have continued if they hadn't arrived like unexpected relatives who then outstayed their welcome. During their stay, Brazilians learned they would always be poor second cousins as long as they were ruled from Europe. So they tossed that monarchy out. I like that. Australia still hasn't tossed the English monarchy out, and shows few signs of doing so.

For most of Antônio Conselheiro's life, the Church and the state were close. Like the Portuguese monarchy, the Brazilian imperial family was pious. Plots against them were rare, and none had much chance of success prior to 1889, when the republicans won out in a fairly sudden and mostly peaceful coup.

During the decades of Brazilian imperial rule, arguments had begun between the states and the Emperor over economic policy and the funding of services such as education. There were also points of contention between Emperor Pedro II — who had taken over in 1831, when his father abdicated — and the Church over issues such as who had the right to appoint clergy. Republican momentum grew and, rather suddenly, Pedro Segundo found himself relieved of his title. By then, the anti-slavery movement had also gathered such strength that the last act of the imperial family was to outlaw slavery. With her father already in Paris, Princess Isabel signed the Golden Law in 1888.

The Church had for centuries neglected the backlands. Priests actively avoided postings to *os sertões*, partly because the Church didn't support the region in any meaningful financial way. Antônio Conselheiro, preaching messianic hope as it neared the end of the century, resurrected the Church's neglected assets and gathered unto him the Church's neglected souls.

Not everyone supported the Republic. Conselheiro mourned the monarchy and railed against the recent separation of church and state in his thundering and mesmerising voice. He roared about the sanctity of marriage, outraged that this sacrament had been hijacked by the republicans. Utterly charismatic, his preaching drained the workers (and a good many recently freed slaves) from the parched land.

Landowners, so recently stripped of their cheap labour because of the abolition of slavery, were now losing their paid workers too. They demanded action from their government. The Church was aware that it had no control over the preacher or his people, and that its failures were among his favourite sermon subjects, so it added its voice to the growing din. A cacophony of self-interested voices demanded that the government *do something* about the Counsellor and his followers. I like to imagine them jumping and up and down with rage like Elmer Fudd, but their demands had much more serious consequences than losing a rabbit.

The Counsellor continued to gather followers with words prophetic and millenarian. In his novel, Llosa paints a compelling character: 'He told them things that they could understand, truths that they could believe in. That this calamity [the drought] was no doubt the first forewarning of the arrival of the Antichrist and the devastation that would precede the resurrection of the dead and the Last Judgement.' He would, he promised, build them a New Jerusalem.

The Counsellor's flock were a motley crew, a diaspora of the poor and lawless who had been displaced by the drought. His congregation grew too large to be nomadic, so he settled them on the banks of the Vaza-Barris River. (The river now feeds the Cocorobó Dam.) Under the watchful eye of their leader, they built Canudos, their New Jerusalem.

The people built houses, schools, and churches; they raised cattle, goats, and sheep. They were married by their Counsellor. He baptised their babies and gave their children first communion. He heard their confessions and read them last rites.

At its peak, Canudos was home to twenty-five thousand souls. But theirs was a spiritual revolution, not a physical one. Conselheiro preached loudly his disapproval of the Republic. Was he, I wonder, baiting his detractors? Or was the government response as unexpected to him as it seemed to me?

Word began to spread southwards: the message arrived that he had gathered up and organised a sizeable chunk of *os sertões* peasant class, who sought a better life. The richer, more refined people of the South didn't want their peasant class to be organised. They were scared of Canudos' continued growth, encouraged by the press, who were happy to play fear-monger. So a military force was sent against the town and its people.

What followed was a holocaust.

But, as with the *quilombo* at Palmares, government victory did not come easily. Antônio Conselheiro's followers met the threat with a mixture of messianic hope and mystic fatalism.

Entering the Canudos State Park, we passed a sign with the fierce promise, 'History Cannot Die!' The guard post was empty. I was happy to see that the visitors' registration book had not even been left outside. Jamison directed his friend to take the dry, dusty path to the right. Occasional cacti rose fifteen feet in the air; low spiny bushes spotted the red dirt.

When Marco parked at a sign that announced the Valley of Death, a shiver ran over me, despite the blazing sun.

The first shots of the war were fired when one hundred and fifty of the Counsellor's followers were on their way to buy wood, with which to build a new church, from a town not too far away. They were kneeling for prayer by the side of the road when the first wave of the government's troops, still sweaty from their long march, slaughtered them like lambs. The soldiers, my research had told me, continued on, hot and tired, knowing little about the terrain around Canudos.

Word of the slaughter raced ahead of the army. They were met by a well-organised mob who used the scrub as camouflage, and sang hymns as they wielded whatever weapons had come easily to hand. Conselheiro's people included AWOL soldiers and outlaws who knew how to turn the escarpment into a fortress, and the army was defeated.

Although Peter and I didn't speak a lot of Portuguese, and Jamison did not speak English, he gave an energetic commentary. He pointed to a depression that was used as a trench in the war. It was roped off, a half-dug archaeological site overgrown by scrubby bush. This excited Peter, who has a deep interest in archaeology; he went off to examine the pits more closely. What were the soldiers thinking as they went up against the townspeople, I wondered, looking around at the dry ground. That they were there to quash a dangerous uprising? That they were safeguarding the nation from moral decay?

'*Faz muito tempo que não*,' Jamison replied when asked how long since the digs had been worked. Not for a while now. 'No money left,' he said before falling quiet.

The Valley of Death, where troops and townspeople clashed, where so much blood had been shed, was silent but for the occasional cry of a goat.

A telegraph system had newly tethered the North to the South, so news of the villagers' resistance reached the authorities quickly. They sent out a second, larger military force. Word of the resistance also reached the city newspapers; metropolitan Brazilians all over the country followed the story avidly. Sending correspondents to cover the war became a profitable business. Twenty-nine new national newspapers were founded in the final year of the war alone. For the first time, a single story dominated the national front page. Urban Brazilians — who would become the most fanatical consumers of soap opera in the world — were riveted by the 'facts' presented: the story of a crazed and dangerous man who styled himself as a messiah, leading an equally mad mob who threatened the very cohesion of the nation.

At the museum, I noted the lack of investment with dismay. There are stories the authorities would prefer not to tell. They wished, I supposed, that this did not appear as an exclamation mark in the national story.

Jamison had stayed with Marco and the car, smoking Peter's cigarettes. Disheartened — surely the people's memory warranted more than this? — I took a photo of a couple of battered mannequins, one dressed in a threadbare uniform, the other in a battered robe. In a paint-peeling cabinet lay replica rubber heads used in the 1997 film *Guerra de Canudos*. They had hollow cheeks, lips drawn back in terror like crude Halloween masks.

In shabby glass cases lay items that conjured the everyday, objects found throughout the region that tugged at my heart: irons for pressing daughters' confirmation dresses, kettles that heated water for tea or to ease the birthing of babies. There was a lock and key from one of the farms that pre-dated the town, perhaps used as a missile by one of the townsfolk. There were nails once used to build a schoolroom. I was finding it just as difficult to believe the slaughter was 'justified' as I had when reading Peter Robb's account of it.

The third attempt to get rid of the people of Canudos involved an army of 1,300. They were equipped with sixteen million rounds of ammunition, an artillery battery, and a squadron of cavalry. Soldiers hauled four cannons up and down the rocky hills. I imagine they cursed their superiors as they wiped the sweat from their brows.

Euclides da Cunha, sent by his newspaper as a war correspondent, revelled in the drama: 'From their nooks and hiding places, from thickets here and there ... the *jagunços* now made their presence known with a sudden burst of gunfire.' Did he forget that these were men and women and children, mothers and fathers, brothers and sisters, fighting for their lives? He described a wounded child: 'For the little one's mouth was a gaping bullet wound from side to side!'

Whether fuelled by desperation or righteousness, the townspeople somehow managed to repel that third assault. Having run out of ammunition, Conselheiro (whose name had by now become employed in the cities to dissuade children from bad behaviour) and his brethren grabbed whatever was to hand. They used pitchforks, spiked sticks previously used to prod cattle, scythes, hoes, washing-line poles, and kitchen knives. Newspapers reported crazy-eyed fanatics throwing stones at the last of the exhausted and retreating soldiers.

The last time the troops were sent against them, the town had shrunk, da Cunha reported. It was now 'largely made up of women and children ... many times above the roar of battle, there would come the sound of piteous wails'. On the fourth assault, the government was triumphant.

Almost no one in Canudos survived.

The press published photographs of the devastation under headlines that proclaimed victory. They showed a robed Antônio Conselheiro, slim and bearded like Christ. They showed the rubble of churches, schools, and homes.

Those bones that were buried — archaeologists have reported finding plenty still scattered across the battleground — were put in mass graves: an extra tragedy in this land where a good send-off and burial are so important.

The image that I find most haunting shows a small herd of bedraggled survivors, flanked by soldiers. The mostly dark-skinned group are bone thin. They sit on — have collapsed upon — the sunbaked earth. Some of the women's heads are covered, and they stare at me through the lens, horror evident in their eyes. One touches a ragged veil to her forehead, covering her face entirely. In front of the women, a few dusky children have been assembled. Their bony knees are drawn to their sunken chests. They stare, hollow, at the camera.

It would be easier to pretend that these sorts of things couldn't happen in my home country. But the look in the eyes of the survivors of the War at Canudos is familiar to me. Australians see it in newspapers and on television in our own fear-mongering media. It is the same look of many of the people who have sought refuge in my country, those our government keeps behind razor wire. It is not only the look of lost hope; it is the look of the betrayed.

Governments and the media have become expert at scare-mongering. It happens every day all over the world. It happens in the United States, where they've built a wall because of the fear of being overrun by Mexicans. It happens in Australia, where we have been made to fear those who come in search of safety. 'Legitimising myths' is a term political scientists use. 'Ideologies that justify discrimination against disadvantaged groups.'

The English language is loveable when it's not scare-mongering — although not so loveable that it should be imposed on people the world over, as seems to be happening. The growing pervasiveness of my mother tongue, while convenient for me, is eroding other cultures and their languages. But the English language is rich; its vocabulary caters widely when it comes to labelling a person or persons in passage: traveller, tourist, nomad, expatriate, diaspora, displaced, exile, migrant, refugee. These are words that can be wielded with specific intent or recklessness, not only by governments, but also by travel writers, as some travel-writing theorists have pointed out.

The nuance is found in the reason for passage. 'Traveller' implies choice, although I'm not so sure that's accurate. 'Tourism' is thought of as pleasurable, even though I've had plenty of tourist experiences that haven't been. Strictly, 'nomad' refers to those who are in fairly constant motion with their herds, but it's often used for travellers the likes of Bruce Chatwin, who wander at will, aiming for aimlessness.

An expatriate chooses, and an exile doesn't. Both technically refer to living outside one's country, and are oft-used as metaphors. I hadn't known that 'diaspora' first referred to the Jewish forced from Israel, but it is now used to describe — most importantly for Brazil — the Africans stolen from Africa. Migration can be forced or by choice.

'Displaced' can be a synonym for 'refugee', according to the Oxford: 'A person who has been forced to leave their country in order to escape war, persecution, or natural disaster.' And that last form of passage — the seeking of refuge — implies hope: that there is somewhere to escape to, worth escaping to. So what does that give us? After all, it won't change the Australian government's anti-refugee policies, leaving such people without hope. I hope, then, that they have faith.

Those few who survived the War at Canudos were asked what Antônio Conselheiro had promised them to engender such faith, loyalty, and determination. Their reply was that the preacher had promised to save their souls. As an atheist (or am I now merely a non-believer, and what is the difference?), I regard religion as fostering hope. The people at Canudos

did not, it would seem, merely hope that their souls would be saved —
they were certain of it. Is certainty, do you think, compatible with hope?

An archaic meaning for 'hope' was a 'feeling of trust'. Trust implies
certainty. Certainty in the order of things is what religion, I suppose, offers
— indeed, fosters. Formal religion is the leading sponsor of continuity,
most noticeably by ritual.

In Brecht's *Life of Galileo*, there is a scene that has haunted me since
I studied the play in high school. I used to think it was just about hope,
as in there is something better waiting for us in the afterlife. While
translations vary, the substance of the scene is that the Little Monk tells
Galileo about his peasant parents, who find the strength, day after day, to
rise at dawn and work until dusk, toiling in the stony soil. Theirs is a bleak
life, the monk says, and their strength comes from routines: 'the routine
of scrubbing the floors, the routine of the seasons … of paying taxes …
and the Bible texts they hear every Sunday'. 'Even,' the monk says, 'the
troubles that come to them are recurrent troubles.'

I can see the attraction of hope — via the idea of an afterlife — but
the Little Monk is talking about order and routine being the things that
get his parents through their days. The concept of certainty and sameness
being reassuring is new for me. But I sit in a position of privilege, as many
in the West do. Note to self: for some, I must remember, sameness and
certainty are synonymous with safety.

Chapter Six

Passion in the Backlands

NOVA JERUSALÉM, PERNAMBUCO

'To sit there and witness all this was such a bizarre and incredible experience for me, seeing the sacred stories with their heroes and miracles ... now being enacted in exchange for a modest admission fee in front of a grateful cinema audience.' Harry Haller (*Steppenwolf*)

The process of tourist-collection took about an hour, but when it was complete the bus sped out of Porto de Galinhas. The popular holiday spot was named 'Port of Chickens' because when slavery was outlawed, slave cargoes were called 'chickens' to disguise them.

The tour guide began to run through which states his new friends were from. 'São Paulo?' More than a dozen hands shot up. 'Minas?' The Mineiros' arms shot high like flags up poles. 'Pernambuco?' There were a few locals. Satisfied, he was turning to the next topic when my neighbour, a middle-aged woman whose thighs oozed out of her short denim shorts like chocolate-coloured lava, asked loudly: *'Gringa?'* Forty sets of eyes turned as I admitted to being an *'australiana'*. The guide looked astonished. Evidently my being there was strange to him. Recovering, he gave a little hop, and said, '*Canguru!*'

In the arid backlands of the Northeast, on the dry red dirt inland from Recife, a Brazilian called Plínio Pacheco built his version of New Jerusalem. It's testament to his commitment: it is advertised as 'the world's biggest stage', and it might well be. The venue attracts an audience of up to eight thousand each night of the eight nights of its Easter season. From all over the country, people flock to see the Passion Play performed by Brazil's most famous soap-opera stars.

The day before, by the hotel pool — it was a holiday weekend, so like everyone else in town I was taking some downtime — I'd been leafing idly through a tourist brochure that listed *passeios*, which strictly translates as 'rides' but is more like 'things to do'. 'Nova Jerusalem': the words were becoming a theme in my travels in Brazil. Those words alone would have been enough to catch my eye, but when they were followed by 'Paixão de Cristo' ('Passion of Christ'), well, my fate was sealed. I went to the front desk and booked the tour for the next day. It seemed I was destined to chase down every religious reference I came across. And it did seem odd, given that I rarely looked at tourist brochures in Brazil.

There are times when Brazil makes me feel like Harry Haller in Hermann Hesse's novel *Steppenwolf*: separate, unsure if he's the subject or the object, as though he's taking it all way too seriously.

I didn't have a rollicking good time playing the party games the guide used to distract his brood from having to watch life on the streets. Having decided that he couldn't communicate with me, the man was content for me to sit out.

Eventually, we stopped for lunch in a bustling market town. Instead of making sure I understood, as Brazilians kindly and often do, I had to run after him once he'd finished giving my tour mates instructions on how to find the bus again after lunch. I was pretty sure I had them, but I wanted to make sure. I'd mistaken 'at one o'clock' for 'in one hour' when collecting my newly mended sandals from the cobbler. The potential consequences were less dire then.

Back on the road, as we caught the first glimpse of turret, the couple in front of me began talking more rapidly and pointing. The breathing of the lava-legged woman quickened. She leaned over the aisle towards her friend as the stone wall came into view.

Disembarking last, I avoided the enthusiastic jostle. They gathered round the guide, who barked a few orders about staying together and not going wandering off. Brazilians make great fodder for tour guides. They seem to love being told what to do in a way that Australians just don't.

I snapped a quick photo of the rows of turnstiles — forlorn now, they would be crowded each Easter when the play was performed — before the guide sailed us through the open gate as if he were the figurehead on the prow of a ship.

This Jerusalem is an empty arena, most of the year, rather than the labyrinth of alleyways that the Old City is. We were led to the base of a tower that was spiked with spotlights and antennas, resembling Bart Simpson's hair. Enya's 'Sail Away' burst suddenly from the speakers above as if escaping some long confinement. The music's grandeur was fitting for such a vast space, but no one could hear as we were handed over to a local guide whose job it was to show us the site.

The new bloke was dressed as someone's idea of how a peasant might have looked more than two thousand years ago. He wore a conical woollen hat and a dirt-brown robe. Although I guess they hadn't, by then, invented mirrored sunglasses.

The man recited his lines as he walked us past a soccer field that probably wasn't part of the set. Stopping us in front of a cave, he told us it was the sepulchre in which Jesus' body is laid. During the show — he waved his hand with a dramatic flourish — its entrance is closed, miraculously, by a rock. He was enunciating so beautifully I could understand easily — until his words were overwhelmed by the roar of a whipper snipper.

I am not the first to point out that in order to begin to understand anything about Brazil, one must understand the importance of their national obsession, besides *futebol*. It is the *telenovela*. The Soap Opera deserves to be capitalised for its role in the national story, for its influence on the national psyche. Airing six nights a week, each *telenovela* generally runs for six to eight months. With storylines that always feature love and betrayal, they usually focus on a couple, one of whom is of a lower social class. Sometimes they are loosely based on history, with a storyline added about a couple, one of whom is of a lower social class. These are called *histórias* or *novelas de época*. Although the former does translate as 'histories', there's usually little about them that could be accused of being factually accurate.

The melodramas attract an audience, both male and female, that regularly numbers upwards of fifty per cent of television sets during prime time. The population of Brazil is around two hundred million. In a nation where there is a television set turned on in just about every shop, bar, restaurant, bus station, taxi rank, kiosk, and hamburger stand, not to mention lounge rooms, that's a lot of sets.

The final episode of the phenomenally popular *Avenida Brasil* gained a staggering eighty-four per cent of audience share. The Brazilian president, Dilma Rousseff, rescheduled a political rally because it would clash with the finale. That last season is said to have earned the equivalent of one billion dollars for Globo, the company that made the program. That's US dollars of course, since we seem to measure everything of value in that currency. Unless a huge soccer match was on, I don't recall ever seeing a television *not* tuned to the *telenovelas* during prime time.

Globo, the Brazilian media conglomerate, is responsible for the bulk of the most-successful *telenovelas*. The programs 'create a space to promote commercial goods'. They don't just mean during ad breaks, but rather by product placement, which, although fairly new in Australian soaps, Globo has been doing for decades. The company sends out a prospectus for each new soap opera, with an outline of the story, together with a list of placement opportunities, to customers such as Procter & Gamble, Lexus, and Banco do Brasil. In the mid-1990s, a *telenovela* with a rural setting called *The Cattle King* included product placement from companies that sold meat and dairy products, seeds, financial services, beer, sports cars, soft drinks, and a cattle vaccine. It's a practice that began in the late 1960s when the leading character — a lovable rogue type — used a product called Engov, sold as a hangover cure.

Globo's *telenovela* department contracts some two hundred writers, one hundred and fifty directors, and more than five hundred actors, and it supplies the lead actors for the Passion Play at Nova Jerusalém. The play's cast — who lip-sync to the soundtrack — are no strangers to passion, having starred in programs with such titles as *Love and Intrigue, War of the Sexes, Stupid Cupid,* and *Ways of the Heart.* For eight nights the stars strut the nine stages, their audience following like a cloud of rapidly banking swallows. Annually, the season plays to more than sixty thousand people; it is, by anyone's definition, a going concern.

To my eye, the stages at Nova Jerusalém verged on the comic and gaudy. The cave that is miraculously closed by the rock looked grey and lumpy, like someone had poured concrete over a pile of old potatoes.

The Temple of Jerusalem is gilded and white, with solemn stone columns of the Doric order. My tour mates rushed to sit on its golden throne, and I offered to play the role of photographer. Snapping away, I thought: was it the combination of history, religion, and *telenovela* stars that made the play so compelling? Perhaps you had to have been brought up on a diet of the three, as Brazilians had, to appreciate it in the same way. I was fascinated, but for different reasons than my tour mates. The idea that someone would think to build such a spectacular theatre in the middle of nowhere, and that people — so many people — would come, astounded me. Couple after couple handed me their cameras and settled on the throne, under an image of a roaring lion. They seemed glad to have found a use for me, this strange woman who travelled alone.

We were led to Stage Number Three, behind which a short man was soaping a bus with a long-handled brush. Number Three is a grand stage with a graceful red-brick proscenium, and heavy metal braziers on the wall that were filled with flinty globes. We were ushered past a stone well, Herod's Palace, and the Olive Garden to The Forum. It is impressive. Two giant robe-draped statues flank the stage, their hands raised theatrically.

As my tour mates headed for the bar, I took my turn to sit on the hard stone throne stamped with 'SPQR', guessing it stood for 'the Senate and the people of Rome'. It rekindled memories of my robed and mesmerising history teacher. A golden eagle was perched atop the throne, its angry wings spread wide above my head as my hands rested on gilded lions. It was easy to be flippant about it, but really, the work involved in creating all this in the middle of nowhere was huge. I enjoyed the quiet for a moment before the peace was ripped apart — again — this time by the metallic whine of a brush-cutter.

Plínio Pacheco, the man responsible for building New Jerusalem in the *sertão*, married into a large family of local hoteliers. For some years, the family had performed the story of Christ wearing their hotel's bedsheets. Pacheco built New Jerusalem in the 1960s, writing the script for the play himself. Each word of his script was taken from the New Testament. (The cynic in me notes that there's probably enough words in the New Testament to allow him to write whatever he wanted.) To date, an audience of more than two million have seen Pacheco's Easter spectacular. The mix of religious story and soap-opera stars prove an irresistible combination for his Brazilian audience who, in 2015, according to Nova Jerusalem's shiny website, numbered sixty-eight thousand and came from twenty-two states.

And spectacular the show would be. Since it wasn't Easter, I could only imagine the five hundred costumed extras who flood onto the stages while a brass-horn fanfare swoops in from the tower-tops. The drama is accompanied by a fully orchestrated soundtrack. The Forum's golden throne, where I was sitting, is where the actor playing Pontius Pilate sits each night in judgement of Jesus. Pilate is conducted to the stage by a cavalcade of chariots driven by large and richly attired horses. Roman soldiers, with red plumage sprouting from their helms, use short swords and golden shields to beat a path for him through the hundreds of peasants, played by hundreds of turban-topped extras.

A tour group of Scandinavians had beaten ours to the bar. It would seem that this New Jerusalem is on some foreign itineraries after all, despite being so 'off the beaten track'. They were staying onsite, at the Pousada da Paixão — the Passion Pousada. I compared notes on the best *caipirinhas* with one typically blond couple. The drinks in our hands were nice enough: the lime juice was a little over-sugared, we agreed, but the *cachaça* — a clear spirit made from sugarcane — was smooth and not too strong.

Suddenly I realised with a spike of panic that I hadn't heard the buzz of my Brazilian companions for some time. They weren't in the bar, were no longer by the pool. Had I been left behind? If so, would there be room at the Passion Pousada for me? But I really needed to get back to Porto de Galinhas, several hours away.

Then our tour guide rushed in, draped in a white robe. Looking harried, he hustled me through the back door and over to the Last Supper that was being consumed on a table-filled stage. Each man, woman, and child had a red or white robe over their clothes. Flushing, I was led to the one vacant chair and handed a plate of half-cold roast, while my neighbour kindly filled my goblet with blood-red wine. Smiling with reassurance, she clinked my glass. '*Saúde!*' we exchanged, and drank.

Interlude

Folk Carnaval

OLINDA, PERNAMBUCO

> *'The true Brazilian ... is an incorrigible romantic — impetuous,*
> *impractical, pleasure-loving, and yet idealistic, gallant and vital.'*
> John Updike

The period between Christmas and Easter is busy for Brazilians. Christmas is, of course, a religious and family-oriented occasion. In Rio de Janeiro, New Year's Eve — the Ano Novo — is celebrated with the Festa de Yemanjá. In Salvador, they celebrate Réveillon, also dedicated to the sea goddess, with mega-parties in the streets and on the beaches. Although these parties merge and overlap, each one attracts crowds that would exceed the capacities of Rio's Maracanã Stadium or the Melbourne Cricket Ground. The Festa de Bom Jesus dos Navegantes, honouring the patron saint of boatmen, begins on New Year's Day, when those who are able to get out of bed watch the flotilla take the image for a sail. A few days later, 6th January, the Day of the Three Kings is celebrated in a more low-key manner across the nation. There are other celebrations during this period: Saint Sebastian's Day, Foundation Day in São Paulo, the four-day Festa do Senhor do Bonfim in Salvador, and all manner of summer festivities.

You might think February would be quieter, but the madness simply marches on. February is the lead-up to the most important festival on the Brazilian calendar: Carnaval, the world's biggest party.

Each year on Australian television, the news channels broadcast some of the highlights of Rio's Carnaval Parade, which takes place in a purpose-built stadium called the Sambódromo. I'd catch glimpses of colour, frenzied and rhythmic movement, and spectacular floats from the comfort of my couch, wine glass in hand. I'd admire the beautiful people, the wondrous costumes, and the dedication and skills of the participants, so evident in their precisely choreographed and enthusiastic steps. But it didn't occur to me that one day I would see it in all its guises and glory.

In Australia, we only hear about the parade that happens at the Sambódromo, and sometimes the Carnaval balls, but not the myriad other ways Brazilians celebrate. There are smaller folk festivals and private parties, special parades for kids, masked balls, ear-blasting pop concerts on both fixed and moving stages, street parties, and beach galas. Brazilians love Carnaval so much — though there are a number who avoid its growing commerciality — they keep extending the period during which it is celebrated.

Carnaval used to be a three-day festival, but now the official program runs to five. Many municipalities expand this with elaborate practice schedules in the lead-up to the big week. Others hold warm-up events — as if a Brazilian ever needed warming up — and previews, as well as cool-down events. Carnaval can, in some places, extend the period of celebration and mayhem to span some weeks.

Brazilian national identity and Carnaval have a symbiotic relationship. The festival is both part of the national identity and one of its major contributors. Brazilians regard the period as their due. They can become someone else and enjoy a time when the rules are inverted, when the poor become the stars of the show. Carnaval is about parading and partying. It is about Brazilian-ness.

In some places you get warning: you can hear the parading mob coming towards you and be ready for them. But in Olinda — as in most historic cities in Brazil — you don't always know when a *bloco*, a Carnaval parading troop, is coming your way.

Two weeks before Carnaval officially started, I was in Olinda, in the northeastern state of Pernambuco, when I heard a sudden but slightly muffled *ra-ta-ta-ta-ra-ta-ta-rat! Ra-ta-ta-ta-ra-ta-ta-rat!* Then a battery of drummers surged through the doorway just three quaint colonial buildings away from where I was standing. On the heels of the drummers, a parade of people in orange shirts spilled into the laneway like a burst water main.

Spotting a shop that offered sequined costumes, papier-mâché masks, and a panoply of noise-making instruments, I ducked inside to avoid being crushed as the *bloco* moved past. It was a fairly typical start to the boisterous parade practice-sessions that fill the streets — laneways, really — of pre-Carnaval Olinda.

Through the open door of the costume shop, I saw a round woman come onto her first-floor balcony. Her small fat dog took tiny, shivering steps after her. Shaking like a poppy in a windstorm, he wasn't sure if he was safer with his mistress or cowering under the bed. She made the decision for him, lifting the dog on one stockinged foot and lobbing him through the French doors.

The passage of the *bloco* took some time. The sound of drums had barely finished echoing when around the corner came the leading edge of another *bloco*. The blue-clad trumpet section skimmed past the tail end of the orange-shirts so closely they could have been baton-passers in a relay race. I scampered across the street to a bar where an audience had crammed in to watch, each person holding a cold bottle of Brahma.

Brazilians like their beer so chilled it is often frozen when served. I was taking a swig of beery icicles when a giant figure lurched into view.

It was dressed in threadbare khakis. Its head, covered by a half-moon hat, was level with the balconies above. Two dark belts crossed in an X over his chest: it was the famous Brazilian outlaw Lampião. Another figure of Brobdingnagian proportions slowly careened into view. Similarly clad, her hair was dark and shoulder-length: the outlaw-ess Maria Bonita.

My original plan, to come to Olinda to see the Giant Puppet Race, had been thwarted because the race wasn't on two weeks before Carnaval, as I had read, but one. I would, however, be able to attend the Virgens de Verdade parade the next day, the kind woman who sold me a ticket to the Giant Puppet Museum said. '*Entendeu?*' Well, yes, the idea of 'Virgins of Truth' — as I mistakenly translated it — intrigued me. But thanks to the *prévias* (previews), I hadn't missed out on something new: the giant puppets lurching down the street were making me feel like Gulliver in a strange new land.

The costumed figures were about twice the size of the men inside them, like finger puppets on a grander scale. I assumed the operators were men by the weight they must have been carrying, as much as by Brazil's famed machismo.

The figures are called *bonecos gigantes* — giant dolls — by Brazilians. They commonly take the form of people who have been newsworthy in the year prior. President Dilma Rousseff features currently; Hugo Chávez and Osama bin Laden have been seen in previous years. Historic and mythic figures are common: Death dancing with his scythe; the famous republican rebel Tiradentes as a cavorting dentist (his nickname means teeth-puller); Brazilian Formula One driver Ayrton Senna; Luiz Gonzaga, 'King of Baião', who transformed folk music into pop. The acclaimed singer was another national hero; his trademark tasselled hat was modelled on that of outlaws like Lampião. The *bonecos* don't just take part in the race; they feature while *blocos* parade through the streets as part of the official Carnaval schedule.

As dusk fell, more *blocos* trundled noisily through town. Pressing themselves into the wall as the parades went by, spectators then joined the tail end, dancing and singing as if Carnaval had already started. Mothers and fathers held excited children. An all-girl troop singing a pop tune were led by tight-bodied dancers, spinning and stepping. They moved as precisely as if they were performing for the judges at the Sambódromo.

A mother helped her toddler to wee against the stone wall of a house. She held his penis gently, between two fingers, as if it were a cigarette.

Satin and sequins, cowgirls and clowns: the *blocos* kept coming, noisy, dancing, and fun, washing through the streets like spring floods. Some were accompanied by more giant puppets.

Darkness had drenched the streets by the time a huge jester swayed by. It was later still when a brash band of teens began playing brassy pop on a corner. Two trumpeters faced off, competing. To see who was the loudest? They were young and shirtless — although one wore a purple cape over his finely muscled torso — and they paused every few minutes to take a swig from the row of beer cans that stood on a cobbled step. They played until the early hours of the morning; I could hear them from my bed.

~

At street parties, and at Carnaval, I have often wondered at the sheer determination of Brazilians to have fun. It seems, at times, as if they have been charged to eke out every last bit of pure enjoyment they can. I have wondered if, perhaps, they are biologically compelled to celebrate. But I'd discarded these thoughts until my recent anthropological reading made them not as silly as they initially sounded.

Social scientists discuss a notion they call 'the obligatory expression of sentiment'. Brazilian anthropologists have applied this theory to Carnaval. It suggests that the sentiments we show are prescribed in, and by, the social order. Thus, at funerals we must be sad; at weddings, happy; at an inauguration, graduation, or commemoration, solemn. And at a Carnaval dance, we should be boisterously happy and ready 'to do anything'. So that explains my hunch: it is *almost* a biologically determined behaviour, and it is a collective compulsion. So even though I enjoy the spectacle, it isn't really that there's anything wrong with me, as Brazilians tend to think, that I don't want '*brincar* Carnaval' — to play Carnaval — as they do, with every ounce of my being. A product of my own society, I'm content with being fascinated by it because in Australia — or my Australia, at least — we don't have that particular obligatory expression of sentiment.

Although I tend to feel better when there's a scientific explanation, it can drain some of the wonder from the world.

~ The Central West ~

Chapter Seven

City of Hope

BRASÍLIA, DISTRITO FEDERAL

'Brasília is the ... triumph of pioneering spirit, proof of the
confidence of the greatness of this country [and a] complete
break with routine ...' Juscelino Kubitschek

When you come into Brasília by bus from the southwest, it can take a while to realise just how different the capital city is. As is usual when approaching Brazilian cities, the first hint of it comes when, from across a field, static metal monsters carrying power lines turn and join the highway. The road becomes more frequently punctuated by petrol stations. Local buses, more battered than the long-distance vehicles, join the outside lane. The undulations of the land, despite being reasonably flat, cause Brasília to appear and disappear like an ephemeral future.

The man mostly responsible for the construction of the capital, former president Juscelino Kubitschek, was another Brazilian whose contribution to the national story is unique. The city he built is controversial: some love it, others hate it. Usually, those who love it are residents. Brazilians argue about whether his creation is a work of art. The former president certainly meant it as such, and in my view it is — after all, you don't have to love something for it to have artistic value. Yet the 'Capital of Hope' has been a topic of national contention since Brasília, the once super-modern city, was built in the 1950s.

Brasília interested me not solely because it is the capital and thus regarded — at least by foreigners — as the 'heart of the nation', but because Canberra, Australia's capital, is a constructed city, too. I'd read that Brasília was 'space-age', egalitarian, and well-planned, and that there were no poor. Brazilians who didn't live in Brasília wondered why the hell I was going instead of spending more time in their traditional cities: Rio, for the samba! Salvador, for the beaches, the music, the culture! São Paulo, the height of chic! Of course I went anyway. In fact, I found myself in Brasília several times, partly from interest and partly because it is the centre of the nation, at least in the sense of being a transport hub.

Although construction didn't begin until the 1950s, the idea for Brasília wasn't new. The 1891 Constitution provided for a new capital, but no leader had yet found the courage — or the time — to build it. Decades before, the capital had come to Dom Bosco, who would become patron saint of the city, as prophesy. While he soared above Brazil's Central Plateau in a dream, a voice promised the Italian priest that there below him would appear 'a Promised Land, flowing with milk and honey'. It would, the voice assured him, 'be of inconceivable richness'.

The Australian capital, Canberra, was chosen, as Australian folklore tells, because neither those who lived in Sydney nor those in Melbourne would countenance the other city being chosen. So Canberra was a capital born of jealousy and compromise. Washington, D.C., was another born of compromise — to placate the southern states and to keep the capital away from the economic elites in Philadelphia and the old capital, New York, as well as from 'potentially volatile constituents', who were demanding back-pay for fighting in the American Revolutionary War. George Washington chose the site for his capital on the Potomac River.

The positioning of Brasília was reasoned and hopeful. Brazil's population had resolutely 'clung to the coast like crabs', as a famous saying goes. The long-held belief was that a capital on the tableland would link the populated coast with the near-empty interior; it would unite the South with the North.

On a map, you can see the site is in the centre of Brazil, more or less. Washington, D.C., was also more or less in the geographical centre of those states that had by then signed up to the union. It's obviously not in the centre now — that crown belongs to a cow field near Lebanon, Kansas. It's impossible to imagine that the US capital would ever be moved full stop, cow field or not.

A central capital is a nice idea, but not possible in Australia, either. That would put it in the middle of the Simpson Desert, where it would kill the world's chance of slowing climate change just because of the necessary air-conditioning. The regions are (in Australia's case) or were (in Brazil's) similarly bereft of people. Despite the Brazilian tableland representing twenty per cent of Brazil's landmass, before the capital landed there it held only six per cent of the population: just one person for each square kilometre; only a little more than for the Simpson Desert. Twelve Brazilian states — states in the North and the West — were technically uninhabited. It meant there was plenty of room for a city. So too, I gather, is there plenty of room to relocate Washington, D.C., to Lebanon, Kansas. The population of that town is two hundred and eighteen.

In Brazil in the 1950s, democracy was a novelty. 'Universal' male suffrage had been introduced in 1889, when the republicans threw out the imperial family. But even dropping the minimum-income test, which had so restricted voting eligibility before the republic, resulted in only five per cent of the population being eligible to vote due to the remaining requirement for literacy (literate women would get the vote in 1932). A few powerful states controlled the government: São Paulo, with its coffee barons; Minas Gerais, made rich by seams of gold; and the then federal district of Rio de Janeiro were primary among them. In 1930, despite losing the election, Getúlio Vargas took power in a *coup d'etat*. He, in turn, was overthrown in 1945, although he would be democratically restored to the presidency to govern from 1951 until his suicide in 1954.

It was during this lull in dictatorships (the military would take over again in 1964) that Juscelino Kubitschek was elected president on a platform of national development and hope. The jewel among his election promises — that which would come to underpin his whole development strategy and make him one of the most famous and popular Brazilian leaders ever — was to build a utopian capital for the nation. It was to be a secular New Jerusalem that would solve all the nation's problems. Kubitschek, painfully aware that Brazilian governments never finished the work of the predecessors (and because democratically elected leaders were not permitted to serve consecutive terms), campaigned under the slogan 'fifty years in five'.

Juscelino Kubitschek de Oliveira's father had been a peddler and a poet, an unconventional man who would have been comfortable in troubadorial times. Kubitschek's mother, widowed at a young age, was ambitious in a bohemian kind of way and encouraged her son to spend their spare *cruzeiros* ordering books from Rio de Janeiro. Deciding he would contribute to society by becoming a doctor, Kubitschek apprenticed in Paris, specialising in kidneys.

The handsome Brazilian was elected mayor of Belo Horizonte, then governor of Minas Gerais, and finally, in 1956, president, two years after Getúlio Vargas shot himself in his bedroom at Catete Palace as leaders of another military coup knocked at the door.

J.K. — 'Jota Ka', as he was called by the people — wanted to build a city that would drag the entire country into the twentieth century. A city that would encourage nation-building. Most cities are a response; Brasília was to be a cause.

If religions provide a way of making sense of the world, J.K. was a secular messiah trying to impose order on it. He wanted the people to see the future in his city and to be modernised miraculously.

The first time I arrived in the city, our overnight bus pulled over to let a woman alight at the side of the highway. The conductor, made invisible by the upturned doors of the under-bus compartment, handed the haggard-looking woman her luggage. They could have been worldly goods: a package wrapped in brown paper and string — a picture, judging by the corner of frame that had torn a hole in the paper; several large plastic-wrapped boxes; and a lamp. Someone new moving to the capital? Riding the bus all the way to the *rodoviária*, I hopped a local bus into what passes for the city's centre.

Brasília was built in the shape of a cross. People will tell you it's the shape of an aeroplane, but what's an aeroplane but the shape of a cross? The government held a competition to choose who would design the city — as the Australian government did for Canberra. Lúcio Costa, the man who won the Brasília competition, said, 'Basically the plan arose from the primary gesture of one who marks or takes possession of a place: two axes crossing at right angles: the sign of the cross itself.' It was a mark of ownership. The sign of the cross, and a symbol of hope.

Brasília is a city that is itself a contradiction: a modernist city, now dated. A city that was clean and shiny, now camouflaged by graffiti. In a country that runs on personal relationships and prizes the family, it is impersonal.

And in a country that is so spontaneous — and now so mobile — in this capital everything is designated and divided. Its residential axis is curved, like a bow readied to shoot an arrow into forever. But the accommodations it provides for its people are ponderous concrete buildings — square super-blocks that loom as large and dark as a pending jail sentence. It was accommodation meant to be egalitarian, but over the last fifty years mansions and sectors of slums have infected the plan.

~

In general, I find the experience of being a pedestrian in Brasília disconcerting. It took me some time to work out why I felt so anxious trying to cross roads. Traffic in Brazilian cities isn't so crazy compared with, say, Jakarta, Hanoi, or Kathmandu. But in planning the city, Costa and his team prioritised the car over the foot, the passenger over the pedestrian. It is not simply that almost nothing is walking distance from anything else, either. Then it dawned on me: there are no street corners at which to cross! In fact, there are no streets at all, only avenues, roads, and *vias*, or ways. On a map of Brasília, you will see that 'access' has been transformed into a proper noun. (Although that is, perhaps, less surprising in a country that has 'shopping' as a bus destination.)

In Brasília, you will find few red lights or stop signs. Traffic is conducted with all the finesse due a concerto, played by an orchestra of underpasses, interchanges, and ramps.

Another strangeness I find is that, due to Brasília's unique and impersonal address system, I become nostalgic for suburbs. Instead, there are sectors. Every sector is designated by an acronym. There is the SPMS, the SGAN, the HCGN. Each has its own dedicated function, which kind of makes sense, but seems to leech all fun out of the world. There's the hospital sector, the sporting-club sector, and residential sectors. Brasílienses take their cars to PLL, the cleaning and lubrication sector; their children to the EPDB, the Dom Bosco Park; and do their banking at SBN or SBS, as the financial districts are known. The tourist will find her room — if she finds it at all — in the Hotel Sector North or Hotel Sector South, and she will see the sights in the Monumental Sector. Said monuments are lined up along the long avenue that divides the city into hemispheres.

If you need to go to the Santa Lúcia Hospital, for instance, it's at SHLS, Quadra 716, Conjunto C. If you don't speak Portuguese, the address makes only slightly better sense translated. In English, it would be Hospital Sector South, Block 716, Complex C. I guess they thought it was clever to have such a different system of addressing that no one — not even the taxi drivers — can easily negotiate the city. Being in Brasília sparks odd emotions: it never occurred to me that one could be nostalgic for a simple address.

Until recently, houses on Flinders Island had no street addresses. Even now, we don't really use them. We all know who lives where, or we give directions by landmark. A letter addressed simply to Bryson with our postcode will find its way to me (although our postmaster might not thank me for pointing this out). If a visitor wants to have a conversation with a local, they just go to one of the shops or pubs, or they stop someone in the street. Little wonder I find Brasília challenging.

The city bus tour that did hourly circuits — there is one in most Brazilian cities nowadays — didn't show up in the hour and a half I waited for it, so I grabbed a cab. The driver, let's call him Eduardo, took me to one of the few monumental buildings not on the monuments *avenida.*

Brasília may be an impersonal city, but it still caters for religion. The radio was playing softly in the Santuário Dom Bosco when we arrived, and three women were sloshing buckets of soapy water across the marble floor. The interior of the cathedral was bathed in bowerbird blues. The blue-stained glass fractured the light, as if the sun was shining through a kaleidoscope. Seated on a pew next to the now-praying Eduardo, I watched the women push foamy waves out the door with long, flat-headed mops. A man was hosing down the marble robes of a statue of Dom Bosco. Head inclined at gentle angle, the statue's hands were joined in prayer. The man pinched the rubber hose in one hand so the flow gained a force more appropriate for cleaning a car than this image of the city's patron saint.

Thousands and thousands of people were involved in the building of Brasília, but three must be mentioned by anyone writing about the city: the President, the Planner, and the Architect. J.K. conceived of and drove the project, Lúcio Costa devised the layout, and Oscar Niemeyer designed its most monumental buildings. It is the work of Niemeyer that visitors like me find so immediately startling: the man preferred to wield a curve than a corner. His work often robs me of breath for a time.

Niemeyer sculpted in glass and concrete. Unlike the Santuário Dom Bosco, with its magical blue light — as if souls were streaming in through the glass — most of his creations don't look like buildings as we expect them. Niemeyer was master of the architectural metaphor. Now a national hero himself, he designed churches with the majesty of crowns and galleries that resemble spaceships; he wrapped parliaments in glass, and crafted staircases that sweep like sonnets.

You have probably seen buildings by Niemeyer, in photographs if not in life. I had not realised that his work was familiar until I found myself in the museum dedicated to him, in the southern city of Curitiba. He built it in the shape of an unblinking eye: two white curving lines meet at each end of a crest that surrounds an ellipse of dark glass. Inside is a wonderland of shape. Niemeyer's black-brush sketches cover the white walls. In pristine glass cases are finely wrought architectural models. His designs have been built all over the world, and prove that buildings don't need to be boring.

When I look at Niemeyer's architecture, I feel as if I've been given a graphic novel when I expected a Penguin Classic. It's modern, sometimes challenging, and often provides moments of magic. Take Rio's Museum of Contemporary Art, which I saw on my very first visit to that city. It stands on the cliff on the opposite side of Guanabara Bay from Rio's *centro*. With its sides sloping down and inward from a flat roof, I can't decide whether it is meant to resemble a UFO, a football stadium on a stem, or a giant gaping grail. Perhaps even an old-fashioned wide-brimmed champagne glass. You travel from the street to the inside via wide looping walkaways that seem designed to disorient you before you see the art inside — if you can concentrate on art when there's that amazing view. Either way, your first sight of it is — or will be — memorable.

Eduardo pulled his taxi into a small parking lot in the middle of the monumental sector, where a giant white dome, smooth and round as a young milky breast, touched the ground. The National Museum used to shine white, but now its surface was coated in a layer of grime. I found it wasn't like most 'national museums' in that it didn't have permanent displays exploring the nation's history. In fact, there was little to see; they were between exhibitions. A small huddle of workers seemed to be discussing how to hang flat pictures on the perfectly round walls. Surely they'd encountered the problem before? It was difficult to make out their words through the echoes. A man sneezed, and the sound exploded around the space like cyclists in a velodrome. Spotlights were small, dark eyes peering from the curved ceiling. It was a strange-feeling space, disorienting.

Niemeyer had made two large emergency doors off-kilter square. It was as if someone had grabbed diagonally opposite corners of the doorframe and pulled.

Born into comfort in a suburb of Rio de Janeiro, Oscar Niemeyer chose architecture over his father's typesetting business. He trained under Lúcio Costa and was commissioned by J.K., when the future president was governor, to design the community buildings for a new suburb of Belo Horizonte. Niemeyer regarded it as his first real job. You can still see them today: a yacht club with tall windows like sails; a dance hall with a sensuous snaking portico mimicking the contour of the lake's shore; a church of four humped vaults and murals of finely stained glass.

My favourite building in Brasília is the Catedral Metropolitana. It reminds me of a crown, but elegant rather than gaudy. With this design, Niemeyer — although himself a committed atheist — reminds us of the majesty of God. Before you Google pictures of it, imagine a high-waisted hourglass or a boned corset. The building is a circle of pointed white columns that have been drawn in high by an invisible ribbon. The tops of the columns splay, tipping their heads back, looking towards heaven, as if in awe. It's pure gesture, like a yoga pose — and is topped by a gleaming silver cross.

Eduardo led me proudly into the bowels of the cathedral. Niemeyer did away with a ceiling; the space disappears loftily above the supplicants. I had to tip my head back to properly take in the soaring ribs that separate waves of stained glass in green and blue.

The voices of a group of schoolchildren echoed as they chattered and pointed. Three men in shorts and soccer shirts knelt in front of a pew.

Sculpted metal angels with fluffy wings floated just above my head, and on one wall were paintings of the Stations of the Cross that might have been done by Marc Chagall but for their heavy brush.

Niemeyer was not only an atheist but also a card-carrying communist until his death in 2012, at the age of 104. In the 1960s, he was forced into exile in Paris — where he designed the French Communist Party headquarters — after Brazil's flirt with democracy was ended by another military coup. J.K.'s new capital was past the point of no return by the time his presidential term was completed in 1961. From 1964, and for two macabre decades, the military ruled from Brasília. It was a period in which thousands of Brazilians were tortured, murdered, or simply 'disappeared'. Juscelino Kubitschek was one such, murdered by the government in 1976, although it took nearly forty years to prove it.

Oscar Niemeyer was commissioned to design a memorial to his friend. Unsurprisingly, the ruling military junta — the very men who conspired to kill J.K. — objected to the giant sickle in which a statue of the former president stands, one arm raised to hail his city. Eventually, Niemeyer was allowed to build it. It was, he said, his first protest piece.

Eduardo pulled into the car park under the controversial statue. Inside the memorial — it is a severe shape, like the bottom third of a pyramid — the usual exhibits commemorated a life. Schoolchildren jabbed at interactive screens, and I could read about J.K.'s life in English as well as in Portuguese. An officiously helpful man in a guard's uniform told me to hold the railing of a very safe-looking staircase. I felt like I was four years old. Or perhaps ninety. Brazilians in uniform can be very authoritarian.

On the upper level you can gaze at glass cases filled with presidential suits and the sequined gowns his wife wore to state balls. In one corner, J.K.'s office had been reconstructed.

The centrepiece of the memorial, Niemeyer's second tribute to his friend, is an ultra-modern crypt. This looked as if it would never date. The circular room was shrouded in spooky red light, cast through a stained-glass scarlet angel. I wondered if the colour was a reference to

Niemeyer's communist beliefs. The red angel stood sentinel, watching over his friend's remains.

Where every other Niemeyer building in the city shines brightly, this room was dark and solemn. I looked at the ebony marble sarcophagus that rests in the centre of the crypt. It is a commanding tribute. Then the stillness was interrupted by a boy of about thirteen chasing another past a sign too fast to notice that it requested silence and respect.

~

It is not an uncommon feeling among travellers, and among those writing about travel, to feel as if they have arrived late. The passing of time is somehow both more and less obvious when travelling. Sometimes you arrive in a place hoping or expecting to see it as it once was, only to find it changed by the passing of time. The aeroplane Michael Palin arrived in to visit the Amazonian Yanomami tribe was greeted with expectation rather than amazement or suspicion, as he might have expected in a previous century. Even Brasília, the passageway to the future, is now rooted in the past. I would have loved to have seen it when it was shiny and new. Instead, today it feels as if it has an edge of desperation, of trying to ignore that for which it didn't plan: the graffiti, the pedestrians, and the poor. Eventually they were forced to deal with the poor: Brasília was planned to cater for 450,000 worker-residents by the year 2000, but it attracted more than two million — many more than there were jobs for — 'prompting the construction of some 16 satellite cities of poverty', as *The New York Times* described the overspill.

Things change with the passage of time, but change can also be forced — or time can be sped up. That's what J.K. did, although perhaps there was a certain time lag, too. Brazil is only now, sixty or so years later, becoming the world powerhouse the former president had in mind.

And in some ways Brazil, I would suggest, is better at change than Australia. The Brazilians have managed to reject monarchies twice; Australia hasn't even managed it once. Despite Australia's White Australia Policy being abolished in the 1970s, the attitude doesn't seem to have changed much, judging by the current policies on immigration and refugees.

It's on Flinders Island that I find change at its slowest. It's a great place from which to observe transformations, be they big or small, elsewhere. On the island, changes — what some might call progress — are small, so gradual as to seem insignificant. Less than thirty years ago, we got our power from electricity generators; now there's a grid that connects most houses to the wooden power poles that have, over the years, gradually studded the landscape. When I was a child, there were no bitumen roads, let alone the white lines that now separate lanes for the almost non-existent traffic. During those same years, J.K.'s New Jerusalem, his 'Capital of Hope', was growing exponentially, like a king tide on a full moon. And, as if in perfect counterpoint, the population of my island home has slowly drained away. In the modern world, people move to cities, and cities are equated with progress. Flinders Island, in contrast, feels timeless.

Chapter Eight

Valley of the Dawn

VALE DO AMANHECER, DISTRITO FEDERAL

'Children! The man trying to escape his karmic goal or transcendental vows will be eaten or lost as a bird trying to fly in the darkness of night.' Pai Seta Branca (Father White Arrow)

Delfino turned off the highway about forty kilometres northeast of Brasília. There, in the centre of a roundabout, was a circle of women and men with their arms raised skywards, their eyes closed. I flapped a hand at him to stop the car. It wasn't so much their stance that I found startling — it was their clothes, which would be more usually found in a storybook.

The breeze blew garish billows of puce, turquoise, scarlet, and green. The women's gowns were sewn with stars and rainbows. One wore a conical princess hat with a long veil that was flying like a flag. Both the men and the women wore vibrant capes; the corners were attached to their upraised wrists, and they filled as if they were sails. There were four men, each in a cape of chocolate, with yellow and lilac crosses sewn onto them. Beneath the capes they wore brown pants and black shirts, their shoulders and pectorals covered in what looked suspiciously like white vinyl bolero jackets dotted with stars. Think *Star Trek* meets Rapunzel.

Judy — a friend from Flinders Island who had joined me in Brasília the day before and wanted me to show her a bit of Brazil — turned to me, eyes wide. Ah, the longevity of first impressions. As a child arriving at the world headquarters of the Catholic Church, my first impression was of a very long queue of people lined up to enter St Peter's Basilica. Years later, when I arrived at the Old City in Jerusalem, I was struck by the Western Wall. When Judy — a lapsed Catholic — and I arrived at the headquarters of the relatively new religion the Valley of the Dawn, I knew that first image would stay with me as long as I had my memory (which is not necessarily a great deal of time, in my family).

Perhaps memory issues are arriving early, because I can't quite remember when I first heard about the Valley of the Dawn. After my interest was aroused, I searched the internet and hadn't been able to find out much more than that it was a new — and for me, bizarre-sounding — religious group that had settled on the Central Plateau. Of late, I've noticed, there's a lot more about them in cyberspace.

The tableland on which Brasília resides has attracted a number of religious sects. They are drawn by the energy that comes from Brasília's artificial lake. The lake, like the futurist city itself, was predicted decades before by Dom Bosco. Another theory is that these groups are a response to the dehumanisation and alienation of the city's people and its attempt to accelerate history. As a non-believer, the latter explanation makes sense to me, but it still doesn't explain the — well, the *extent* of the cult's beliefs, its fantastical elements. Perhaps I shouldn't be too hasty to discount the first explanation.

These figures at the roundabout who struck me were, I soon learned, a group of mediums whose task it was that day to strengthen the vibratory fields around their compound by channelling energy from the spiritual plane.

The Valley of the Dawn (Vale do Amanhecer) is the most colourful of the region's millenarian sects. The little I had found about them hadn't quite prepared me for how costumed they'd be. Judy was impressed too — her face had a broader-than-usual grin on it. But not everyone was: Delfino, it was clear, wanted to drive straight past them.

The Valley of the Dawn was founded on this land in 1969 by charismatic leader Neiva Chaves Zelaya. It offers healing services to all those who seek them. Boasting more than eighty thousand trained mediums worldwide, among the central concerns for the cult are the 'science' of manipulating energy and the 'liberation of karmic debt'. Is it not obvious I'd be intrigued?

In photos, Tia (Aunt) Neiva, as she came to be known, looks a lot like your stereotypical gypsy and is looped with jewellery. Like so many who settled in the region — like Delfino, too — she was drawn to Brasília during its construction phase, in search of work. As a professional truck driver, she carted cargo across the country: an unusual enough occupation for a Brazilian woman even now, let alone in the 1950s.

Tia Neiva was unusual, as well, in becoming a religious leader. Most of them in Brazil, as worldwide, are male. In 1959, the woman began to see spirits and to hear voices. Soon, she perfected 'soul flight' and spent her nights surfing the astral plane. Each morning, she woke in her own bed after taking instruction from her guru, Humahá, who resided — still resides, perhaps — in Tibet. In 1968, Tia Neiva met Mario Sassi, who helped her to write up the Valley's 'doctrine', extrapolated from her visions. By 1969, she was the clairvoyant messianic leader of the Valley of the Dawn, with Sassi her 'secretary-general'.

Delfino had drawn his mouth into a thin line when we were only a few kilometres out of Brasília, after I asked if he knew much about the sect's doctrine. At first, I took his shake of the head as mere scepticism, but it was tinged with disapproval. Some years before, he said, he brought his wife to a healing session here. He had hoped they would be able to cure her cancer. It was plain that neither the doctors nor his Catholic God had succeeded. I was struck dumb, feeling naïve; until that moment it hadn't really occurred to me to consider the people who might actually rely on such cures.

Although impatience isn't a common trait among Brazilians, Delfino was tapping his hand on the car roof as Judy and I snapped our cameras at the costumed folk on the roundabout. We returned somewhat sheepishly to the car and he drove us through the golden archway, with bright symbols of sun and moon, that let visitors know they'd arrived at the Vale do Amanhecer. Letting us out near a billboard-sized Jesus, he asked how long we'd be. I quashed a niggle of irritation — if he wanted to leave so soon, why did he bring us? — and tried instead for a Brazilian-style shrug.

The population of the town grew from four hundred in 1981 to some eight thousand ten years later. It nearly didn't get a chance to: the government threatened to flood the valley. The rapidly expanding capital needed all the drinking water it could get. Just before her death in 1985, Tia Neiva predicted that the government — newly democratic again by then — would relent and that the president himself would see the legislation through that would save the community. Two years later, President José Sarney, who had taken over when president-elect Tancredo Neves died suddenly before taking office, flew in by helicopter himself to deliver the good news to Neiva's eldest son, who had taken over as leader from his mother.

The Doctrine of the Dawn tells of three races of spirit beings that — or who — over the last thirty-two thousand years made the earth fit for human habitation. Tia Neiva and her mediums belong to one of these spirit races, the Jaguars. In our tendency towards scepticism, Judy and I were decidedly in the minority in the valley: over the decades the town has grown to hold twenty thousand followers, many of whom commute to Brasília for their mainly menial jobs. Their website says there are more than six hundred Temples of the Dawn across Brazil. The religion allows Brazilians to indulge their love of dressing up and pursue their fascination for the supernatural. There are also a dozen chapters of the sect in other countries, including a couple in the United States and one in Japan.

Beyond the robed image of Jesus — which looked rather like it was cut from a giant children's book — a yellow-and-purple ellipse, and other of the sect's symbols, we saw a young man who had rested his bicycle against the temple's stone wall to better oil its chain. Judy and I were drawn past him by the noise from inside, and we swapped a glance that, at least on my part, was full of trepidation.

As we entered the temple, the guard spread his hands to us in welcome. He looked at my camera and gave a shake of his balding pate. Judy had sensibly stored hers away. He wore the uniform of brown, and his white vinyl bolero jacket was pinned with a golden star, but was missing a cape. Without it, he looked like a sheriff: a kind of happy, seven-dwarves type of sheriff. I began to feel as if I was on the set of a strange, not-quite-futuristic, badly scripted television show, or perhaps in Hermann Hesse's Magic Theatre.

The sound in the temple was spellbinding: overwhelming and inescapable. Imagine a weave of murmuring, muttering, ranting, raving, smacking, snapping, and slapping, underpinned by incessant babble. It was an aural kaleidoscope of echo that is with me still today. Sound can do that. In her book *Warning: the story of Cyclone Tracy*, Sophie Cunningham comments that in the years after they survived the cyclone, people forgot myriad other details but they all remembered the noise. The confronting din inside the temple forced itself around the cavernous space with the power of the Southern Ocean working its way through a blowhole in the side of a cliff.

The temple itself was built in the sacred shape of an ellipse and divided roughly into areas. Along each side were small chapels, and in the centre was a huge table, around which sat a dozen or so initiates. Standing over them were half a dozen men and women in white. Judy and I watched, sneaking glances at each other as if we were children in a kindergarten during 'quiet time' — though it was far from quiet. A man traced his hands around a bowed head, and his arms flowed from shoulder to fingertip, before he went on to the next person. He was manipulating energy sent from the spiritual plane. I couldn't help thinking: do people really pay for this?

The folk at the table were silent. It was from a room beyond them that the sound was coming. One man's voice dominated the cacophony; it rose and fell, in a raw, almost primitive chant, sending shivers along my spine. 'Ay-ay-aiee,' he chanted in what seemed to be some kind of glossolalic trance. 'Muuunnn-*ya*!' The last syllable cracked like a whip. He punctuated each sound with a deep, sonorous slapping. The closest my mind could come to making sense of it was a demonic version of a Maori haka.

On the walls, among the symbols and the photos of spirits in their human forms, were photos of the prophet Tia Neiva, her eyes as dark as an owl's. You can see the smile that appeared in photos of her younger days became rarer in later years, when tuberculosis took her in its grip. In each picture, you notice her eyes even before the bouffant of black hair that unfurled from her forehead like a crest, or the grand robes that fell to her feet.

Delfino appeared at my elbow, clearly wishing to hurry us along. He led me to the back of the temple, where a statue of a tall Indian stood, haloed by a headdress of white flowers. He reminded me more of the stereotypical 'American Indian' than a Brazilian *índio*. Judy trailed behind, a crease wrinkling her brow; she was not keen to be moved on by Delfino, either. Reincarnation is a central tenet of the Doctrine of the Dawn: the Indian was Pai Seta Branca, Father White Arrow, spirit of light and leader of cosmic beings. His incarnations include St Francis of Assisi (a particular Brazilian favourite), the African deity Oxalá, and the last Inca king, Túpac Amaru. 'Religion is a way of making sense of the world,' I could picture my old philosophy lecturer saying, as his exuberant passage to and fro across the front of the lecture theatre mesmerised me. I wondered what he'd make of this.

The discordant chorus was making me edgy, and so was Delfino. I waved him off and gestured to Judy. Do we head for the mediums? She shrugged — in for a penny, in for a pound — and I led her to the small queue outside the room where the smacking and snapping, murmuring and howling, was coming from. This room, I guessed, was where the mediums were working. Judy was standing behind me, looking as calm as always, while I shifted from foot to foot, nervous, hoping they weren't going to slap me.

Peeking around those waiting in front of me, I spotted eight or ten seated figures in the dark room. I was impressed: we have only one doctor on Flinders Island. The mediums' eyes were closed as they rocked back and forth, emitting murmurs and exclamations. At the far end of the grotto was the source of most of the noise. The man was striking his chest extravagantly with the palm of his hand, chanting and rocking over a bowed supplicant. It'd be just my luck to get him, I thought, as punishment for being sceptical. He looked thoroughly possessed. What, I wondered, was he feeling? What was he believing? God, what if it's true and they really can heal? What if they find something wrong with me? What if ...? The voice in my head was incessant.

I was embarrassingly close to fleeing, but suddenly it was my turn.

The attendant dropped the curtain behind me and asked how many mediums I wished to see. I turned to consult Judy, but she was behind the curtain. Putting on my brave face, I plucked the number two out of the air, although the truth, of course, was none. The woman gave me no hint whether she thought that was not enough or too many. Taking a pinch of what looked like salt from the proffered bowl, I touched it to my temples, in what I hoped was a correct interpretation of the attendant's gesture. Then I was led to a woman in a stiff white robe. A purple-and-yellow sash was slung across her chest, a white star pinned to her left breast. She thumped the star loudly with her hand several times as she contacted the vibratory plane before passing her fluttering fingers over my upturned palms. Her murmuring was unintelligible, swallowed by the acoustic bedlam of the echoing chamber. Suddenly she stopped beating her chest, took my hands, and lifted them, first to my forehead, then to my heart, finally dropping them and falling silent. As if a switch had been shut off.

The attendant came over and led me to a similarly dressed man who performed more or less the same strange but painless ritual. The second time I caught the words for 'salvation' and 'believe' but felt no discernible difference except a kind of guilty bewilderment. Praying for my soul? Beside me the bellowing man fell thankfully quiet, and I escaped into the plaza before he could start up again.

It turns out that there are two types of healing work performed by the mediums. Both involve the manipulation of energy recruited from the astral plane. One uses the energy to heal those on Earth, like the mediums in their cave-like temple. The other uses energy to heal those on a less tangible plane. These mediums try to cure the malevolent spirits that are apparently responsible for most of the maladies suffered by many, including 'schizophrenia, cancer, epilepsy, and a variety of obsessions'.

While the mediums work in the temple to heal mortals, the spiritual plane, where the malevolent spirits are to be found, is accessed from an arena in an elaborate and theatrical ritual. As if Tia Neiva had read the collected works of Mircea Eliade, the arena is called the Unification. At the heart of the arena is a lake in the shape of a six-pointed star. It is there that a rite called the Consecration takes place up to three times a day. Members of the public are allowed to attend, although this has not always been the case. The mission of the Consecration is 'to intercept an enormous space ship that arrives at scheduled times, called an Amacê, and to direct it into a position above the Star'.

Delfino had not told us about the Consecration. We heard about it from the shopkeeper who sells liturgical items in the Valley. She looked under-dressed, with merely a floral cotton dress covering her voluminous form. From her, you can buy sequins and tulle, beads and chiffon. I bought a full-colour book that elucidated the levels and sub-levels of the doctrine's complex hierarchy, as well as explaining — in great detail — the different symbols, uniforms, badges, and accessories that identify each level. Judy said she was tempted by a ream of tulle in a particularly blaring shade of blue, but it wouldn't fit in her suitcase. I wasn't entirely sure that she was joking.

Delfino sighed with annoyance. If we wanted to stay for the Consecration, he said irritably, it would cost us more. Scowling, I wished, not for the first time, that we'd taken a bus instead.

For the Consecration we were dressed up, too. A white half-cape was tied around Judy's shoulders and then my own. She shrugged and grinned while I giggled like a child on school dress-up day. My costume: World War II nurse. After a siren blasted, we were led, along with six other pairs of visitors, through two sets of ceremonial gates. The gates seemed to have a cleansing function, and before we passed through them, we each took a pinch of salt and swiped it on our temples and tongue. Two men in chocolate-coloured uniforms deposited us onto concrete seats with a finger to their lips. Matching movements. Like Tweedledee and Tweedledum, I thought, but thin. Each seat was designed to accommodate two, and were placed at various points around the star. We had to peer over our shoulders to watch the beginning of what to me looked more like pageant than religious ritual: at the 'radar command post', a man who looked like a Catholic priest, despite his medieval robe, was pairing up the brightly costumed mediums, who began to march towards the Unification in two snaking lines.

The female mediums were dressed in flowing tulle, chiffon, and satin, sprinkled with sparkles and beads and stars. Veils flowed over their capes, cascading down their backs like waterfalls. Female mediums are usually the type called Incorporators, or Moon Masters. Of the group in front of us, there was one male Incorporator, designated by his green, rather than brown, cape. Male mediums are generally of the type called Doctrinators, also Sun Masters, and their capes shimmered in the breeze. The pairs took up positions near each point of the lake, this sacred space that they call the Shooting Star. I squirmed, caught between fascination and disbelief.

The Incorporators stood closest to the water, forming a rippling rainbow. It is these mediums who will reach out to the spiritual plane, casting out 'magnetic nets' to catch the malevolent spirits. As they raised their costumed arms, I turned to Judy with a look of amazement. But she was staring at the mediums who were entering their trances, with their partners watching over them from behind. I wagered that Judy's thoughts were on a similar plane to mine: how on earth do they do this three times a day? It looks like it would only be fun the first time, until your arms hurt from keeping them raised.

And were they really in a trance? Did they truly, privately believe that there is a 'factory of forces' in a spacecraft that becomes caught above the star-lake? That spirits are caught and rehabilitated by educating them as to what they are and how to liberate themselves from karmic debt? Was there a whole world out there that I simply wasn't seeing?

Focusing on one medium who looked like she was only in her late teens, I tried to imagine her training at medium school, studying for her 'master's degree', which would qualify her to be a 'medium of the current'. She had obviously graduated, since she was simultaneously standing by this lake and plunging across the spiritual plane. Was there a topic called Energy Manipulation 101? Maybe it wouldn't have been much different from my own master's degree but for the subject matter. Assuming they weren't actually channelling or delusional, did each of them think they were the only medium failing to achieve true possession? Was each one forever waiting to be 'found out', or did they get together at night and laugh about those who had sought their help? I knew that feeling — like you were pretending to be someone you weren't, that others were achieving something much more easily and doing it better than you, that you were overreaching and at any moment people would realise that. Sian Prior had those same uncomfortable fears, as she confided in her memoir, *Shy*. Deciding I didn't want the answers, I surrendered to the spectacular performance and its mesmerising, silent story of supernatural forces, ending always in the triumph of good over evil.

There was no applause at the end, no encore. The Doctrinators gently woke the Incorporators by passing their hands before them, behind them, and around them until the Incorporators weakly opened their eyes.

In their pairs they filed out, the farthest first, with each group they passed falling in behind like mourners exiting a church after a funeral. Following a silent instruction, Judy and I also left the arena, our backsides more than a little relieved.

Like me, Judy was quiet as Delfino drove us to Brasília airport, where we were due to take a more mundane form of transport. We were going over the experience in our minds. Trying to make sense of my feelings, I wondered why I had been more than mildly uncomfortable rather than content with my utter fascination. If religion is a way of making sense of the world, I have since concluded, the folk of the Valley of the Dawn live in a completely different and much more colourful world to mine and, curiously, I find myself ever so slightly envious of that.

Chapter Nine

Replaying the Reconquista

PIRENÓPOLIS, GOIÁS

'The Brazils are thoroughly Catholic — perhaps there are no countries,
save Spain and Italy, that can be compared to them.' Ida Pfeiffer

After the Pope divided the world in two and allocated half each to Spain and to Portugal, he bade them claim it for the Catholic Church. I imagine he had a map on the wall of his office, which his people shaded in red and in blue. The red signalled non-Christian lands, and were fair game: the veins of the world would be filled with the blue blood of Christianity.

In 1500, Captain Pedro Álvares Cabral arrived after his fleet was blown off-course on its way to India, and he claimed Brazil for Portugal. I imagine on that map on the wall of the Pope's office, his cardinals would have sketched in Brazil's coastline — 7,491 kilometres of it — and shaded the country in blue.

Having arrived by bus alone, and with my room not quite ready, I wandered the streets of Pirenópolis in search of something interesting to eat. Local cuisine can highlight the familiar or exemplify the strange. It can serve not only for comparison, but also to provoke nostalgia. Some of my best travel memories are of food.

I spotted a picture of a crusty pie on a menu board outside one restaurant. A similar image was printed on a banner hanging on the wall next door. The national dish of Australia — if we have only one — is the meat pie. Like all good things, people can't just leave it alone. It now comes in all sorts of tasty flavours, such as cheese and bacon, chicken and camembert, or lamb tandoori. On Flinders Island, our bakery wins prizes for their wallaby and red-wine pies. Those, of course, I miss the most.

In Australia, the pie is as ubiquitous as the hot dog in the United States, the croissant in France, and the hot chip in Britain. Travelling in Brazil, I felt homesick — what the Brazilians call *saudade* — for pies. So I headed up the steps of the second restaurant. '*Tá em falta,*' the waitress said after I'd finally caught her eye: they had none left. Same story next door. The *empadão* was proving as elusive as a Himalayan snow leopard.

The restaurants had sold their pies to the tourists who had flooded into town for Cavalhadas, which I'd read about from home. There wasn't a lot of information on the internet, but it seemed to be a three-day jousting festival, where 'knights' re-enact the battles between the Christians and the Moors — the re-conquest, or Reconquista. The festival was now in its 195th year. I'd heard something about these sorts of re-enactments happening in Spain and Portugal. But it turned out I was in for a surprise.

Further down the road, I was weaving my way around the restaurant tables that spilled across the street when the air was suddenly filled with the sound of hooves rhythmically striking stone. The sound was almost overwhelmed by a bell, rattling maniacally. A horse cantered around the corner. She was draped in yellow from her long neck to her round rump. Turning, she bore her rider away, up the hill towards the church, moving at a graceful lope.

But her rider was no knight. Like the horse, he was costumed in yellow silk. He wore a bovine mask with two enormous horns curling from his head.

After they crested the hill, all that remained was the echo of hooves and the discordant bell: *clop-clank-clop-clank-clop-clank*. Horses I was expecting, dressed-up horses even — but on an arena, rather than cantering through town. (I wondered just how many permits you'd need to canter through public streets at home.) Medieval knights, yes; mad cows, no. Was I in the right town?

In order to get the attention of Brazilian serving staff, it is useful to be adept at the hiss. I am constitutionally unable to do this. In Australia it would be regarded as rude, but it is perfectly acceptable in Brazil. So it took me some time to get the attention of the waitress to ask if she had any *empadãos* left. She did, and kindly recommended it without *guariroba*, the type of palm heart being *amargo*, bitter. She screwed up her mouth in a way that suggested it was the cause of the delicate lines around it. A hiss, so brief it might have been flatulence, was emitted from the man at the next table and drew her away.

It wasn't the first time that day I'd been reminded I didn't fit in. As I checked into the hotel that morning, the receptionist had asked where my husband was. She had looked startled when I told her I was travelling *sozinha*. It was the middle of the university semester; Peter had, by then, begun a degree in archaeology. Then she denied having received my reservation until I showed her the confirmation email on my laptop. Had the booking really not come through, or was the notion of a lone woman too — what: confusing, confronting? It certainly challenged her expectations.

Hoof beats began to bounce off the buildings again. Around the corner trotted a dirt-grey workhorse. She was blanketed in silver. Her rider wore checked blue-and-yellow pyjamas. His head was covered by a black hood, with stark circles for eyes and two rather ghoulish slashes for a mouth.

The effect was chilling and demented.

The devil has played a major role in everyday life in Brazil. These strange *mascarados* wear the horns of an ox, the face of a wild cat, or other frightful masks, a helpful plaque by the tourist office informed me after lunch. The masks were originally intended to scare off the devil.

The devil still dwells in Brazil, but only the more evangelical religions regularly draw attention to the fact these days. And the *oratórios* — small shrines or altars — that used to ward off bad spirits are now more usually pressed into service to pay homage to the saints. You see these cupboards or niches filled with religious statues and symbols in towns, beside roads, on hillsides all over Brazil. I love them: they pepper the countryside with stories.

Masks don't feature greatly in my own culture, either — not physical ones, anyway. Until recently Australians didn't even do Halloween. The mask provides the opportunity for anonymity. An attractive notion. Wouldn't it have been great to grow up with a tradition of masks? Not least when it came with the opportunity to ride a horse through town, dressed in swathes of green silk and wearing metre-long horns studded with roses — as did the next rider to ride by — and with no one looking at you askance!

After my *empadão*, which was delicious, I headed to the arena they call the Cavalhódromo. In the streets around the Cavalhódromo, vendors were busy setting up tarpaulin-covered stalls.

Brazilian festival crowds require much by way of infrastructure. Under shade-cloth gazebos, the legs of portable barbecues were yet to be snapped into place. Some sheltered flat-metal grills that looked like they could, indeed, feed an army of hungry knights. In an empty lot, I watched a jumping castle slowly distend, inflated by a device that looked suspiciously like a vacuum cleaner. On the concrete floor of the service station, next to an inflatable slide, lay the torso of a mechanical cow. There was more than one stall in which a man unpacked bottles while his wife wiped out a blender with a damp cloth before she turned to cut up fruit.

Brazilians are expert in the art of the street party.

Cavalhadas begins in the afternoon of the Sunday fifty days after Easter. It shouldn't have surprised me that I hadn't managed to get anything as mundane as an accurate start time from either the internet or those I'd asked — including my friend at reception. (She had become more amiable once she was forced to label me a 'guest'. She'd even sent her daughter to my room with an extra towel should I wish to use the pool.) The *móvel* date — the date that depends on the religious calendar, not the one on my fridge — is common to Brazilian festivals, and so, it appeared, was the movable start time.

The Cavalhódromo is an open-air arena, and there was already a crowd, buzzing with anticipation, when I walked in. I squeezed into a spot in the grandstand next to a thin man with a child on his lap. Although the slope of the stadium was between me and the sun, the shade didn't stop my blouse from growing damp. Beer-sellers slipped among the crowd like crabs around rocks. I signalled to one and he balanced his white foam box on one knee, lifted the lid, and handed me a dripping can of Skol. People chatted and pointed, hailing friends they probably saw yesterday with the enthusiasm of the long-lost. Parents hoiked squirming toddlers higher on their laps. On the edge of the arena, I spotted the teenage daughter of my receptionist in a milkmaid costume, waiting her turn to dance around a maypole, tapping on her mobile phone expertly.

The marked distinction between the house and the street in Brazil is also evident in the penchant for private boxes at the Cavalhódromo. Beneath the towers at both ends of the arena (the red Moors and the blue Christians) are private boxes. They provide the control and safety of the home in a public place. Not simply a symbol of status, the boxes are a foil to the chaos and anonymity of the outside world. In the private boxes are individuals, social scientists would say. In the grandstand, as in the street, I was simply part of the crowd.

Then the gate at the Moors' end opened, and the chaos of the street erupted onto the arena as a storm of *mascarados* raced in. These masked and costumed figures were on horseback, churning up the neatly coiffed grass. The field was suddenly filled with maniacal faces; the air, with a cacophony of cowbells. This was a re-enactment of the Reconquista? As so often happened in Brazil, my ears began to ache. On the field, I could see that every rider was masked, and some of the horses as well. The bodies of about one third of the horses had been swathed in different materials. The colours of their wrappings covered the spectrum: pale green silk, rich reds and golds. Those with shrouded horses wore the masks with the curling horns. Other horses were bare but for a sack or blanket. Their riders were more simply attired too: some in shorts, some shirtless, many with two riders, both barefooted and riding bareback. It was more like I expected of Halloween than the Pentecost.

The most finely attired — those sporting the huge horns — definitely looked to be riding the finer horses. Class evident on the field? They raced up and down in anarchic circles, like ants swarming their nest. Befuddling me further. The commentators began to ask them to leave; it was time for the knights to appear.

Weaving a path through the spectators and out the front gates in search of food, I found a street party in full swing. Revellers slurped from plastic cups brimming with fruit cocktails or from cans of beer. In various states of dress, they bopped along to music pumping from car speakers. After grabbing a hot dog and returning to find a seat in the front row, I found I hadn't missed much: the commentators were still imploring a few dozen errant and crazed-looking riders to clear the arena.

On Flinders Island, hot dogs (as well as pies) are a favourite. You see them at almost every event: markets, concerts, sporting events, fundraisers. I enjoy them too, but they are generally served as a fat frankfurter in a piece of bread, and simply don't compare to the Brazilian hot dog. The hot dog in the United States is closer. In Brazil, the bun is piled high with extras: peas, pickled carrot, onion, tomato, and cheese are most common, usually with little potato chips criss-crossed like matchsticks on top. A Brazilian hot dog includes most of the major food groups.

Whether it's in a restaurant, on a beach, or at a festival, Brazilian food is everything that, say, Japanese food is not. I love both kinds. Japanese food is about smallness, about delicacy. It is, as Roland Barthes has pointed out, rarely cooked. He described how his dinner tray was presented in Japan: 'It is a frame containing, against a dark background, various objects (bowls, boxes, saucers, chopsticks, tiny piles of food, a little gray ginger, a few shreds of orange vegetable, a background of brown sauce).' They are 'bits of food' and 'slight in quantity'.

Brazilian food could never be described this way.

You'll have heard about the great Brazilian barbecue restaurant. There's nothing delicate about it. Waiters weave their way to your table hefting great skewers of beef and pork, poultry and lamb. The next skewer to pass you by might be threaded with stubby sausages, chicken livers, or nuggets of kidney. Some restaurants provide you with a map of a beast, so you can identify which part of the animal you are being offered. The map is carved up into regions labelled rump, chop, brain. It looks like a jigsaw puzzle.

Brazilian lunch is pretty serious, too. It is commonly offered by the kilo. Great buffet tables stand in the centre of the restaurant, heaving under pots of stews; platters of grilled meat; kettles of black, black beans; and a colourful palette of salad. You can load your plate at the bain-maries that warm steaming rice, red-splashed spaghetti, meaty lasagne, mashed potato, and the odd green or orange vegetable. Japanese food might prolong your life, but Brazilian food is the stuff of life. Even the hot dogs. I'd finished mine by the time the arena was cleared for the knights' entrance.

The women of Pirenópolis had obviously spent weeks — months — dressing their men for this event. I assume it was largely the women dressing the men because gender equality in Brazil is a veneer. Sure, it's been strengthened by the election of the country's first female president, Dilma Rousseff, a sometime Marxist revolutionary who had been jailed and tortured under an earlier regime. Her re-election — against another female candidate — means that she has now been elected for the maximum number of allowed terms. That's twice more than the first female Australian prime minister (Julia Gillard wasn't elected to her brief time at the post), and the United States is yet to have a female head of state, although Hilary Clinton might change that. In Brazil, gender roles still tend towards the traditional.

I had, of course, expected costumes, but not as lavish as these. The velvet measured and cut by the local women was abundant. They had sewn on sequins and embroidered hats. They'd placed beads, trimmed fur, bent metal, glued glass, coaxed feathers, punched buttonholes, and curled brims. Not a seamstress myself, I was almost overcome with awe.

What happened next was also unexpected: I got bored.

The magnificently attired riders rode up and down, one at a time, from each end. And up and down, and up and down. For the first set of twelve passes, one red and one blue-cloaked rider met in the middle of the arena and lifted — lifted, rather than even brandished — a stick about two metres long. It was meant, I guessed, to represent a lance. For the next set of twelve passes, they followed the same process, this time holding long-nosed pistols. When they passed each other in the middle at a gentle canter, the knights discharged their blanks at the ground. The final set of twelve passes — yes, I was counting — involved the brief wave of a short sword. No instant gratification here. No need for televised debates about Brazilian children's over-exposure to violence at popular festivals. Because the Iberians have a solid tradition of bullfighting and other bloodthirsty events, I had been expecting a melodramatic pantomime of aggression. I had anticipated the meaty clang of shields, the dramatic ring of swords. I yearned for the rise and fall of the crowd, united in their cheers of victory or sighs of lament.

Brazil had managed to confound my expectations again. I had assumed the knights would provide the main pace and focus, but the *mascarados* were far more entertaining, if not as sumptuously costumed. Of course, I was the only one surprised.

Looking around, I suddenly realised that the people beside me weren't really watching the arena. Feeling slightly foolish, I wondered why I hadn't taken my cue from them. While my attention was focused on the arena, I was missing the show. The crowd, too, was more entertaining than the supposed main event. Young males — I think they were male — were strutting past in silk jumpsuits. They wore masks with mouths stretched into insane grins; many practised their air-guitars. A figure sauntered past wearing what in Australia we would regard as a convincing bank-robber's costume: a uniform of brown-and-green camouflage pants and a white-eyed black balaclava. A boy — I guessed he was a boy from his size — in a Dracula mask grabbed his satin-covered crotch with one hand and performed a series of energetic hip-thrusts to entertain the crowd. A trio of robed figures came past, sporting the disconcerting faces of Edvard Munch's *The Scream*. And, judging by how many sightings I had of him, Elvis had not left the building.

As at most events in Brazil, the vendors were worth watching, too. They swung poles above the grandstand crowd that glittered with cellophane bags of potato chips and fairy floss. Bottles of water and cans of Coke and beer were pulled from buckets. Taking advantage of the weather, a hip-looking man carried a board stuck with sunglasses. A man, thin with age, hefted a carousel dancing with small plastic toys. I bought a DVD of the previous year's event as an ultra-light plane buzzed over the arena.

A plump, sad-eyed woman, who had covered her breastfeeding baby with a face cloth, vacated the space above me. She seemed to be the only lone person — if you didn't count the baby — in the arena other than me. Still not used to the press of people, I lifted myself into her seat to give my legs respite from being bumped by passers-by.

~

'Rockets are to the Brazilian calendar what exclamation marks are to the correspondence of a *debutante*,' Peter Fleming wrote in *Brazilian Adventure*. Fleming must not have corresponded with many Brazilians: they use exclamation marks too, when they can't use pyrotechnics.

I was woken by rockets the next morning at dawn.

Cavalhadas is but part — the most popular part, judging by the attendance — of Festa da Divino Espírito Santo, a religious festival that was brought from Portugal, probably in the early nineteenth century, although it has roots in the fourteenth. Like so many things brought from Portugal, it was not only adopted but also adapted in Brazil.

The rockets were announcing the imminent start of another feature of the festival: the Imperial Cortege. The procession was departing from the house of the Emperor around breakfast time. The Emperor of the festival is chosen the previous year, in a lottery drawn by the town priest. The Emperor is charged with the organisation of — and with raising funds for — the next year's festival. It could be a lean year at home if your father was chosen Emperor.

With a later start, I found that the second day of Cavalhadas was much the same as the first. At least until the Christians won, the Moors agreed to be baptised, and the two teams congratulated each other, pumping hands and slapping backs.

The Jesuits told the story of the Christians and the Moors to the native peoples they were trying to convert — until the time of the Marquês de Pombal, who effectively ruled Portugal in the third quarter of the 1700s, expelled the Jesuit order from the entire Portuguese empire. So Cavalhadas is a three-day parable. While the Moors were being 'baptised' by the local priest, I made my way down to the arena to join some of the locals who had walked onto the arena to get a closer look. But the man guarding the gate turned me away with a look that suggested I didn't know the right people.

That night my hotel was full, necessitating a move, and I discovered that the theatricality isn't confined to this time of year. You can stay in a castle when you visit Pirenópolis. I mention this not necessarily by way of recommendation. The Castle of Romeo and Juliet has been constructed in brown render and thin pale brick. The turret rooms are large enough for a family of six. Giant plaster urns perch on the parapet. By the pool, two sets of ornate stairs ascend. Each level zigzags, crossing like arms in an embrace. The top landing cries out for a wedding. After I checked in, the receptionist told me there was a *barzinho*, a 'little' bar, 'right outside my room'. It was open in the evenings, she said, although I never saw evidence of it. People were too busy buying their cocktails from the tarpaulin-covered bars that had temporarily made the street home. The *barzinho* was supposed to be in the stone-cobbled courtyard into which, if this were a real castle, or a movie set, horsemen would ride with relief, having just crossed a drawbridge that would be rising above a moat.

I was not unhappy about the bar remaining closed, needing all the help available for my beauty sleep: the mattress was so thin I was thankful that management had not thought to put a pea under it.

~

The last day of Cavalhadas dawned perfectly once more. Again, I was woken by fireworks. Finding a seat had been easier on the previous two days. Today was to be a competition between the blue and the newly baptised red. A priest in black trousers and a shirt shifted to make room for me. The priest on his other side — he must have been hot in his robe — regarded me with a look that made me feel like a scientific specimen. I felt vaguely disrespectful sitting skin-to-skin with a priest. On my right was an under-dressed woman — she looked barely past puberty but for her breasts, which bulged each time she lit a cigarette to share with her boyfriend.

The first round of competition involved target shooting. Somewhere in the world there is a factory that manufactures hollow plastic heads, stamps them with neat buzzcuts, and sends them to Pirenópolis for twenty-four knights to shoot at with long-nosed pistols. Two squat men took turns at running up and down the now-dusty arena — three days of hosting horses' hooves had cleared it of grass — to replace the heads on the poles when one was hit.

The crowd favourite was the ringlets. Each knight used their 'lance' to try to spear a ring the size of a child's hand. Every time a knight succeeded, one of the squat men dragged a ladder under a tall metal arm — it was shaped exactly like the gallows in a game of hangman — and replaced the ring on its hook. The success rate was roughly fifty per cent, and when a knight snared a ring, we cheered mightily. The victorious knight then took his token to bestow on some favoured person in a private box.

Once the games were over, the knights took their leave and paraded proudly through the streets of Pirenópolis for the rest of the mild evening. The *mascarados* trotted around in bands as darkness fell and the church bell called final Mass.

By close of Cavalhadas, I had tried many *empadãos* in Pirenópolis. Not just because the pie is tasty. In Brazil, most often when you look at a menu, the best dishes are only offered in a serving for two. The *sozinho* — or *sozinha* — diner is restricted to the list headed '*Executivo*', which most commonly offers a slice of lasagne, meat, or fish, with chips and vegetables. Although those dishes make me feel at home, they don't do a lot for my search for something new. So the single-serve *empadão* suited me well, with its round pastry and filling of chicken, sausage, egg, potato, corn, and precisely two green olives. Perhaps Anthony Bourdain had the *empadão* in mind when he observed that 'Good food is very often, even most often, simple food.' And, as so often happens the world over, the best simple food was found in a nameless joint tucked away on a side street.

Cutting into my last pie, I watched as the *mascarados* left town, one by one or in posses. The *clop-clang-clop-clang* would stay in my head for some time. I thought about the fact that the odd detail is sometimes more memorable than the most lively of spectacles. There was the female soccer fan in Foz do Iguaçu who bought Cokes for the street urchins who had crept under the side of the marquee to watch the football game. The man on a dusty bus journey standing in his Sunday best for four hours. He was barely out of his teens and his round face hinted at a native bloodline. For the entire journey he kept one hand clamped around the strap above his head, while the other clutched a pink rose in a clear-plastic sheath.

Or the sight that will stay with me more than any other from my time in Pirenópolis: the man in the pizza restaurant who spent the entire night with his pudgy hand caressing his far-from-comfortable date's silk-encased breasts as she sat opposite him at the table next to me.

~

But for a quirk of fate or some arbitrary lines on a map, the Portuguese might have shaded Western Australia in blue. Australians, too, might have been celebrating the triumph of the Christians over the Moors. Instead, the British marked it as their territory, in pink — the colour we shared with Canada, India, and some of Cameroon, to name just a few cousin-colonies. I'd always been taught that pink was used because it was the colour of the Tudor rose, but a Google search presents an alternative suggestion: that it was used because it was cheaper to print than red. But the British were as determined as the Portuguese to claim the land and convert native peoples to Christianity — that, or wipe them out. As I've said, there are many parallels in the stories of Brazil and Australia.

The festival in Pirenópolis celebrates conquest over the infidel and the claiming of land for the Portuguese empire. I notice that the land-claiming itself, and the initial triumph of Christians over the native peoples of Brazil, is not 're-enacted', as indeed such British conquests are not in Australia. This is something I'm especially conscious of, living on Flinders Island.

Although the first sighting of Australia was recorded in 1606, it wasn't until 1788 that the first British settlers arrived on the east coast of the continent. There were soldiers, convicts, and entrepreneurs. As in Brazil, relations between the invaders and the indigenous peoples — who had been in Australia for more than forty thousand years — began amicably enough, but it didn't take long before the original inhabitants began to object to the theft of their land. So began a long series of often-brutal battles across Australia, none more brutal than that which became known as the Black War. The Black War ended with the near-complete eradication of the Tasmanian Aborigines.

As with mainland Australia, Indigenous populations had lived in the islands now known as Tasmania for thousands of years. Much longer, in fact, than native peoples had lived in Brazil. They had been isolated on the island when the land bridge that linked it to the mainland was flooded by sea when the last Ice Age ended.

The state of Tasmania's first European settlement was in 1803, with a party that included twenty-one male and three female convicts, soldiers to guard them, a stonemason, a shopkeeper, and a surgeon. Although the Indigenous population fought valiantly, it didn't take long for the whites to decimate them. Wooden clubs and spears tipped with flint were no match for the usurpers' gunpowder and lead. The genocide was astonishingly swift. By the end of thirty years, ninety per cent of the Tasmanian Aboriginal population had fallen victim to modern weapons or unfamiliar diseases against which they had no resistance. The remainder were transported to Flinders Island, where they were forced to live in exile. Many died there, too.

In the 1990s, there was a re-enactment of some of this history on Flinders Island. It was for a scene in a film called *Black Man's Houses*, about the doomed settlement. I helped my Aboriginal friends into their costumes and watched as they formed a ragged funeral cortege. At sunset they trudged along the ridge of a hill, silhouetted against the sky. They walked to the rear half of the cemetery, where, in the 1830s, there would have been mounds of dirt from too many recent graves. The cemetery is still there, not far from the reconstructed chapel. The re-enacted funeral procession was lead, of course, by a 'priest'. A member of the race whose very presence in Tasmania was a death sentence for its people. Not history worth romanticising or celebrating, but worth remembering.

Chapter Ten

Peddling Hope

ABADIÂNIA, GOIÁS

'A civilisation does not reveal its true meaning unless it is grasped through its mythical vision.' Roger Bastide

'Remember keep your eyes closed … concentrate on the current.' The voice was seductive and awash with Celt. It had repeated the instruction so often it was almost hypnotising. Almost.

'Feel the energy,' it crooned. 'Feeeeed the current.' I flexed the cheeks of my aching butt; those in the know had bought pillows to ease the effects of the adamant pews.

Most *estrangeiros* who come to see the man they call John of God will fly into Brasília's Presidente Juscelino Kubitschek International Airport. They are gathered up by their guides and popped into buses and driven to Abadiânia. The majority of Brazilian visitors arrive in bus groups and stay each night in the nearby metropolis called Anápolis, where the accommodation is not priced for foreigners.

Abadiânia is really two towns. From a public bus boarded in the capital, I'd alighted in the Abadiânia that looked pretty much like any Brazilian town, although perhaps more sparsely populated. Its inhabitants were obviously in the lower income tiers. The town was separated from the mystical Abadiânia by National Highway 060. It was lunchtime, and the dusty plaza was silent and empty. Not a taxi to be seen, nor a map on a wall to show me where to go. A vendor was gathering her wares — sweets, phone cards, plastic dolls, and the like — so she could close her kiosk window, but she was happy enough to call me a cab.

People come from all over the world seeking to be healed by João de Deus (John of God) — or, rather, to be healed by whichever spirit possesses him that day. Now, I like to think the best of people. I like to think that most of us treat one another fairly, with respect and honesty, and I'm not one for ridiculing another's beliefs. But this visit was always going to test someone who likes stories but prefers her explanations supported by scientific evidence.

The story of John of God goes like this:

He was born João Teixeira de Faria in 1942, in a town not far from the current location of the healing centre. The son of a tailor, João was nine when his family had the first inkling that something supernatural might be going on with the boy. He was visiting his older brother's house in a nearby town when he predicted a storm and insisted his family flee to safety. Forty homes, including that of João's *irmão*, were destroyed. Prophesy became a lucrative sideline for the family coffers.

I'd been fascinated simply by João's name, John of God, let alone his profession, since I first heard it. It sounded mysterious. Hearing that a friend of a friend had visited the healing centre, Casa de Dom Inácio de Loyola, I tried to find out more about it from him. But this acquaintance wouldn't reply to my messages, which made me more intrigued.

In the First Current Room of the Casa, I realised my left ankle was draped over my right and hurriedly set them side by side — before the voice could remind me that crossing anything inhibits the flow of energy.

The crossing of arms, legs, shoulder straps, and, of course, ankles is forbidden in the sanctuary. My body, however, kept forgetting. I couldn't quite decide whether my ankles, legs, and arms crossed so often in everyday life or if my body was rebelling against the rules.

There were about one hundred of us arranged as an audience, which was unsettling because we had to keep our eyes closed. 'Even a slit of an open eye can disturb the vibration and undo all the good work you've done,' we were cajoled. The idea was for those of us in the First Current Room to contribute energy to the invisible Current. The medium was sitting on a throne-like chair around the corner, in the Second Current Room. The energy would feed the spirit that — or who — was inhabiting him. The energy would provide the strength to diagnose and treat the long queue of people that stretched left to right in front of the pews in front of us. That we were not supposed to open our eyes to see.

The spirit — the Entity, as he is called when using the medium — could use the energy to perform visible or invisible surgery. This had been explained by the staff in our introductory session that morning in the sanctuary's main hall. They had also explained the rules. The voice repeated these in an endless spool of melodic instruction. The Entity would, apparently, be simultaneously sending energy to us in a kind of symbiosis that I couldn't quite grasp. I couldn't *feeeeel* anything, except my aching backside and no small amount of boredom. Unable to resist, I cracked an eye open.

Shutting it before I was chastised, a ghostly image remained hovering on my retina. The queue of supplicants were like statues carved of snow. The wearing of white is mandatory at the sanctuary, where between two hundred and two thousand come each day to seek healing by, or the blessing of, the Spirit of the Day. My term, not theirs.

'Episematic' is not a word I knew before I went to Brazil. It's a zoological term to describe colours or markings by which species recognise one another. Not that it's needed on this side of Abadiânia; everyone is there for the same reason.

My weight shifted to my left butt-cheek and, flexing the right, I hoped it would be closer to the smaller number today. Three hours must have passed since we filed into the room. At our doctor's surgery on Flinders Island, Dr Alex sees maybe a couple of dozen people a day. Plus his hospital round — if there's anyone in the hospital. The thought of the thousands seeking medical attention here was challenging on more than one level.

The centre is named for St Ignatius, founder of the Society of Jesus. He's one of the most commonly incorporated of the spirits. Incorporation is something done by companies in my world, but it's a word used by a number of spirit-obsessed groups in Brazil. Mediums don't like to say they're 'possessed' by a spirit — the spirit 'incorporates' in them. I have discovered a whole new language since coming into contact with spirits. Even the word 'obsession' has a different meaning to the one I'm used to.

A strangled cry erupted from the Second Current Room. I couldn't tell if it signalled anguish, pain, excitement, or hope. Was it, perhaps, a yelp of success from one of the ashen posse who, that morning, had been sitting waiting patiently at the head of the queue in their wheelchairs? I lifted an eyelid: a bloodless-looking man was being carried through a side door to what appeared to be an infirmary.

Medium João, as he is known when not incorporating a spirit, is in residence in Abadiânia Wednesday through Friday each week. That is, when he is not travelling the world on healing missions. The former farmer and car salesman visited Sydney in November 2014, holding a mass healing session at the Sydney Showgrounds. It was 'a three-day prayer and meditation event' run by a company called Eventopia. He gets around: only a month before, he held five days of sessions in New York. But usually, Saturday through Tuesday he lives with his wife in Anápolis.

That morning, a Wednesday, I had left the stark sanctuary of my room at The Enchanted Pousada, to join the steady trickle of chalky figures who were drifting in ones and twos towards the Casa. The slow white swarm moved as if drawn by some unseen force. In my white pants and top, I followed along, feeling like an extra in an episode of *Doctor Who*.

Most visitors to the Casa have a guide who shepherds his or her charges and explains the rules and procedures. Mine was called Cecilia; I had found her online. If you don't have a guide, you can buy a manual from the Casa shop. It's available in a range of languages.

Every morning at eight, and every afternoon at two, the guides herd their charges into the main hall until it overflows into the courtyard, to listen to the same spiel I had heard that morning.

Each introductory session went pretty much like this:

After the Lord's Prayer, a man in a white coat — the kind that doctors don't often wear anymore — tells us that we are threads of light. Into a microphone he speaks about his ex-wife, who was cured of breast cancer by the Entity. It was the same story, more or less, told in a different language by staff members each day.

Usually you walk back to your accommodation, but if you have just undergone a visible or invisible surgery, he says, you must go by taxi, no matter how short the distance. Then he reels off the rules, which include post-surgical procedures:

You are not to eat pork for four days post-surgery.

Chillies and hot sauce (nearly every table in Brazil is set with hot sauce on it) might stimulate sexual energy, and are likewise forbidden.

No exercise for eight days.

No alcohol or sex for forty days.

Vegetable soup, made in the Casa kitchen, will be delivered to you at your *pousada*.

You must not leave your bed for twenty-four hours (I wondered about going to the loo). During this time you must not read, watch television, or use the internet.

Now, I did want to 'pass before' the Entity, but what if he (no female spirits are incorporated by the medium) ordered surgery for me? I didn't want to be disrespectful, but I *couldn't* follow all these rules. Apart from the reading, the hot sauce, and the alcohol, Peter was due to arrive in a few days; I hadn't seen him for months!

Cecilia, a Swede so pale she could pass for albino, tried to calm my 'what ifs'. She had not been offended that I was not a believer. The Entity helps believers and non-believers alike, she assured me. And surgery didn't hurt. And he won't order surgery if there's nothing wrong with you; he'll probably just prescribe some herbs to take, she said. You see, the Entity sees you as a kind of hologram, or an X-ray in three dimensions. That is how he knows what's wrong.

Cecilia had not had surgery herself, but she had been cured of the terrible depression that had threatened to end her life. Then she fell in love with Arturo, one of John of God's most trusted assistants. A medium himself, Arturo was furthering his study at the night school for mediums in Brasília. I was too polite to ask her if the curriculum prescribed a textbook called 'Spiritual Surgery 101'. Nor did I ask what they discussed in bed at night, despite burning to know. I was fairly sure it wouldn't have been as mundane as whose turn it was to put out the rubbish.

Scientists have recently suggested that there may be a gene — they call it the 'God gene' — that affects our propensity to believe in the supernatural. I quite like this explanation. It makes sense to me.

Once we were released from the First Current Room, five and a half hours after we entered, I went in search of some lunch.

A petite woman with greying hair and eyes so blue they were mesmerising asked to join me at the table in the café. Usually I find that Germans are reticent until they get to know you. This one, however, proceeded immediately to tell me her story. The purpose of her first visit to the Casa was to take before the Entity photographs of her disabled niece and nephew (the Entity heals by proxy if you can't make it in person). The Entity had taken the photos, laid them on top of a pile of other photos, and proceeded to inform the woman that her niece and nephew were, in fact, her own parents reincarnated and that they had given her up for adoption because they couldn't afford to feed her. She said all of this in a conversational tone, as if she was talking about the weather. Then she abruptly left the table and wandered off up the street, leaving me with more questions than answers.

How John of God became a medium was like this:

When he was in his teens, João came across a beautiful woman bathing in the river. The pair talked away a pleasant afternoon. The next day, João returned to the river but found only a brilliant shaft of light. Then a woman's voice spoke his name. The voice — the medium later identified it as Saint Rita of Cascia — bade him go to the Spiritist Centre of Christ the Redeemer. Upon arrival, João fainted, and awakened to the news that he had cured some fifty people while channelling a spirit who incorporated in the medium for years to come, that of King Solomon.

The Entity performed no public surgery while I was there, visible or invisible. On occasion, Cecilia said, the Entity wields his scalpel live on the stage in the main hall. But they screened some operations to occupy us as we waited in the queues. Visible surgery looks pretty gruesome. You can watch it on YouTube. I watched the screen with mounting terror as the man snipped a bulging bowel with small scissors. He used a hook to pull an obstruction from a woman's nose, and then coaxed a lump from a ropy bicep. Crikey! What if he wanted to do that to me?

You can spend a lot of money at the Casa. There's a shop with tables so laden with tall shards of crystal, they look like futuristic cities from a science-fiction movie. The crystals have been blessed by the Entity, as have the bottles of water on sale that staff constantly recommend you drink. There are John of God DVDs, CDs featuring music and prayer from the Casa, and books in several languages about the medium. A DVD and a biography entitled *John of God: the Brazilian healer who's touched the lives of millions* saw my Visa charged US$90. Thankfully after that I didn't have room for any of the rings, gemstones, pillows, triangles (the Casa's sacred shape), rosaries, necklaces, and bracelets on display.

At Cecilia's suggestion — and hoping she was on commission — I shelled out for a double session on a crystal bed. Over a massage table, seven alien-like arms held seven crystals, which hovered to form a 'healing modality'. For forty minutes, the crystals winked at me like a coloured chain of stars as they were shot with light. Rather than making me feel balanced, cleansed, and that my body's 'energetic template' had been restored, I stumbled out of the room feeling as if I'd sent every last bit of my oomph to the Entity. Perhaps he would restore me when I saw him.

The afternoon sessions began with the Lord's Prayer, the stories, and the procedures and rules. As in previous sessions, the staff arranged us into groups they called 'timelines'. Think *Groundhog Day* meets *The Time Machine*. Cecilia had handed me a card that allocated me, because it was the first time I was to go before the medium, to the first timeline. So I joined the queue to walk through the First Current Room to meet the Entity. There were different timelines for surgery and for repeat visitors.

A woman in a white coat tracked along the queue, pressing a button on a small mechanical counter with her thumb: *clack-clack-clack-clack*. I heard her report that there were three hundred and thirty-four in the first timeline. Cecilia had told me the Entity gets grumpy when there's a miscount.

The queue moved surprisingly quickly, but there were about three hundred people before me. I was a captive audience for the repetitive words from the woman on stage, who was relating stories of success and reminding us to be 'mindful' of those around us and to keep our positions in the queue. A message from the Casa manager was relayed: people going down to the cleansing waterfall were asked to wear appropriate clothing. 'Some,' she said, 'are going down there' — she paused, pursing her lips — 'scantily clad.'

Almost hypnotised by the repetition, I didn't notice the queue slowly advancing. There, suddenly, was John of God. Tall and fleshy, he sat on his throne-like chair receiving the sick, the maimed, and the faithful as a king greets his subjects. Then it was my turn, and I was tongue-tied. Cecilia rushed up. She grabbed his biography from my hand, opening it at the page where an ink-stamp had been placed, ready for his signature. She held it in front of the medium, who scrawled something on it, and then on top of a pile of slips of paper: a prescription of herbs to be purchased for US$25 from the Casa pharmacy. He handed it to me. I grasped his big pudgy hand, noting that it was uncomfortably warm and soft before being drawn away by Cecilia.

The visit had lasted nine seconds.

There's a documentary film called *Marjoe*, from the 1970s. Marjoe Gortner was made an evangelical preacher at the age of four. He tells the story of how his parents taught him, rehearsed him, for the role. When he was six, he walked into newspaper offices in towns all over the country, announcing, 'I'm in town to give the devil two black eyes!' Marjoe said he studied performers with charisma, and pinched mannerisms from them, such as Mick Jagger's hippy strut.

His parents devised signals for him as he preached: his mother would say 'oh, Jesus' if he was going too slowly. When she said 'praise God', she meant her son 'had the people where you need them, you'd better take an offering and raise some money'. His mother sewed extra pockets into his suits to better collect the cash that rolled in. Marjoe continued preaching into his young adulthood. He found an invisible ink that turned red with sweat, so he painted a cross on his forehead that would slowly appear midway through his sermon, as a kind of stigmata. In his early twenties, a crisis of conscience made him give it up, and he told his story for the camera.

I can understand the attraction of the evangelical churches: gospel music is compelling, the sense of belonging reassuring. I can also see the attraction of healers such as John of God: they offer a sense of possibility. They offer hope. It is not simply that I am reluctant to believe people will seek to dupe others for their own crass benefit, but that I see the possibility their services might help, at least psychologically. Recently, medical researchers discovered that paracetamol, commonly prescribed by doctors for back pain, works no better for back pain than a placebo. But they didn't say it didn't work at all.

The image I'm most unable to shake when I think of John of God is not from the Casa but from my final night in Abadiânia. I had just ordered dinner at the Saint John Pizza Café when a small, sleek dog trotted in. Not much more than a puppy, he looked to have some Jack Russell in him; probably some dachshund as well. He weaved through the forest of ankles made by a table of Casa volunteers who were celebrating a birthday. A couple of them bent down to scratch his ears, and he trotted amiably back towards the street.

Suddenly the little dog barked sharply — viciously — and snapped at his tail. He chased himself around-and-around-and-around-and-around in quick tight circles, snapping his teeth as if possessed by a dog-spirit.

This didn't look like any game.

He gnashed, he growled and bit at his tail, spinning so fast he became a blur. Then he stopped. As suddenly as he had started.

Neither staff nor the other diners gave him a second glance. I was halfway through my second pizza slice when the dog, who'd continued to happily wander in and out of the restaurant in the lull between demonic storms, started up again. It wasn't a Hanna-Barbera moment; all comic element was absent. If his teeth had reached his tail, he'd have drawn blood. And to this day I still wonder whether the dull thud of fear I felt that night was due to not knowing what was going on, or because I had begun to wonder if the dog might be some demonic counterpoint for the good that is said to be done at the Casa.

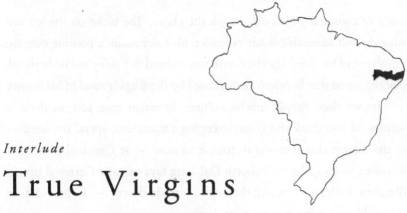

True Virgins

OLINDA, PERNAMBUCO

> *'Everybody likes Brazil and we want the Brazilians to come out.'*
> Alan Hansen

Startled by the sudden toot of a horn, I spun around to see a battered white Kombi van, its rear end weighed low. A man of maybe eighteen was leaning from its side door, yelling, *'Gelo-Gelo-Gelo!'* He bit hard on the *g*. I scooted around vendors as they surged forward, waving *reais* for bags of ice, and nearly bumped into a barbecue that had been set up on the footpath outside the home of another enterprising soul.

I pulled out my camera to take a shot of the line of *vendedores* and their white foam boxes, which lined the seawall for as far as could be seen.

'Ai-ai-ai!'

I turned around again — at this rate I'd get dizzy. A middle-aged man in a short blue satin skirt, capped by a blond wig, grabbed his two mates and spun them round to pose for my camera. Think cheerleader crossed with gorilla. Marvelling that his tight white satin blouse hadn't yet split with the strain of containing his bulk, I took the photo. The bloke on the left was wigged in an admirable shade of scarlet, his hairy paunch pouring over the waistband of his skirt. The third man was encased in a shiny red body sheath that suggested that he wasn't embarrassed by the shapely swell of his breasts.

Despite their deeply macho culture, Brazilian men love to dress as women. If you think this is too sweeping a statement, spend the week — or the month that it seems to stretch to now — at Carnaval sometime. Brazilian anthropologist Roberto DaMatta says because Carnaval inverts Brazilian society — turns the world upside-down — it provides an acceptable space for men to cross-dress.

Everyday life for Brazilians involves a complex set of relationships and responsibilities not necessarily of people's own choosing. It is full of patronage, hierarchies, and kinship. People are forced to don uniforms that at once define roles and responsibilities, make similar or hide. Carnaval is all about choosing: who you will 'play' Carnaval with, how you will dress — if, indeed, you will dress at all. The *fantasia*, as a costume is called, allows a freedom of expression Brazilians find missing in day-to-day life. Carnaval allows the poor to be rich, the downtrodden to be free, and men to become women. It is something of a relief valve. Brazilians will tell you they work hard all year so they can play at Carnaval time. It's a right, a rite, and part of the national psyche.

One of the biggest *blocos* can be found by the beach in Olinda a week or two before the official start of Carnaval. It is called the Virgens de Verdade: Real (or True) Virgins. What did the organisers think they were doing by promising that the virgins are 'real' or 'true', I wondered. One could be forgiven for thinking that the name referred to a religious sect.

Having not been successful in obtaining a certain start time, I'd arrived early in the day. The road was already warm as I walked along the seafront, past the section lined with *camarotes*. Most of these private boxes were 'all you can drink' affairs and boasted the initials 'VIP'. It felt like being on a Formula One circuit with spectator stands looming on each side of the tarmac. Archways of scaffolding catering for advertising and television cameras straddled the street. Many of the private boxes sported the red prawn logo of Pitú *cachaça*. *Cachaça* is the national fire water, a drink made from sugarcane; the fact that it is devoid of colour attests to its lethal qualities. It goes great with crushed limes and sugar in the national cocktail, the *caipirinha*.

Clear of the *camarotes*, the road was edged by the solid line of vendors' styrofoam boxes. They were end-on-end like a long train track, with sellers sprawled behind their wares on the low seawall. I could have, had I been inclined, bought my own foam box, preloaded with beer cans to sell. I passed a couple of harried-looking officials; the one with a clipboard moved ahead, leaving her colleague to slap a sticker on the vendor's foam box, clearing it on behalf of the department of health.

My t-shirt was becoming damp with sweat, and I envied a man who was tying up a hammock in the shade of his carport; he'd have a prime and cool view.

Continuing on, I weaved my way between a short, thin man pushing a trolley holding a stereo several times his size, and a plump woman balancing a bag of ice on her head. A guy in a floral skirt with a ribbed tube-top — it wouldn't have been out of place on my ten-year-old niece — stopped for a photo. After I took it, he asked, '*De que país?*' I answered; he gave a little hop, said '*Canguru!*', and wandered off up the road.

Then a couple posed before I could move on. He was in a short skirt with a white bikini bra with red crosses on the cups. The woman rested her hand on his hirsute belly lovingly while I clicked away. I was assaulted by a mental image of this woman chasing her 'nursey' around the bedroom, Bennie Hill–style.

In Australia, we have the Sydney Mardi Gras. It's the nation's gay-pride parade, although some heterosexuals take part as well. In the big cities of Australia, as in most Western cities today, it's not all that unusual to see men dressed as women, or effeminate-looking men.

But the True Virgins event was no gay pride parade. It was more akin to the time two local blokes turned up in wedding gowns for the Flinders

Island Running Festival and raced in them. Since I was busy trying to run the five-kilometre circuit, I'm not quite sure how the fishermen and the farmers reacted to the prank.

It was while walking beside a trio of gents in brown miniskirts and the half-moon hats that the bandit Lampião and his *cangaceiros* had worn that I spotted, looming in the distance, the hulking shapes of semi-trailers. What, I wonder, is the collective noun for a group of semi-trailers? In *Arabia*, Jonathan Raban, like a number of other travel writers, quotes from *Alice in Wonderland* to help convey moments of amazement or confusion. What were such trucks doing at a cross-dressing parade? As I walked up to the lead semi — it towered over me — I felt as if I had drunk Alice's potion and shrunk, as she says, 'like a telescope'.

In Brazil, it is not uncommon to see trucks carrying musicians in various parades and processions. Trucks take on the role of mobile stages, and are usually decorated only a little more simply than Carnaval floats. I've never seen trucks used in this manner in Australia. And this was the first time I'd come across this giant version of the *trio eléctrico*. They were also mobile billboards, decorated in advertising, and they were huge. Each was an entire theatre: stage, dressing room, sound and light operating box, props room, and wings in one.

Mostly when I think of rock concerts, mobility isn't the first thing to come to mind. The expectation is that an audience sits or stands in front of — or perhaps around — a stage. Or they dance in front of it, like the entire audience did at a Pink concert I went to in Melbourne once. If there's more than one band or musician, they perform their set sequentially, as each band finishes its allotted time. They thank the previous act and start playing. There are also festivals, where there is more than one stage and the audience chooses which stage to go to.

In Brazil, the *trio eléctrico* provides an opportunity for a different relationship between a singer and her audience. And it gives the audience a whole new dynamism.

I had just managed to find a slither of shade cast by a street lamp when

I felt the beat of the first rock song hit me. Teenagers — some of them in onesie animal costumes — swarmed the base of the truck. Weren't they hot? I was sweltering.

Circling around half a dozen plastic tables where old men played crisp games of dominoes, I finally got enough distance from the speakers that I could breathe. The semi began to move forward at a pace barely faster than a glacier. I'd counted ten trucks; it was going to be a long parade.

How did Brazilians cope with such noise? Maybe it's something you get used to. Maybe my hearing is better. Maybe it falls under the theory of 'obligatory expression of sentiment' that dictates delirious and boisterous fun at Carnaval time: you must enjoy super-loud music. Or maybe in Brazil you are born enjoying loud music.

One of the things I love about Flinders Island: there's rarely anything louder than the lunatic laugh of a kookaburra or the low rumble of a boat engine. I guess, like my bloke, Peter, Brazilians are desensitised to loud music. Listen to it loud enough and you start to lose your ability to hear.

On the second stage, Elba Ramalho, the 'Queen of Forró', appeared. Bodies streamed towards her truck. While admiring their fortitude, I scuttled further away to ease the sensation of her sound check. Her 'um-dois, um-dois' slammed into my liver like the quick 'one-two' of a boxer's mitts. A guy in a devil's mask performed a nonchalant somersault on the sandy concrete in front of me. As the truck moved off, the staff of a street-side café crowded onto their verandah, clapping and dancing to the music.

A tall roadie had been standing on top of the driver's cab, outside the safety rail that wound atop the truck like a halo. As the rig inched forward, he gathered the power lines that sagged across the road between power poles. They would otherwise have been snagged by the height of the truck. He held the cables high in a thick-gloved hand, first climbing over the safety rail and then taking mincing steps across the stage as the truck rolled on beneath him. Recently, three revellers were killed by power lines when a Carnaval float collected them. The Queen of Forró didn't miss a note as she ducked under the cables; I could see the roadie admonishing her: *'cuidado'*, take care. Bobbing up again, she kept on singing, and peered over the rail to her adoring fans below.

Every fifteen minutes or so, the next truck in the queue began to move. I wandered off to find one of the seventy-seven buses that the municipal government boasted they put on to help the audience get around. They also promised they'd hand out thirty thousand condoms. Carnaval is a busy time for local governments.

The first truck was just passing the last of the private boxes near the finish line by the time I managed to get there. The viewing platforms allowed their members to be at the same height as the performers.

In the street, I watched, fascinated but not boisterously happy. I was trying not to get drenched in beer, trying not to get bumped — or humped — by fairy-winged folk. It was, indeed, like the crowd had an obligation to enjoy themselves. In Australia, it's not so usual to see men dancing alone, or even with other men in discos or concerts outside the gay clubs. Brazilians are not so silly. Everyone — wigged, winged, or otherwise — danced with everyone else. Men in tulle sambaed with one another, teenagers topped by golden crowns ground their groins together, fairies humped legs and smacked bottoms in an orgiastic frenzy of musical mayhem, and all under a shower of beer.

And there were still two weeks to go before Carnaval.

~ The Southeast ~

Chapter Eleven

The Virgin
Who Appeared

APARECIDA DO NORTE, SÃO PAULO

> *"'Do it," Emilia said, her cheeks hot, "and I'll throw your saints
> in the outhouse."'* Frances de Pontes Peebles

There are many Brazilian women whose good works and achievements
are celebrated, although they are less commonly commemorated with
their own memorial site than men. Sister Irmã Dulce worked with the
poor in Salvador and was beatified in 2011. María da Penha fought long
and hard for the first Brazilian laws against domestic violence after she
was shot by her husband in 1983 while she was sleeping. When she
returned home from hospital, he tried to electrocute her. Law 11.340 was
enacted in 2006; it criminalised domestic violence in Brazil and became
known as the María da Penha Law. Dr Zilda Arns Neumann, an expert
on infant mortality, worked with the extremely poor and the indigenous.
Dr Arns was killed in the 2010 earthquake while helping people in Haiti.
A campaign for her beatification is being mounted.

A huge proportion of good works in Brazil are credited to the intervention of Nossa Senhora Aparecida: Our Lady (Who) Appeared. She is — other than the president, perhaps — the most visible female figure in Brazil. And not only has there been a fine memorial sanctuary constructed in the state of São Paulo to honour her; it has grown into an impressive and well-attended complex. The tension between the shrinking Catholic Church membership and the growing Evangelicals often plays out there.

The Santuário Nacional de Aparecida is a shrine to the patron saint of Brazil. It is in a town roughly halfway between Rio de Janeiro and São Paulo in the region of Brazil they call the Southeast. The Southeast is a lot more populated than the North or the Northeast or the Central West. People from all over the country make pilgrimage to the site, to pay their respects and to petition the image that resides within it. Each time I have been there it has taken my breath away.

The shrine has a glossy multimedia website, its own radio station, and a television channel that broadcasts across Brazil. From any hotel, no matter where I was, I could watch Mass broadcast live each day. I checked out programs called *Welcome Pilgrim*, *Think Like Jesus Thought*, and *Taste of Life*. The latter features advice on a range of matters: rights and duties, manners, food, craft, health, culture, gardening, and floral arrangements are among them. The kindly young face of Padre Evaldo César on the telly became the only familiar feature of my ever-changing hotel room.

The basílica is big by any standards. A few facts: it can fit more than sixty thousand worshippers, ninety-three times the population of Flinders Island, inside its walls. Its annual number of visitors recently topped ten million. The nave is one hundred and seventy metres long. The complex spreads over eleven hectares; it is too big to take in during one visit.

In the town where I live, there's a small brick church built around the same era: the 1970s. It's small by anyone's standards. When we have funerals there, we park our cars on the road's verge, one behind the other because there's too few to bother with a car park. Then most of us stand outside the church, hands clasped solemnly, in sunshine, wind, or rain. We strain to hear the service and the hymn music through tinny speakers borrowed from local musicians, the interior being barely big enough to seat the family of the deceased. Visitors to our town easily miss the church; it's small and blends into the bush.

On my first visit to Aparecida do Norte, my friend Judy came with me. She asked how we'd know when to get off the bus. I didn't think — even in Brazil — something so large would escape us, but said that I had spotted two women who looked to be going there and we could follow them. They wore freshly ironed dresses, not a button out of place. They had been chatting to each other quietly, comparing photos of toddlers. When the women rose, we followed. The bus pulled clear of the bus stop to reveal the basílica. Like the Rock of Gibraltar, it loomed at the other end of a vast strait that was the Fatima car park.

Don Watson wrote of the United States, 'It's a country where God is in the storm and the pancake batter. He is present at rodeos and in football stadiums, where national and college teams — in breach of their Lord's injunction to pray privately and without display — go down on their knees, hold hands and pray together.' He could have written those same words about Brazil.

Some more facts: four thousand buses can be parked in the Fatima car park. There is also parking for more than six thousand vehicles in car parks named Matheus, Marcos, Lucas, and João. (The same names, incidentally, that in English my parents had shortlisted for my baby brother — curious, given their lack of religion.) Hundreds of wheelchairs are available for free use by visitors. In just one of the many ablution blocks, I could choose from forty-six basins in which to wash my hands. The Little Saint, as the image is known, is only as long as my forearm, but she commands a lot by way of infrastructure. Little Saint: Brazilians love to use the diminutive. Aleijadinho is the little cripple, Ronaldinho is a soccer star. The spelling changes with gender.

Like the basilica in Belém, this one was purpose-built to house the statue — or the 'image', as one Marian scholar reminded me, in a rather prim email, they preferred to call her, as if there was something wrong with the word 'statue'. She takes the traditional guise of Our Lady of Immaculate Conception and plays a large role in the national story. Pilgrims come to ask her for — and, more commonly, to thank her for — her help. The image herself, the Little Saint, also has an interesting story.

In October 1717, the governor of São Paulo was due to visit the region, an occasion that demanded a feast. But no fish had been caught in the river for months, and when news of the governor's impending arrival reached the townspeople, they looked at one another in despair. The fishermen poured their hearts and their nets into the Paraíba River and hauled them up empty. Conceding defeat, all but three — Domingos Garcia, João Alves, and Felipe Pedroso — pointed their bows for home. The three had decided on one final cast, and were drawing their net's empty folds into the boat when they felt an unfamiliar weight. With what I imagine was quite a thud, the headless image of the Virgin landed. With their next cast, they hauled in her head. Their third cast completed the miracle, and the boat was filled with fish. It is a story re-enacted, and the feast replicated, each October on the Santinha's Feast Day.

Security these days is tight around the Santinha. She stands in a high nook, behind toughened glass. Judy and I joined the lines of pilgrims who were funnelled past her by stainless-steel rails. Though lapsed, Judy crossed herself reflexively. Vigilant guards watched the praying throng. Before you knew the Santinha's story, you might think the security excessive.

Although there has long been tension between the Protestants and the Catholics in Brazil, two particular incidents between them polarised the nation. The first was in 1978: as Mass was being said, the Little Saint was snatched from her niche by nineteen-year-old Protestant Rogério Marcos de Oliveira. At that moment, it is said, lightning flashed across the valley. Chased by priests and pilgrims, the young man dashed the image to the ground, where she shattered into one hundred and fifty pieces. The

Santinha was restored at the São Paulo Museum of Art. The painstaking work took thirty-three days. I wonder what sort of burden the artist took to bed each night.

A Protestant desecrated the patron saint for a second time in 1995. It was on the Santinha's Feast Day that a pastor of the rapidly growing evangelical Universal Church of the Kingdom of God kicked a replica of the image on national television.

It sparked uproar from the North to the South.

Brazil's Catholics lobbed eggs, fruit, and vegetables at branches of the Universal Church and the offices of Rede Record, the evangelicals' television station. Thousands of protesters took to the streets, brandishing pictures of their saint. Pope John Paul II counselled his brethren 'not to answer evil with evil', but popular Catholicism in Brazil has often been at odds with the Vatican.

The incident became known as the 'kicking of the saint' and dubbed the beginning of a 'holy war'. The somewhat-chastened pastor said he was objecting to the faith that millions of Brazilians put in the Nossa Senhora when they ask for her help. He was sent to work in the United States. For his own safety.

The pastor wasn't wrong in his facts: millions do ask the Santinha for help each year. And although evidence of their success is on display in the basement of the basílica, the stories like Delfino's, when prayers have not been answered, are not. I learned what the body parts I had seen in the cart and the replicas people carried in Belém were: tokens of gratitude.

The subterranean Sala dos Milagres — the Room of Miracles — is also vast. Uniformed attendants accept thousands of tokens of thanks each day on behalf of their small saint. There's no possibility of them all going on display, so I wondered whether they were recycled or stored somewhere else, or whether there was a massive landfill somewhere nearby. Perhaps a combination of the three.

There are various ways in which you can convey your thanks for a miracle. Most ecologically sustainable — and in keeping with the times

— you can text-message your thanks and see it scroll live across the basílica's television screens. You can leave your gratitude in cash or by credit card at the counters dedicated to donations. Or your thanks can be more symbolic, and might be put on display in the Sala dos Milagres.

On entering the sala, I found myself under a canopy of crutches, no longer needed. They dangled from the ceiling like a forest of trees and cast a dappled light over a row of mannequins dressed in the uniforms of Brazil's armed forces. To my left, on wall-to-ceiling shelves, people had thanked Our Lady for their good fortune by constructing elaborate model houses and painting them in blue and pink and brown. On the larger shelves were ornately carved churches. In a tall glass case was evidence of how grateful Miss Brasil 2007, Natália Guimarães, was for her title: her glittering sequined gown was accompanied by a busty portrait.

The white walls held photos, letters, and artificial limbs. There were toys, trophies, and banners of thanks painted by church and school groups. A kayak hung next to a surfboard. In a corner, someone called Lucas had left his motorcycle with a hand-scrawled letter in which he thanked the Santinha for his life. Hard to argue with so much evidence of the good works of the patroness of Brazil.

This is the world's second-largest basílica and the world's largest Marian shrine. They refrained from building a bigger basílica than St Peter's, although I suspect the temptation must have been great.

There is plenty to do after you have paid your respects to the saint, while you are between Masses, while you are waiting for your prayers to be answered. You can visit the Marian museum, chat with a Marian scholar, or take the lift to the top of the shrine's eighteen-story administration building to take in the 360-degree view of the town. From there you can see the Footbridge of Faith, which will lead you to the Old Basílica. You can look out over the many, many hotels and see the Stations of the Cross that lead the way to the Morro do Cruzeiro. The hill is topped by a giant cross.

You can also shop at the basílica's store. It sells vials of holy water, DVDs, books, pens, tea towels, prayer cards, and all manner of souvenirs with an image of the image on them. I found an Aparecida cushion irresistible, as well as a copy of *O Milagre (The Miracle)*, a movie that some millions of Brazilians saw when it premiered in theatres across the country. I also bought a wax liver, hoping it might act as insurance.

And if those activities weren't enough, you can light a candle in the Sala das Velas, visit one of the bookshops, or buy a second-hand confirmation dress for your daughter. And that's just what's available in the basílica itself.

If you bring your family, you will be grateful that there's much to entertain them in the surrounding complex. Taking the long, covered walkway that leads to the Pilgrim Support Centre, I passed taxi ranks, information booths, and a bank of cash machines. The open-sided building is shaped like a cross. At the centre is a food court, although none of the food on offer would earn a tick from the Australian Heart Foundation. A dozen long buffets provided lunch *por kilo*. You could load your plate up with meat from the grill or with *feijoada*, the national dish that — as if it didn't have enough fatty calories and fab flavour — is often topped with crunchy pork rind. You might put some token salad or a few soggy carrots on your plate before taking it to the counter to be weighed. If you, or your children, don't want your food by weight, you can choose a Bob's Burger (the Brazilian fast-food chain is ubiquitous) or even a Big Mac. Having satiated my hunger — *feijoada* is so tasty it has become a regular feature of my dinner parties on Flinders Island — I went window-shopping. The aisle to the south led me past a couple of dozen shops to the giant convention centre. The shops were small, but bountifully stocked. I could buy Bibles and sunglasses, toy trucks and car stereos, figures of Jesus that acted as decorative sheaths for giant candles, binoculars, beer mugs, and fluorescent-green fishing rods — even suitcases in which to carry my booty. Windows displayed Aparecida umbrellas with the saint's image on each panel; she decorated night-lights and glittering capes. We were in Gaucho country, as an ornately embroidered saddle reminded me. Then a child walked past me brandishing a shiny toy horse that every few moments emitted a melodic and maniacal neigh.

The western aisle led to the Aparecida aquarium. On its facade was a mural in which a triumphant fisherman held up the image as if she were the World Cup. I wandered east to the fun park, where I could have ridden the Looping Star rollercoaster if I hadn't feared losing my lunch. Then it struck me that it was likely that someone had changed the date on the Utopia 2100 Ghost Train when Judgement Day didn't arrive with the new millennium.

As a child in Australia, my family went on the same pilgrimages to the 'big' attractions as other Australian families. We visited the Big Pineapple, the Big Merino, the Big Koala, and the Giant Worm, just to name a few. Given that ninety-two per cent of Brazilians nominated a religious affiliation on the most recent census (sixty-eight per cent chose 'Catholic'), I supposed it was not surprising that Brazil might have the 'Big Basílica'. They have a 'Big Christ' too, of course — He overlooks Rio. But at our 'bigs', the most we might have been offered was a five-minute documentary on the life cycle of the koala, or a ride on a small steam train through a pineapple grove. And our 'bigs' generally only sold instant coffee and lukewarm pies. The ticket-seller would do double-duty serving food. She always looked like she hated children as she passed icy-poles across a glass panel in the counter, beneath which lay a pineapple or a worm on a keychain and a few dog-eared postcards.

In Aparecida do Norte, there was so much to do, buy, and eat, it would take days to partake of all on offer. I felt vaguely blasphemous wondering how much this impressive complex made for the Church each year. It's not so surprising that the evangelicals call it 'the shopping mall of faith'.

But the fast-growing Evangelical movement in Brazil is not far behind the Big Basílica when it comes to large places of worship. In Salvador, one of the first buildings you notice when you arrive at the station from which long-distance buses come and go is the Universal Church's colossal cream-coloured centre for worship. It dominates the landscape with its kitsch Romanesque columns. It is testimony to what one social scientist called 'the market-like competition for adherents'.

In São Paulo, the Universal Church has built a mega-church to rival the one at Aparecida do Norte. Bishop Edir Macedo, the Church's founder — said to be worth some US$950 million — boasted: 'Following the guidelines contained in the Bible, the UCKG will build a replica of Solomon's Temple in the city of São Paulo, Brazil.' And so they have. Except that the Temple of Solomon — which was destroyed in Jerusalem in 587 AD — was thirteen metres high, and the bishop's temple comes in at several times that. It towers over the suburb of Brás. Like the basílica, it shouldn't be easy to miss.

Or so I had thought when I had tried see it while it was still under construction.

I had approached the single taxi at the rank outside the Brás metro station and asked to be taken to the Temple of Solomon. The driver looked blank, and I hadn't thought to get an address for it. It was supposed to take up two entire blocks — surely everyone in Brás would know about it. I spotted three cabs parked outside a coffee kiosk. This time, only two of the cabbies looked blank, and I hopped into the car of the third, apologising for interrupting his coffee break.

While asking for the help of Our Lady of Aparecida doesn't come at a cost (although donations are welcomed), the Universal Church works on the idea that if you donate money to it, God will grant your wish. The more, the better. This has made the Church — and its bishop — very, very rich. But not rich enough to finish the Temple of Solomon on schedule, it seemed. When I went to the site, the building only six months from its then-advertised completion date, I could see little evidence of workers, or much by way of a building behind the graffiti-covered fence.

As with Catholic churches, there is a Universal Church in every town in Brazil. You will recognise them from their slogan, which, when translated into English, has a nice rhythm to it: '*Jesus is the man*'. But most of the churches are shopfronts, not replicas like the temple, which is made of stone imported from Jerusalem and can seat ten thousand, on chairs imported from Spain. The temple was built on more than seven hectares, an impressive amount of space given that it's in the middle of one of the world's largest cities. But it would appear they'll need lots of space: membership of Brazil's evangelical religions grew some sixty-one per cent in the decade to 2010.

The Temple of Solomon was built to celebrate its bishop rather than a saint, but at both it and the basílica, performance is important. The natural showmanship of Brazilians outdoes anything we do in Australia — or, I contend, in the United States and the United Kingdom. Even the more boisterous modern churches, such as the evangelical Hillsong, can't really compete. Ida Pfeiffer, an Englishwoman who visited Brazil in the mid-1800s, was of the opinion that for Brazilians, religious ceremonies are attended 'merely for the sake of amusement', and certainly most ceremonies I've seen have been entertaining.

At the Temple of Solomon, the charismatic theatricality of Bishop Edir Macedo is an attraction. But at the basílica, the Little Saint is the star of the show, and at no time more so than her Feast Day. Each year a pageant is performed that provides more colour and movement than a football Grand Final in Australia or, perhaps, Independence Day parades in the United States.

The Feast Day is preceded by a novena. Each of the nine Masses is choreographed with all the panache of a Carnaval parade. One year during a novena, Our Lady of Aparecida was delivered to the altar by a giant hand sculpted from styrofoam. The following day, the Nossa Senhora was accompanied down the aisle by an abstract figure I had trouble, initially, identifying. Eventually I realised it was the pregnant Virgin Mary; it could have been designed by Pablo Picasso or Juan Gris. Her arms encircled her womb, on which a foetus had been painted. It was a small representation of Jesus, complete with umbilical cord. The priest took the Nossa Senhora and placed her on a platform held aloft by four figures sculpted from purple neon tubes, from where she oversaw the saying of Mass. Pilgrims watched the arrival of their Santinha with tears in their eyes. I could see why the Protestants might accuse them of idol-worship.

It is a bone of contention between the Vatican and Brazilian Catholicism that devotions are so often turned into something of a show. The fluid border between the sacred and profane has engaged many studiers of Brazil. And until travelling in Brazil, I had never thought of church as a place to be entertained.

My personal favourite of the novenas that year was worthy of an Olympic opening ceremony and starred Padre Evaldo César, the kindly-faced priest from my hotel-room television set. He was mid-sermon when he was interrupted by circus music — *dunt-da-na-nah-nah, dunt-da-na-nah-nah* — and a dozen white- and golden-robed angels came roller-skating down the nave's central aisle. On the heels of the roller-skating angels was a float bearing a giant golden chalice, slowly spinning, in which sat a teenage girl who shone with beauty. She brandished a large Bible like it was a scorecard, before handing it to the priest with a bow.

~

In Brazil, I often feel like the Elizabethan travellers must have felt when they first came into contact with diverse forms of religious practice. Even those that I thought were familiar are rendered strange. They offer a sensory pageantry that's sometimes overwhelming.

And I can see a few reasons why the Vatican might feel challenged with regard to popular Brazilian Catholicism: it's not solely the issue of idolatry. Popular Catholicism in Brazil seems to have put the Virgin on more or less equal footing with Jesus. But you'd think the Vatican would applaud the entertaining nature of Brazilian Catholicism, given that it attracts a larger audience for them in a world where the number of Catholics is shrinking fast.

Chapter Twelve

The Little Cripple

ESTRADA REAL, MINAS GERAIS

'Journeys are the midwives of thought.' Alain de Botton

The only complaint you'll hear me make about Brazilian bus travel is that the *rodoviárias*, the terminals for long-haul buses, are usually on the outskirts of cities and towns. Unlike boats or trains (although Brazil is notably light-on for trains since the British stopped building the railways), buses don't take you to the town's beating heart. Yet when I arrived at Ouro Preto's terminal, it was easy to see why the bus didn't go to the *centro histórico*: the streets of the former state capital are best suited to mountain goats.

Ouro Preto is a mountain town in the rich state of Minas Gerais, at the head of the Royal Road. It's a region you come to, as I did, for its beauty and its history; the town is on the United Nations' World Heritage List. At the beginning of the eighteenth century, in the heady days of the gold rush, it was more crowded than Rio de Janeiro, Buenos Aires, or New York. Its cobbled streets spread up the sides of a valley like veins. Talking points include not only impressive colonial edifices and old stone churches, but also a modern hotel that the town's authorities allowed to be built on the main street. It was designed by Oscar Niemeyer, of course. Most of his buildings I find both beautiful and challenging, but it was immediately obvious why the hotel in Ouro Preto wasn't one of his most famous works: it stuck out like a teenager's first pimple.

Gold was discovered in the mountains of the state of Minas Gerais in 1695, sparking a Klondike-style gold rush, good fortune that would last more than a century. In 1940, Getúlio Vargas' New State regime commissioned the internationally famous Austrian writer Stefan Zweig, still best known for his fiction, to write Brazil's first comprehensive history. It was an exercise in nation-building.

Zweig reported scenes similar to those Australian children learn about our own gold rush days, and kids from the United States learn about California: tales of hard lives, sudden riches, prostitutes, and price hikes. 'Adventurers, beggars the day before, strut about in gaudy velvet clothes … A pretty *mulatto* girl costs more than the most expensive courtesan at the King of France's Court.' Mining is still evident in the Minas Gerais region today: giant machines devour whole mountains, excreting them into gargantuan peaks. As in Australia, mining has been an important contributor to the national economy, and an efficient wrecker of landscape. And in both countries, as in the United States, the discovery of gold had a large impact on the national story.

The gold rush began and ended while Brazil was a Portuguese colony. The taxman dispatched The Royal Fifth from the Casa de Contos, the Counting House, which still stands today. Like its neighbours in the square, the building is whitewashed stone, sprinkled with tall shutters more like doors. Its shingled roof slopes up towards a central turret-like room — the perfect spot for snipers. The Royal Gold was hauled along what was soon called the Royal Road, which had been built over trails originally hiked by the Tupi people.

The miners came up with an array of inventive methods for tax minimisation. They buried their gold in pottery jars. They bartered with gold dust, hid nuggets inside religious statues, and made lavish donations to the Church.

The brotherhoods who ran the churches in Ouro Preto used their wealth to construct more churches, with which they hoped to distract their rapidly growing congregations from lives of pure debauchery.

Minas Gerais has supplied such a significant number of Brazil's heroes, I sometimes wonder if it's congenital. National heroine Chica da Silva I mentioned earlier: she began life as a slave and ended it owner of a diamond mine. Former president Juscelino Kubitschek was born in the state capital. Brazil's most famous Spiritist-medium was incarnated as Chico Xavier in the state's north. So, too, Carlos Luz, Brazil's shortest-serving head of state. He was president for two days after Getúlio Vargas shot himself, and before being deposed by his minister for defence. Minas Gerais was the birthplace of the 'king of football', Pelé, arguably the world's most famous Brazilian, and the internationally celebrated artist Lygia Clark. And, before her bones were excavated by archaeologists, the state was the resting place of 'Luzia', Brazil's oldest human remains.

The dentist nicknamed Tiradentes — 'teeth-puller' — earned his place in the pantheon of Minas' most famous by being hanged, drawn, and quartered. He was one of the leaders of Brazil's first republican uprising, and the royal family, who hadn't yet fled from Portugal to Brazil, used Tiradentes to show their subjects the consequences of suggesting Brazil mightn't want their rule. His corpse was tied to four horses and pulled apart in the square in Rio de Janeiro that would eventually be named after him.

The beautiful colonial town now called Tiradentes is further along the Royal Road from Ouro Preto. It is a drawcard for tourists, but there is another — and at least as famous — favourite son in the region. Aleijadinho: he is known by only one word in Portuguese, like a modern megastar, like Madonna, Pelé, or Cher. There is no town named after him, only a small museum, wherein lie some of his metacarpal bones and a single vertebrae. When I came across them, I was aghast that some of the remains of the man who is probably Brazil's most famous artist would be left in a corner on a dusty wooden shelf, like a full stop forgotten from the end of a sentence.

Although he was born Antônio Francisco Lisboa, schoolchildren learn about Aleijadinho, a nickname they translate as Little Cripple, although the artist wasn't afflicted by the degenerative disease until he was forty or so. It took me a while to get my head around the name. In Australia, it's not considered politically correct to refer to someone's stature or their disability. Brazilians have few such qualms, and given the propensity to refer to colour and race, perhaps it's more surprising that they don't call him the 'Little Black Cripple'.

The gold rush was well underway by the time Antônio was born, the product of a union between a celebrated architect and his African slave. As Brazil had the highest rate of manumission in the world, it was not unusual that the illegitimate boy was freed upon birth. Manuel Francisco Lisboa, himself the designer of impressive and imposing churches along the Royal Road, armed his son with a chisel and hammer and packed the boy off to some of his better-known sculptor friends for training. Antônio developed a lavish style, carving 'monuments of piety' in wood and gold and soapstone.

Soon, Antônio was receiving commissions from the local brotherhoods to sculpt statues and altars, chapels and portals, and to carve biblical scenes to adorn naves and facades. He took the regional baroque/rococo style to extravagant levels, creating columns, towers, and temples, shaping ornaments, fountains, and figurines. He chiselled reliefs and frontispieces; he hewed pulpits, pilasters, and parapets, as well as oratorios and sarcophagi, to adorn churches along the Royal Road. You will see some of the work of Aleijadinho if you visit the Museum of Sacred Art in São Paulo, but most of it is still in situ along the Royal Road, the Estrada Real.

During their lifetimes, Michelangelo and Leonardo da Vinci grew both rich and famous on the proceeds of sacred art. They also worked in a range of other areas. But Aleijadinho's story is quite different. It took a century or so for the Little Cripple to become more than a footnote in the national story. Yet when he did, he became a major character.

When President Vargas commissioned Zweig to craft a history of Brazil, he wanted to create, promote, stimulate, manipulate — chose your own verb — Brazilian national identity. A decade before, Gilberto Freyre's *The Masters and the Slaves* touted Brazil as a flexible and humane country where intermarriage between races was proof of its racial democracy. Zweig seized upon the Little Cripple to reinforce this idea.

But Zweig's is not the only account of the artist's life that fails to mention that, because of his race and colour, Aleijadinho was paid a paltry sum for his work. Despite his talent, he was only commissioned via a middleman, and was refused entry into the influential artists' guild. During his lifetime he was accorded little respect. Some authors of the time blamed the artist's very disease on his racial 'impurity'. What the disease actually was has never been certain — leprosy or syphilis seem the most likely. Little wonder, I suppose, the work that I've seen is far from uplifting. Its emphasis is on the dark: angles carry skulls, Jesus seems always to be gushing blood, Mary never looks serene; even cherubs seem to be scowling.

When I imagine scenes from Aleijadinho's later life, during the years he was damaged by disease, my mind creates a montage, as if the Stations of the Cross have been recast from the more sensational accounts of his life:

The first image shows a squat man with dark springy hair and a badly trimmed beard mounted on the back of a black slave; Aleijadinho's thick arms are wrapped around the slave, his backside in a sling, his wrists fastened across the slave's muscled chest with cuffs made of leather.

The next scene, dimly lit, shows the slave with one bare foot extended to step with care on the cobbles.

Then they have turned a corner, having narrowly avoided colliding with a bonneted woman; she looks breathless, frightened; her hand clutches at the cross hanging at her bosom.

The cross is raised to her lips; the slave has stepped around her.

She has turned and now holds the cross aloft, a shield between her and the men who have continued into the night.

The slave has arrived beneath a freshly whitewashed church, edged with the tan hues of natural stone; steps rise to a patio that leads to the church's front doors.

The slave's moonlit shadow rests on the pair of wooden doors.

Inside the church, the slave stands beside a pew; the leather ties are a tangle on its wooden surface; a brother in a dark robe is loosening the swaddling that supports Aleijadinho.

Aleijadinho sits on the pew, holding forth one stumpy arm; the leather strap lies limp over the slave's upturned palm like Dali's melting clock; the brother is reaching for a chisel.

The brother is flinching slightly as he holds the chisel's hilt against Aleijadinho's wrist; several fingers are missing, and in places the skin has frayed; the slave is wrapping the long leather ties around and around, binding chisel to wrist.

The slave is binding a pad of wool over Aleijadinho's knee; the brother watches on, looking slightly less queasy; in his right hand he holds a second pad; a hammer has been bound to the artist's other arm; the binding is solid like a gauntlet anticipating a hawk's landing.

The slave's swarthy arms are setting Aleijadinho on a rung of a wooden ladder, as if he were hanging a picture.

The artist has steadied himself, kneeling on the rung, arms splayed like a crab; his 'thick, protruding, Negroid lips' look to move in silent prayer; his 'inflamed and ill-tempered eyes' are fixed upwards, upon an angel half-carved in wood.

The brother and the slave watch from below; the artist has climbed level with his latest work; wood shavings fill the air as he wields the tools to carve the angel with an almost demonic passion.

Prejudice and discrimination, two unfortunate traits of the human race practised against anyone considered not 'normal'. And that's how we justify our prejudices and discriminations. They're understandable, perhaps. I guess it is 'normal' to be wary of those not 'normal', those who are different or strange.

But, as a notion, I find 'normality' challenging. It saps my energy. Travelling, surely, is attractive partly because one can escape what is 'normal' in one's life. And we can be reminded that 'normal' is relative. Mark Twain said: 'Travel is fatal to prejudice, bigotry, and narrow-mindedness ... Broad, wholesome, charitable views of men and things cannot be acquired by vegetating in one little corner of the earth all one's lifetime.' One needs be able to compare 'normals'.

In Australia, I am 'normal' — or, at least, 'the norm'. If you believe our government and our media, at any rate. I am white, English-speaking, right-handed, middle-class, and almost precisely the average weight for an Australian woman. I even have the most common blood type.

Although technically Australia is a multicultural society — we have some two hundred and fifty nationalities — in reality I am, or I represent, the expected. The government and the media — or at least the gatekeepers of the media — are made up, mostly, of other people like me. And they'd like it to stay that way.

Among travel writers I am also fairly typical: white, Western, Anglophone, middle-class. Although I'm female rather than the more-typical male (so perhaps this book is doomed to the half-of-a-bottom shelf reserved for 'women's travel writing' in bookshops).

It is people who make you 'normal' or make you strange. I was normal until my family moved from Melbourne to Sydney and was suddenly surrounded by kids who thought I was not. Those kids had never experienced another 'normal'. The primary differences were that I was from Melbourne — a serious sin; never underestimate Sydney–Melbourne rivalry — and middle- rather than working-class. In Australia, we like to think we're a classless society but we're not, of course. Prejudice is a universal practice.

Sometimes it can produce some interesting results. Aleijadinho seems to have poured all of his anger and distress due to his difference, due to the prejudices of the townspeople, into his art. That is what made him, and his contribution to Brazilian identity and culture, all the more unique, and today his art and his difference are celebrated in Brazil.

In his essay collection *Testaments Betrayed*, Milan Kundera examines a number of French translations of a passage from *The Castle*, a novel that Franz Kafka wrote in German. Kundera, himself from Czechoslovakia, discusses the tendency of translators to impose their own assumptions, prejudices, and foibles on a work. Even when a literal translation is available, says Kundera, they often deviate from it. In one example, Kafka had deliberately repeated a word that should, according to Kundera, be translated as 'strange'. All three translators of Kafka chose to avoid the repetition of 'strange'. Was it the word or its repetition that disturbed them? All three changed Kafka's meaning, and all three interpreted the word 'strange' differently. So even the very word 'strange' is different for all of us according to our preferences, beliefs, and prejudices. In Brazil, I am, literally, *estrangeira*, foreigner, stranger: certainly not normal. Other people make you — and me — strange.

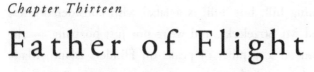

Chapter Thirteen

Father of Flight

PETRÓPOLIS, RIO DE JANEIRO

'One posthumous sign of a man's greatness is that his corpse does not
make it into the grave in one piece.' Paul Hoffman

In a corner of an upstairs room at the aerospace museum on the outskirts
of Rio de Janeiro is a glass case. Not an unusual item to be found in a
museum, of course.

Inside the glass case is a statue of a naked and winged Icarus. His
muscles are taut with the effort of holding up a giant sphere. The metal
of the sphere is punctuated with holes, which represent stars, too small
to see through, but form a reasonably accurate depiction of the celestial
skies nonetheless. A plaque will tell you that inside the sphere is another
sphere, made of crystal, in which rests the once-beating heart of the
famous Brazilian inventor Alberto Santos-Dumont.

The road to Petrópolis wraps tightly around the mountains in
the state of Rio de Janeiro. I was reading about Dona Flor when my
stomach began to protest. Jorge Amado — the famous novelist is one

of the world's best-known Brazilians — gave Dona Flor not one but two husbands, and I was keen to see how that played out, but for now I had to bow to the pressure of the mountains and put the book back in my pack.

I've often wondered at which point hills officially become mountains. On Flinders Island, we call our highest point a 'mountain'. It's probably just a great looming hill, but 'hill' is a label with considerably less gravitas. It's called Mt Strzelecki, and we're not just boasting — the great explorer climbed a number of peaks on Flinders Island. Made from large slabs of granite, from the top you can see the Tasmanian mainland on a clear day.

The mountains that cradle the town of Petrópolis, however, are tall — the highest is over two thousand metres — and green and lush. There was a noticeable change in temperature from Rio when I climbed down the steps of the bus.

Petrópolis is the attractive town to which the Brazilian imperial family repaired when the city heat made Rio too challenging for their olfactory senses. First Dom Pedro Primeiro and then his son, Pedro Segundo, ruled from Petrópolis' Imperial Palace. It is now a museum.

My nose, too, had been looking forward to relief. The smells that waft around some Brazilian cities — and Rio especially — can still be challenging.

I took a cab to my *pousada*, which was quaint but un-imperious, despite it being named after the royal family. The young man who checked me in looked at me suspiciously. '*Só um?*' he asked, peering around for a husband, or at least a clandestine lover. Ulysses left his wife Penelope at home for years to go exploring the world; was it so outrageous that I had left Peter to keep the home fires burning?

Then a stocky, greying man appeared and, after tut-tutting his son, asked if I knew that the municipality had cancelled next week's Carnaval in Petrópolis for financial reasons. It was unclear if it was my single status that had prompted the enquiry. Then he took my bag and led me down a dark passageway to a room so tiny I was reminded of Mark Twain's ship's cabin: 'There was still room to turn round in, but not to swing a cat in, at least with entire security to the cat.'

Another lone traveller, Alberto Santos-Dumont didn't do things in a typically Brazilian way, either. And, like me, he was obsessed by motion, by the notion of passage. Known as the 'Father of Flight', he was another national hero born in the state of Minas Gerais.

Although his achievements are known internationally, the Brazilian's fame outside his own country is not on par with the United States' Wright brothers, despite being the first man to fly 'heavier-than-air vehicles' in controlled flight. He controlled flight, bent it to his will. The achievement was huge.

Brazil isn't known for supplying the world with inventions, though it has some notable ones to its name. Manoel Dias de Abreu invented a useful type of radiography to screen lungs for tuberculosis. German-Brazilian Andreas Pavel invented the Walkman. French-born Brazilian Hércules Florence invented photography in Brazil at about the same time as it was invented in Europe, but because he never published his findings, the fact is little recognised. The achievements of these Brazilians are totally eclipsed by those of Alberto Santos-Dumont.

Early on, the inventor worked out how to send balloons so high they slipped into space. By changing their shape to the more aerodynamic ellipse, he invented the dirigible. He was living in Paris when the Aéro-Club de France offered a prize for circumnavigating the Eiffel Tower along a seven-mile aerial racetrack within a half an hour. In 1901, piloting a powered airship, Santos-Dumont claimed the prize of eleven thousand francs and began dining at Maxim's.

Deciding that dirigible flight — lighter-than-air flight — was like 'pushing a candle through a brick wall', he turned his mind to heavier-than-air machines. He made the first public flight of a powered aeroplane in Europe in 1906, and won other prizes, including for the first flight over one hundred metres in a powered aeroplane.

In Paris, he became legendary. Parisian bakers put his face on their gingerbread men. His 'look' — elevated heels, broad panama hats, and a handlebar moustache — was adopted by fashionistas. He lived on the Champs-Élysées, and in demonstration of his height-obsessed eccentricity, he hung his dining table by wires from the ceiling. He used stilts to sit at it until one day it collapsed, spilling his dinner guests to the floor. When he got a craving for a coffee while aloft, he tethered his balloon to his weathervane and popped inside to make one.

A small man, Alberto Santos-Dumont constantly strove to escape the nickname 'Petit'. He wore hats that made him look taller, and commissioned tailors to cut his suits to disguise his stature. And, after he returned to Brazil in 1928 hailed as a national hero, he built a tall house, high in the mountains, which he called 'The Enchanted'. It is now a museum.

Most Brazilian residences are jammed up against one another and shut away from the street, whether by fence or facade. Typically, a Brazilian house (outside the *favelas*, at least) has an intermediary zone between the street and the home immediately behind said fence or facade. Such a space — it might be a drawing room or a secure verandah — works as a passage, a place to pass through if you are a resident, or where visitors can be met. It is a mediating space, like an airlock. Occasionally, you can see into it through the verandah bars. You might see a couple observing the realm of the street from the safety of their rocking chairs. You might see the family's best china displayed in glass cabinets. In city *centros*, the realm between the street and apartment is mediated by foyers and doormen.

I noticed, as soon as it came into view, that the house that Alberto Santos-Dumont built was different. He perched it high above the street, and there is no fence to speak of. The mediating space between house and street is a steep staircase. The home is small — I felt big inside it — and you walk through the door straight into his lounge room. The walls are covered in memorabilia: photos show him with dark hair lacquered to his head, in stiff, high collars that he wore in order to look taller. The inventor had all the mod-cons: a wooden telephone hangs on the wall. In the bathroom is Brazil's first hot-and-cold running shower. He built an outdoor staircase to the roof to better observe the skies.

In his last years, the famous Brazilian was horrified to see his beloved aeroplanes used to make war. The fact that President Vargas was using aeroplanes to bomb a pro-democracy movement that had become vocal in São Paulo, together with a series of fatal accidents in aeroplanes, including in one named after him, made Alberto Santos-Dumont sink into depression. He ended his own life with the help of two red Parisian neckties hung from a hotel-room door.

You have to travel back to Rio de Janeiro to visit the grave where most of Alberto Santos-Dumont's remains lie. It is a grave he dug himself. The inventor personally selected the site, dug the hole, and re-buried his parents in it. He left space for himself, for when the time came to join them.

But his heart was stolen, literally, by the doctor who certified his death.

Eventually, haunted by remorse, the doctor tried to return the organ to the aviator's family, who refused it. The government stepped in and, after commissioning a suitably respectful and commemorative vessel in which to preserve it, stowed the heart in the display case in the Museu Aeroespacial.

The Brazilian emperor Pedro II and his wife also had disrupted interments. They died in exile, but their bones were eventually returned to Brazil with the remains of their daughter Princess Isabel in 1921. The princess was a favourite dining companion of Santos-Dumont; she predeceased him by eleven years. Now in Petrópolis, the royal family lies in state and suitably commemorated.

Before leaving the mountain town, I walked along the canal to the old stone church to pay my respects to the royal remains. Behind a set of bars that would be respectable in any prison, they rest in shiny white-marble sarcophagi. Their slightly spooky death masks stare at the ceiling. I was still trying to translate the words on the headstones when a busload of Brazilian tourists streamed through the doors, and I slipped out and headed for the bus station.

Historian Martin Thomas describes the long and fractured battle of Arnhem Land's Bininj people to bring home the bones of their ancestors. The bones were hidden in an attic at the Smithsonian Institute's National Museum of Natural History. It took some ten years of lobbying before the first victory, one that was quite bizarre and unacceptable to the Bininj: the Smithsonian agreed to return two-thirds of the bones. In his essay, Thomas doesn't say which two-thirds, or how the Smithsonian decided which bones would go home, and my imagination offered a bizarre image of a child-like divvying up. I found out later that it was, in fact, even more appalling: the Smithsonian had actually kept certain parts of certain people. Skulls, apparently, were especially prized.

The Smithsonian was eventually shamed into releasing the last third of the Bininj ancestors. Martin Thomas recorded their journey as they were sung home. The Bininj interpretation of the world — I trust I am reading this right — says that death does not sever the link between body and soul. That one's remains need to be put to rest in one's own territory, one's belonging place. That territory is where the spirit will remain. The bones seem to act as an anchor and a salve for the spirit.

It was hoped that if the returning and re-burial ceremonies were scrupulously performed by the Bininj, the spirits of their ancestors would rest, rather than restlessly stalk the earth.

Science writer Paul Hoffman, who wrote a biography of Alberto Santos-Dumont, doesn't say why the inventor's heart was stolen. Nor does he say why the aviator's family refused its return. But there it sits, un-beating but respectfully encased, in the Museu Aeroespacial, twenty-five kilometres west of the rest of his remains in the Saint John the Baptist Cemetery in Rio de Janeiro. Yet I can't help wondering if Alberto Santos-Dumont's spirit is soaring the skies or pacing the earth in agitation. Christianity — he would have been raised Catholic, and there's a Catholic university named after him — of course, advocates a severance of body and soul. I couldn't help noticing, though, that the cross on his tomb is quite small, and overshadowed by a life-size statue of Icarus.

Chapter Fourteen

Dictated by the Dead

UBERABA, MINAS GERAIS

'Sometimes anonymity is the child of real understanding and true love.' The spirit Emmanuel (via Chico Xavier)

Imagine: a man sits alone at a kitchen table. In front of him is a stack of paper that his right hand scribbles upon with a pen, line after line of handwritten Portuguese. He pauses, only for a moment, when another man approaches and whips the top sheet of paper away to reveal a fresh sheet. The writer continues on, writing-and-writing-and-writing. Imagine him writing like this, night after night after night.

My taxi had the lingering smell of a urinal. The driver did a U-turn next to five homeless men forming a neat row of hummocks, each under a dirty blanket on the footpath outside the *rodoviária*, where my bus had terminated. Arriving around five in the morning meant there'd been some time to kill waiting for daylight. I had sipped tea and nibbled *coxinhas,* one of the ubiquitous range of fried snacks that Brazilian kiosks offer for breakfast, shivering slightly in the unaccustomed coolness of the

177

bus station. But the tea was hot, and the teardrop-shaped batter that surrounded the chicken kernels was tasty. As soon as it seemed late enough, I left my bag with the luggage-checker, slipped into the back of the taxi, gulped, and cracked open the window.

Paulo knew where Chico Xavier was buried *'por certo!'* His own father was buried in *'no mesmo cemitério. Entendeu?'* The same cemetery, I did understand. Paulo pronounced Xavier 'Shavier'. The *x* in Brazilian Portuguese is called a 'shiss' (and pronounced 'sh'). A cheeseburger is called an X-burger because 'cheese' and 'shiss' sound the same to Brazilians. I do like that. Then Paulo asked me where I was from and yes, you guessed it, if he hadn't been driving he would have given a little hop. He did say — in what might even have been an Australian accent — 'kangaroo'.

Paulo played the role of tour guide proudly, walking me down a long, straight row of mausoleums, pointing out the grand resting-places of prominent local families. In Brazil, they invest in their dead, as historian Robert M. Levine noted: people 'sometimes sold nearly all of their possessions to pay for the funeral of a loved one'. Funerals are elaborate, lengthy, and solemn. A good burial is crucial. Some of the tombs were of a size that living families would be grateful to reside in. Although it would be dark inside, if the straight panes of concrete, marble, and granite were anything to go by.

Turning the corner at the end of the row, Paulo escorted me past some tombs that were merely head-height: the middling classes, perhaps. He stopped by a glass-wrapped room on one corner of a T-intersection. Queues could form in three directions — and regularly did on Chico Xavier's birthday and the anniversary of his death.

The early-morning sun was shining sharply through the windows. I could see inside only by shading my eyes and stepping close to the glass. The tomb was part tribute, part display case.

Francisco Cândido Xavier was another famous Brazilian born in Minas Gerais. Before he died, and against competition the likes of J.K., Aleijadinho, and Alberto Santos-Dumont, he was voted Mineiro of the Century by seven hundred thousand of the state's newspaper readers.

When Xavier was alive, he was given the keys to innumerable cities, in Brazil and abroad. He has appeared on stamps and was even nominated for the Nobel Peace Prize. What made him interesting to me was not those things, nor that he wrote more than four hundred books (rather a staggering number to me, who has written just one). Or even that his books have sold more than fifty million copies, enviable figures by anyone's standards. It's that he claimed that it wasn't he who wrote the books; rather, they were dictated to him.

By the dead.

In the tomb was a large writing desk, its surface carefully covered with books and pamphlets like a neatly quilted tablecloth. Sitting at the desk was a bronze statue. Chico's left elbow rested on the table with firm weariness and, as if he had just lost someone dear, his bronze fingers cradled his brow. His right hand gripped a bronze pen: his most famous pose. Three pots of flowers had been placed under the window by well-wishers. Their perfume was sweet, as gay as their tidy orange wrapping.

'Chico' — 'Sheeko' — is the diminutive form of 'Francisco', and so he was called by the whole of Brazil by the end of his ninety-two years. One of nine children, Chico was born in Pedro Leopoldo, near the site where South America's oldest human remains were later found. His father sold tickets in an illegal lottery, the infamous Jogo do Bicho, the 'animal game'. In Brazil, you grow up having your favourite of the twenty-five animals, 'beginning with an ostrich and ending with a cow'. Each animal represents four numbers between one and one hundred. If you don't have a favourite, you look for signs from the heavens as to that week's winners.

Like seeing signs, being visited by spirits is not, as you will have gathered by now, so uncommon in Brazil. Thus, although Chico's mother lost her corporeal form when he was five, Chico still saw her regularly. By the time he left school at age thirteen, he'd been hearing voices and seeing spirits for a while, to the disgust of his teachers and the derision of his classmates.

In the film *Chico Xavier*— which, depending on your sources, between two and three million Brazilians saw in the first month of its release — he is portrayed as a *mulatto*-haired younger man by an actor with an intensity of look that his agent may have described as 'smouldering'. The actor's coif sits above his head like Bart Simpson's. In later years, Chico's hair began to recede, and he donned a wig that looked — in both the film and in real life — like a 1970s comb-over. It was the subject of much teasing by his mentoring spirit, Emmanuel.

One of the scenes in the biopic tells of the time Chico's father took him to the local brothel to lose his virginity. It was fairly common practice then, but instead of being introduced to the joys of sex, Chico led the women in a prayer circle. He would remain famously chaste all his life.

Beside the tomb, Paulo stooped to pray in front of a bronze bust depicting Chico in his later years. He crossed himself and looked up to see if I was ready to go. On my tiptoes, I was trying to get a look at the covers of the books lying on the desk.

As a schoolchild, Chico 'psychographed' — Spiritists prefer this word to the academics' term 'automatic writing' — essays. One such essay won an honourable mention in a state competition. Was it cheating when you plagiarised the words of a spirit, I wondered.

Chico's first commercial publication was *Poetry from Beyond the Grave*: 259 poems by fifty-six writers, including by some of Brazil's most famous dead poets. He would go on to channel the literary works of more than five hundred spirits, crediting them with authorship and reminding those who were sceptical that the Ten Commandments were 'spirit-writ' by Moses.

One of Brazil's leading literary theorists, who reputedly confirmed the authenticity of Chico's work during his own time on the physical plane, joined the pantheon of Chico's spirit-authors after he died. He dictated five books to the medium in as many years.

The theorist's widow, not one to let her scepticism get in the way of fiscal opportunity, decided to take Chico to court. If the words were actually her husband's — as Chico claimed — then she was due a cut of the royalties. The court dismissed the case, saying it had no way to prove or disprove the matter of authorship. The judge continued, in a statement perhaps designed to set precedent, that regardless of the matter of authorship, the dead don't need royalties.

Chico Xavier's extraordinary popularity wasn't due so much to his literary output as his help in keeping mourners in touch with departed loved ones. From all over the country, people travelled to queue patiently outside his home for his weekly public sessions. The medium would channel messages, writing at extraordinary speed. As well as his books, over his lifetime he is reputed to have produced ten thousand personal messages from the dead. The letters usually provided enough corroborating detail to convince the living of their authenticity. Indeed, academic studies have analysed such messages. One recent study assessed the accuracy of the information in thirteen letters and explored 'the possible explanations for it'. The results of the investigation found the information — generally regarding the deceased's life and family — was 'accurate and precise'. Yet the study's authors acknowledged (somewhat reluctantly, from my reading of it) that they could not 'rule out the hypothesis that the participants' wishes that these letters were genuinely authored by their beloved … might have misled them to distort their memories of what they have actually communicated to the medium before he psychographed the letters'. They still managed to conclude that 'normal explanations for it (i.e., fraud, chance, information leakage, and cold reading) are [only] remotely plausible'.

The people kept on coming despite the protests of Chico Xavier's detractors. The matter of authorship was hotly contested, even among the medium's family. His nephew publicly called him a fraud. In an effort to avoid a family split, Chico moved south, to the small city of Uberaba. There's no explanation as to why he chose Uberaba, and no reason became apparent as Paulo drove me around.

We took photos of each another by the bust of the famous medium, and then Paulo walked me back to the car via a row of knee-high but still marble-covered graves. In the taxi, I cracked open the window again and hoped it wouldn't be a long ride to Chico's house, which had been turned into a museum. The house reminded me of rocky-road chocolate — little rooms attached briefly to each other, all brown and marshmallow. An ode to the 1970s.

Paulo and I signed the register — he'd never been inside, he said — and walked down a short corridor lined with collages of grainy photographs in matching wooden frames, a patchwork of the past. In apparent testimony that all book proceeds were given to charity, many photos showed rows of children standing at a long table, each paired with a soup bowl. In other images, people, dressed in their raggedy best, queued along one — or sometimes both — sides of dirt roads in small towns. The photos attest they came in droves, from wide and far, to receive letters via the great medium, arriving in wagons, in trucks, by bus, and on foot.

Also in the museum were the books Chico produced: nearly five hundred of them. The medium's most constant companion was his 'spirit guide' and author, Emmanuel. After Chico's dis-incarnation, Emmanuel joined the pantheon of spirits that visit upon John of God. Emmanuel's past incarnations include the founder of the Jesuit missions in Brazil (St Ignatius of Loyola, also a regular of John of God's), and Roman senator Publius Lentulus. Chico received a number of books from Emmanuel, beginning when the medium was in his late twenties. These works were mostly historical novels, set in Roman times, 'notable for their lurid sex scenes'.

When he first appeared by Chico's side, Emmanuel gave the medium three rules for his mission: discipline, discipline, discipline. In pictures, Emmanuel is depicted in a long white robe. Certainty surrounds him like a glowing halo.

The most prolific author to write with Chico's hand was called André Luiz. The most famous of all of Chico's books is 'written' by that spirit. *Nosso Lar* ('Our Home') is the first book in a series of nine. It was made into a film called, in English, *Astral City*, a more descriptive title to the uninitiated.

In the novel, André Luiz, recently deceased after a long illness, awakens, weeping 'copiously', to a strange new world. A doctor during his most recent incarnation, André remembers nothing about the spiritual plane from previous dis-incarnations. He is full of wonder and questions, writing in a flowery style that is more likely to be appreciated in Brazil than in Australia. Take this: 'We must wash our face in the sweat of the world and break the chains of hatred, replacing them with the sacred bonds of love.' I can't take issue with the message, however.

The worlds of *Nosso Lar* are as elaborate as those of Dante. Here is a snapshot of *Nosso Lar*'s workings and its philosophy, as I interpreted it:

Our life on Earth is but one of many incarnations. The central and lasting plane is not the earthly one but the spiritual world in which rests Nosso Lar, the spirit city that is a transition zone. Through performing good works, spirits evolve from that plane, climbing a heavenly ladder to higher realms. In Nosso Lar, 'nearly everything', André observes, 'seemed to be an improved copy of Earth'.

The 'colony' seems somewhat over-governed: there are seventy-two ministers in six ministries, some linked to the 'terrestrial sphere' and others to the 'higher planes'. Newcomers are put to work in the ministries of assistance, communications, or elucidation to prepare them for their future planetary tasks.

Anguished beyond belief by his confusion and consumed by a somewhat-belated concern and longing for his family, André laments to his kindly spirit-guide Clarêncio that 'the storm of my complaint had led my mental boat to the wide ocean of tears'. Patting his shoulder comfortingly, Clarêncio tells André that his feelings are the 'result of a faulty religious education' and not to despair, as he can be healed by 'transmissions of spiritual and psychic energies' called magnetic passes.

A precursor to Chico Xavier, a man known as the Father of Spiritism, who wrote under the pseudonym Allan Kardec, experimented extensively with magnetic passes in the 1800s. You might have heard of him; I had not. Kardec was a highly educated Frenchman who began to study those phenomena that 'unite the physical and spiritual worlds'. Kardec wrote many books about Spiritism; *The Medium's Book*, a handbook for channellers, is the best-known. Although Kardec and Xavier are often spoken of in the same sentence, after years of speculation most now agree that Kardec was not reincarnated in Xavier. A pity: it would have had a nice symmetry.

From the Ministry of Communication, in an attempt to assuage his anguish, André sends a letter via a spirit-writer much like Chico Xavier to his family on Earth.

André craves permission to go to the Ministry of Elucidation, hoping to delve into their filing department's stores of memories. He meets up with his mother, who tells André that his father, although outwardly faithful, pious, and hard-working, had 'maintained clandestine liaisons' during his last incarnation on Earth, and as a result has been left in the Umbral — a kind of purgatory — with the 'multitudes of wayward spirits'. Given that extra-marital affairs are said to be something of a national sport in Brazil, I wasn't surprised to learn that it's quite crowded in the Umbral.

At times the workings of Nosso Lar seem like an attempt at institutionalised socialism: inhabitants work eight hours a day 'in the collective interest' and earn 'hour-bonuses'. These 'individual service coupons' can purchase a better house, clothing, and more.

Some may argue that Chico Xavier and his work have been derided by more than a fair share of sceptics, but he found plenty of acceptance, too. A Brazilian court hearing the trial of eighteen-year-old José Divino Nunes, who was accused of shooting his best friend, accepted as evidence a letter that the dead victim dictated to Chico. 'We were just playing around,' read the letter, 'thinking about shooting somebody's reflection in the mirror when I passed in front of my image reflected in the mirror, [and] the shot hit me. If anybody should ask forgiveness it should be me — I should have been studying instead of fooling around.' The charges against José Divino Nunes were dismissed by the judge. His finding noted: 'We must give credibility to the message automatically written by Francisco Cândido Xavier where the victim recounts the event, exempting the defendant from any guilt.' Chico provided evidence at three more murder trials that resulted in the acquittal of the accused or a reduced charge.

Standing on the cream linoleum in Chico's living room, by the velour-covered lounges, I was surrounded by images of the medium. Portraits show he was an odd shape. His broad shoulders were like ski slopes, falling steeply from his neck as if to better shed the weight of the world. His round, combed-over head was like a personal invitation to cartoonists, suggesting it might wobble off his long ropey neck. Nearly blind, Chico's eyes were hidden behind dark glasses.

On one wall hung forty or more of his trademark hats, a perky combination of beret and cap. The wardrobe's door had been replaced with glass to display rows of suits sheathed in plastic. In a room the size of a cupboard was his bed, so smoothly made I was sure it had been ironed. Both bed-ends touched the walls, his austerity plain.

It's not surprising Chico Xavier is a national hero: he assigned the royalties from the sales of his books to provide welfare for those in need. He lived on his small government wage and, later, a pension. A raft of organisations were — are — funded by the books: they provide for soup kitchens, housing for the aged, clothing for the needy, care for the orphaned, and Spiritist Centres for the soul.

Paulo and I had the museum to ourselves for nearly an hour when we were swamped by a busload of Brazilian tourists. They oohed and ahhed and pointed to the tea towels, t-shirts, and handbags. They bought keyrings and pictures of Jesus and Chico Xavier hugging one another, as well as postcards, plates, and busts. They admired the Chico Xavier clocks and the Chico Xavier jewellery boxes. All this before they'd even seen the exhibits.

Paulo weaved his way outside to get the car while I tried to work out which books to buy. The shelves held hundreds of Chico Xavier titles in a multitude of languages. There were poetry and novels; children's picture books; manuals, history texts, science books; and, of course, religious doctrine. One of his friends estimated that Chico had spent seventy-three thousand hours as a medium in his first forty years of writing, and that's on top of his day job as a government clerk. Little wonder, perhaps, that the medium is most depicted hard at work, pen in hand, at his desk writing books for the spirits.

The choice was too hard. I grabbed a couple of DVDs, paid, and went out to find Paulo waiting for me in the loading zone.

The notion of reincarnation is a comforting one. It's certainly more attractive than simple nothingness. For both the living and the dying. But I rather like the belief of some of Australia's Indigenous that the spirit lingers in its homeland. As is clear from Martin Thomas' essay, 'Because It's Your Country', that's why it is so imperative that all stolen bones be returned to Country. 'Having the bones here it means that you've got the man still staying in his own territory ... I can call to him any time because I know he's here,' the Elder Wamud tells Thomas. Comforting to think my home might still be my home after I'm gone. As with the planes of the Spiritist religions, there can be interaction between the worlds of the living and the dead.

Chapter Fifteen

Candelária Massacre

AVENIDA PRESIDENTE VARGAS, RIO DE JANEIRO

'In Brazil the man behind the wheel has the right-of-way. If the pedestrian is too old or too slow, já era, *he's history.'* Alex Shoumatoff

Avenida Presidente Vargas leads you into Rio de Janerio. When you arrive by air, you will travel on it, whether by bus or by taxi, whether you are staying in the *centro* or down Copacabana way. The end — or rather the beginning — of the broad avenue appears as suddenly as an exclamation mark on the shore of Guanabara Bay. Like the Avenida in Belém, it is named for Getúlio Vargas, Brazil's longest-serving president.

When you watch the Carnaval parade at the Sambódromo, you will likely find your seats in one of the grandstands just off the avenue. Half of the road will be closed to traffic, designated 'float parking'. The floats will be tantalisingly, frustratingly, hidden under huge tarpaulins so as not to spoil the surprise. Maracanã Stadium is on the same road, although it has, by then, changed its name to Avenida Osvaldo Aranha, after the Brazilian president of the United Nations General Assembly, who shepherded through the vote to create the state of Israel. Also on the Avenida is the site of one of Brazil's least-proud moments, where, in 1993, eight children were shot by police as they slept on the ground by the Candelária Church.

Ever since working with *The Candelária Massacre* by James McQueen during my time as a literary agent, I wanted to see where such a thing could happen. I wanted to find the memorial — surely there would be a memorial — that commemorated the eight short lives. I looked for it one September, as the annual Independence Day Parade was assembling behind the Candelária Church; the military was readying itself to march along Avenida Presidente Vargas. I had planned to visit the church, the murder site, before watching a parade that, if it included the police force, might just have included some of the perpetrators.

Street children are not an uncommon sight in the streets and on the beaches of Rio de Janeiro. Many prefer to make the streets their home to escape the dangers of the *favelas*. In the early 1990s, a group of children, sometimes as many as seventy-five, made the plaza outside the church their home. A couple of times the group had to move elsewhere after they received death threats from plain-clothed police, members of the *extermínio*. The *extermínio* — death squads, often made up of military police — made money on the side, paid by local businesses to 'pass the mop', as the local saying went.

In their little community, as Julia Rochester observed in her book *The Candelária Massacre,* the kids tried to live life normally: 'They mapped out kitchens and living rooms in cardboard and played at mummies and daddies.' They followed the Orixás, as well as the Christian God. There were two leaders in particular: Come-Gato (Cat-Eater) and Turinha, boys who dressed as girls, in halter tops and skirts. At age twenty, Come-Gato would be the oldest victim that night. The older took on the role of parents, ensuring the younger were fed and clothed. The children washed their clothes and bathed in the fountain outside the church. The day before the massacre they'd made a trip to the beach.

The children slept spread around the plaza, 'some of them on their backs with their arms above their heads like babies'. Someone had given them a bunch of blankets in institutional grey, although Rio never gets what I would call cold.

A car stopped in the plaza; plain-clothed military police got out. One thing they were seeking that night, it came out later, was revenge because some street children had thrown stones at police cars. One officer pissed against a pillar for so long that surviving children remembered the stream with awe. Then the gunmen spun around, shooting at whichever boys appeared in their sights. Come-Gato was shot in the eye, though he didn't die immediately. He was, reportedly, the primary target. There was a suggestion that he owed one of the policemen money. 'Pimpolho' (Little Pimple or Little Man) was eleven. He was shot as he ran to seek the refuge in the arms of his 'mother', Beth. When the policemen's car took off, some of the children were dead. More would succumb to their wounds. Small bodies lay, as if strewn by a storm, across the grimy black and white tiles of the plaza.

There are photos from that night. Some show the dead. But one, in particular, stays with me. It shows the living: a group of obviously shell-shocked children, mostly boys, with tight black curls. Their small hands are clutched around the grey blankets in which they huddle. Some have shrouded their heads, using the blankets as hoods, as if to hide from some threat now unseen. In the centre of the group is a woman, her slim arms encompassing as many of the children as she can manage. The kids and the woman gaze in the same direction; I imagine it is where authorities are attending to bodies. A soft and deep sadness is evident in the eyes of the woman. But it is the look in the eyes of the children that strikes the chord of familiarity in me. It is the same look as in the photo at Canudos. It is the look of the survivor and the look of the betrayed.

The Candelária Church is a beautiful large baroque building of grey stone. As is usual in Brazil, it is filled with pews and ornate sacred art.

In front of it is the small plaza. I walked three times around the church and the plaza, looking for a plaque on a wall, a sign, a statue, some acknowledgement of the events of 23rd July 1993. But it wasn't in any of the places I expected it, and I shook my head and turned toward the parade.

~

Independence Day, 7th September, is celebrated across Brazil. In Australia, we celebrate the day the country was 'discovered', forgetful of the fact that the land had been lived in for over forty thousand years before the arrival of migrants. Brazil gets around the problem by keeping Discovery Day low-key and making Independence Day the day of national hoo-ha.

Earlier, I'd seen municipal workers setting up rows and rows of bleachers along the central boulevard in Brasília, forming grandstands from which the locals could watch their parade. It was immediately apparent, as I approached the starting point for Rio's parade, that authorities expected far fewer to attend the annual celebrations here: only one seating-stand had been erected. Obviously, most Cariocas honoured the holidays in their usual fashion — with a trip to the beach.

Taking my cue from others, I ducked under the rope, which had been — for reasons not readily apparent — tied around the trees lining the southern footpath of the avenue. Crossing four in-bound lanes entirely bereft of traffic to the centre pedestrian path, I could see close-up the gathering troops who filled the *avenida*'s outbound lanes. There were more paraders than spectators, despite the city topping six million residents.

While, from my foreigner's point of view, the Brazilian military have been primarily responsible for the more dramatic and heavy-handed episodes in the national story, the recently crafted 'National Strategy of Defence' notes that Brazilian national identity is fundamentally entwined with the armed forces. Forças Armadas do Brasileiras has more than three hundred thousand members and can call upon around two million reservists, with a government expenditure in the vicinity of fifty billion US dollars. Military service is mandatory for men; women can choose to join up. Compulsory national service provides more conscripts than needed for national security, so the plan is to have the surplus perform social works, a benefit to the community, which will also help in 'reaffirming the unity of the nation'.

A boy of about five sat on his father's shoulders, not really listening as his father identified the different legions. Each section had a unique uniform and was accompanied by a marching band whose members were polishing their brass. Some corps were in camouflage, some wore green berets, and others dressed in red and white.

One Brazilian anthropologist has used the Independence Day parade to contrast Brazilian society's behaviour with that of Carnaval. Certainly the contrast is marked. The Carnaval de Rua — the parties and the parades that fill the streets of almost every Brazilian town each year — is much more casual and fun and, it would seem, much better attended.

The hotel staff had thought the parade would begin at eight, but by nine there was still no sign of rousing cheers. A blonde woman clad in motorcycle leathers sauntered up and handed me her camera with an enquiring smile. Then she strode, in her knee-high boots, to pose between two handsome young men in dress uniforms. After I returned her camera, she turned to thank the men. I could see she was wearing a vest that proclaimed membership to the Caveiras Aladas Motorcycle Club of Rio de Janeiro.

Then the sound of motorcycle engines ruptured the air. The woman bolted like a startled colt between two companies of Brazilian Navy, heading towards the sound. With my interest in the array of different uniforms, I hadn't noticed there was another parade about to start.

A couple of hundred bikers — many on Harleys — moved off slowly down the service lane, engines thundering. Much more quietly behind them ambled civilian groups. As they passed, I could identify youth clubs and charities, sporting teams and folkloric groups. The Lion's Club wore brown vests over their casual clothes, sporting their insignia. A white flag announced the Rotarians, and behind them drifted the Legion of Goodwill.

There were school associations, a few gaggles of scouts, and church groups, moving past, one after another, like a lazy river on a summer's day.

A wave of brassy notes streaked importantly down the avenue as buglers called for their troops to form up. With the small crowd of onlookers, I wandered along the military line as army, navy, and airforce rushed to their places. Each placed their left hand on the shoulder of the man or woman in front of them, confirming their correct position. Thus, section by section, company by company, they strode up the *avenida* to the pomp and ceremony of their brass band and *rat-a-tat-tat* of their drummers. Left-right, left-right, left-right.

One thing military parades have in common with Carnaval is that both are loud. More than once I had to put my hands over my ears as a band marched past. And again I could only admire the scope for dressing-up that Brazilians have. In Australia, our military uniforms are, well, uniform. There's nothing surprising about them. Perhaps it's just their familiarity. Past me were marching a platoon of cadets — I guessed they were cadets from their fresh faces. Their uniforms were neat navy suits, trimmed with sky-blue and buttoned in brass, but it was their hats — helmets, I suppose — that impressed me. They were shaped like cake tins, and waving from each helmet was a short plumed decoration, the colours of a blue and red macaw. These ornaments looked like nothing so much as one of those crazy-coloured cylindrical icy-poles that my nieces enjoy no matter how cold the weather, and each one wobbled crazily with every stride.

~

Every country has stories about injustice. Australia is no exception, and one particularly shameful episode in the narrative of our nation played a major role in my life, although thankfully from afar. My father left his job as one of Melbourne's leading lawyers to become a writer. He began investigating a notorious and complicated miscarriage-of-justice case that took thirty-two years to be made right. In the meantime, it destroyed, or irrevocably altered, a great many lives. And the authorities — the very people we look to for protection — were to a large extent responsible.

In August of 1980, a baby called Azaria Chamberlain 'disappeared' — was taken by a dingo — from the tent in which she lay sleeping. The baby was not found; no dingo was caught. Azaria's mother, then a Seventh Day Adventist, failed to cry for the cameras, opting for a stoicism common to her brethren. Although she couldn't begin to imagine what they were, her God would have had his reasons. This failure to perform according to the expectations of the police, the media, and the Australian population essentially led to Lindy Chamberlain being charged with the murder of her daughter.

My father wrote a book about the case called, depending where you are from, *Evil Angels* or *A Cry in the Dark*. It won some of Australia's most prestigious literary awards. It was made into a film starring Meryl Streep and Sam Neill. And eventually it helped to prove that Lindy Chamberlain was innocent. She had spent two and a half years in Berrimah Prison before they released her; eventually her conviction was overturned.

It was a case in which evidence was falsified, or interpreted either incorrectly or with extreme prejudice. How, I kept asking my father during the trial and afterwards, how could this go on in Australia? Australia — like Brazil — is a democracy with proper judicial processes, where 'innocent until proven guilty' is supposedly paramount. Where people aren't supposed to rush to judgement, or take the law into their own hands. Just as I ask myself how those Brazilian policemen could murder children in cold — or hot, for that matter — blood.

It's not only the authorities, though. The media dehumanised Lindy Chamberlain. It made her into what psychologists call an 'outgroup member': 'utterly different from the rest of us'. Her 'strange' religion was highlighted, her slightly odd manner of expression, her accent, her apparent lack of grief at the death of her daughter. It provided Australians with a sense of 'moral disengagement', which meant we didn't feel much by way of sympathy for the grieving mother. And we didn't look at the evidence too closely.

The process of dehumanisation goes some way towards explaining why the human race put up with slavery for so long. It explains — but doesn't excuse — why many Australians are not more sympathetic to the plight of refugees. During much of Brazil's history, and especially during the War at Canudos, backlanders were portrayed by the newspapers as sub-human. So, too, the children who lived at Candelária. The colonel in charge of the investigation said with some sadness: 'People thought of it as a decontamination.'

Street Carnaval

RIO DE JANEIRO

> *'I have felt like a Brazilian only twice. Once, at Carnival, when I danced the samba in the street. The other, when I beat Julie after she betrayed me.'* Paul (*O País do Carnaval*)

I was fairly sure that Lesley, a close friend from Tasmania, had not expected to be offered a plastic penis within moments of getting off the airport bus in downtown Rio de Janeiro. After all my time in Brazil, I wish I could report taking it in my own stride, but instead have to admit to being a bit startled.

Lesley was with me to experience Rio during the five days of Carnaval, when the city streets are filled with fantasy and soaked in urine. Next morning, we were in the *centro* when we found ourselves in a swamp of people wearing all manner of costumes that featured black and white polka dots. It was eleven in the morning and suddenly it was impossible to move — or to hear. The plaza above Cinelândia metro station had turned into a giant mosh pit. I'd heard about Rio's infamous street parties, but nothing prepares you for the real deal.

There was no room to dance individually to the music that was booming from the giant speakers surrounding the stage. Luckily most of the black-and-white-clad crowd knew the steps. They sambaed collectively, a little forward and a little back, like an enormous wave lapping at shore. One of my sweaty shoulders was stuck to Lesley's sweaty shoulder, the other against the tanned bicep of a man with a dummy in his mouth and a nappy over his nether regions. Brazilians are comfortable in skin-to-skin crowds in a way most Australians are not.

With a roll of my eyes — the music being too loud to speak, and unable to lift my arm to point — I suggested to Lesley that we find somewhere a little less pressing. I felt like an orange being squeezed.

Brazil's tourism authorities do not advise you about just how difficult it is to perform normal activities during the festive period. Sure, we were in town to play Carnaval, but also to see the sights: the giant Christ that watches over the city, his arms outstretched and welcoming; the twin domes of Sugarloaf Mountain, under which Charles Darwin lived for a time; Maracanã Stadium and Copacabana Beach, to name the most obvious.

The first difficulty came after we got off the bus at Cinelândia, the night before Carnaval officially began. Men in overalls were hammering huge wooden boards over the shop fronts. My agitation grew as we walked past boarded-up building after boarded-up building: we needed, most desperately, a bank. I had a few *reais* from a previous trip, but not nearly enough to get two of us through the next five days, especially at Carnaval prices.

Then we came across a tall board that was propped open on the foot-path, like a giant door from *Alice in Wonderland*. Spotting the yellow-and-blue logo of the Banco do Brasil, we scuttled inside. The ATMs allowed us each to withdraw only two hundred *reais* — then about US$100, or £60 — so we used every card we had, exited, and watched as the bank was boarded up behind us.

Carnaval originated a few centuries ago in Italy before it spread throughout Catholic Europe. The word itself comes from '*carne vale*', a 'farewell to meat', as Catholics demonstrated their piousness during Lent by forgoing pleasures such as meat, dancing, and alcohol. There's a certain logic in the idea that a period of abstinence should be preceded by a period of over-indulgence in the things one is giving up. Or followed by it, as some other religions do. Eid al-Fitr, the festival that follows Ramadan, comes to mind. Even though most Brazilians no longer observe Lent in the historically prescribed manner, it doesn't seem to matter. As I've said, modern Carnaval is, for Brazilians, a right as much as a rite.

The festivities run from the Friday to the Tuesday immediately before Ash Wednesday, first day of Lent, and so may fall in either February or March. It is both ironic and typically Brazilian to have a profane festival with a date prescribed by the religious calendar. Indeed, Carnaval seems to define 'profane': it is a word that drips with naughtiness.

Not only is Carnaval 'master-less', the Brazilian scholar Roberto DaMatta tells us, and inverts the usual hierarchies so prevalent in Brazil, but also it is about what goes on 'below the waist'. Which explains, I suppose, why penises and cross-dressing are such favourites at Carnaval time. Most other Brazilian festivals are concerned with the soul.

Lesley and I pushed our way out of the plaza and into a side street. The black-and-white-themed *bloco,* Cordão da Bola Preta, is the largest and oldest of Carnaval de Rua. Later, I read that nearly two million people had flooded into the heart of the city and flowed down its arteries. Little wonder I was uncomfortable: that was nearly four times the population of the state of Tasmania!

In the relative calm of the side street, we watched as a tall man, quick and graceful, led dancers in a complicated set of steps next to a battered Kombi van. They stepped left, stepped right, crossed over, jumped, and spun. The side door to the van was open, to better broadcast music from the oversized stereo. The dancers knew the words — I guessed it was the *bloco* anthem.

We watched with rapt attention as passers-by joined in the dancing without waiting for a pause in the music. They just slipped into the next step as if they'd been dancing it their whole lives. They probably had, I realised with awe.

In Brazil, smells often waft up from the overstretched sewerage systems that writhe under city streets. But Rio smelled more than usual as we walked around in search of food. For a while, I was perplexed by the puddles that lay in dimples in the footpaths near the boarded-up buildings. It hadn't rained, and if the streets had been washed they should have dried off in the midday heat. But the extra-strong odour should have given it away.

Most of the city was encased in boards; all we could find open was a McDonald's. The city — actually the country — shuts down because *everyone* expects the Carnaval holiday (even if they disapprove of Carnaval). I pointed to a photo of a hamburger that looked as though it might have contained not merely cheese and meat. The girl, looking like she definitely didn't want to be working, pointed to a tray of burgers to her left, saying, 'That's what we have.' The limited service they were offering during Carnaval didn't include vegetables.

Outside again, almost every single Carioca (as the people from Rio are called) we saw wore a *fantasia*. After we were swept down Avenida Rio Branco by a bunch of Harry Potters, a swarm of witches stopped for my camera. But the costumes weren't always instantly recognisable. There were Supermen in skirts instead of red shorts, green frogs sporting human bottoms made of such shiny plastic they caught the sunlight, and a bloke in bunny ears wearing only budgie smugglers. (If you're not Australian, you might need to Google that one.)

The first Carnaval in Rio is thought to have been in 1723, when a cobbler called José Nogueira de Azevedo led a group of his friends through the streets all dressed up and playing 'drums, tambourines, pans, and whistles'. Groups of aristocrats took up the idea and began parading. There were *ranchos carnavalescos*, as the more working-class processions were called, and *cordões*, less organised revelry of masked and costumed folk. As samba became the national dance in the earlier decades of the twentieth century, it became fundamental to the festivities. The *cordões* (meaning 'cord' or 'cordon') became *blocos*, many of which are still cordoned by a rope today.

Although not far from the *centro*, Copacabana was friendlier for a couple of Australians a little overwhelmed by Carnaval. The banks weren't boarded up (though I only found one that hadn't run out of cash in three days of trying), and the restaurants were open.

We headed for the beach. Should I buy a hat? I wondered, perusing a vendor's display board. On the board hung panama hats, miniature top hats, and headbands with pipe-cleaners spiralling crazily from them. The vendor also sold all manner of souvenirs inexplicable to me — keyrings with cockroaches attached to them, just to name one. I was tempted by the hand puppet that stuck out its tongue like a flytrap. My youngest niece had just the right amount of devil in her for that.

And there was a fine range of penises: you could buy a hat with a penis standing to attention from your forehead. Or a plastic hand-gun with a penis for the barrel. You could bash your friend over the head with a giant inflatable penis. When it came to penis merchandise, the fun you could have during Carnaval seemed endless.

I was still worried that we wouldn't have enough money to see the festival out. On Avenida Nossa Senhora de Copacabana, I stopped a man clad in an orange nun's habit to ask if any of the ATMs were open. He pointed south and asked where we were from. Upon hearing that we were *australianas,* he solemnly declared '*canguru!*', lifted his wrists towards his chest, and gave a little hop.

The *blocos* in Copacabana were more manageable. Lesley and I joined in, dancing along the streets on the outside of the rope that cordoned the *trio eléctrico* and the *bloco's* members.

Over the course of the five days, I lost count of how many *blocos* we danced with, or how many street parties we drank a beer at — more than four hundred are registered with the municipal authorities — but we'd soon learned the form the festivities took.

A typical *bloco* parade at Copacabana went something like this:

Led by an ambulance and a police car, the group — usually a couple of hundred or a thousand people — walks and dances down one side of the street. When people stray over the white lines to the other side, where the traffic is so very patiently trying to squeeze past, a policeman waves them back across. There is no hint of exasperation or reprimand from the authorities at the recalcitrance, as there would be in Australia. Nor do they ask for the volcanic volume of the music to be turned down because the neighbours are complaining. The band, on the top of the truck, plays all manner of instruments: bells, drums, ukuleles, accordions, maracas, electric guitars, pianos. (How did they get a piano on top of the truck?)

The lead singer of the *bloco* might be straddling a giant can of Antarctica beer or sitting on a throne. The *bom-bom-bom* of the drums reverberates. The *porta-bandeira,* at the front of the parade, holds the *bloco*'s flag high with pride. She is like a mermaid on a prow. Inside the cordon, which serves to keep the public away from the slowly turning wheels of the truck, people wear some form of episematic uniform, such as green t-shirts and headdresses of bright feathers. Most have uniforms and themes, but they don't seem to mind people joining in willy-nilly.

I learn quickly to wear closed shoes. Sneakers are popular, because they keep your feet dry, protect your toes from being stood on in the crush of a parade, and are cushioned for hours of dancing. I walk or dance on the side, near the front of the crowd — not in front of the speakers, where I might become hearing-impaired. Some people tug eskies of beer behind them like toy trains, or hoisted on one shoulder. We carry only what money we need and leave everything not absolutely necessary at the hotel, safe from pickpockets. We also carry coins because even when Brazilian vendors aren't dealing with Carnaval crowds, they never ever seem to have change.

On the final night of Carnaval, the man dancing along in front of us was dressed in a fluorescent pink singlet and a white tennis skirt. During a lull in the music, he waved his tennis racket enthusiastically at Lesley and yelled in English over the din, asking for her name and where she came from. She told him. But instead of the usual response, the man blushed and bolted away like a startled deer. It took a while for it to occur to us that he'd misheard her name and misread our relationship. Brazil might look to throw off its conservativism in favour of the excesses of Carnaval, but it is not, it would appear, all that far from the surface.

Back to the North and the Northeast

Chapter Sixteen

Dancing with the Gods

SALVADOR, BAHIA

*'The city of Bahia, black and religious, is almost as mysterious
as the green sea.'* Jorge Amado

'*Cuidado!*' a voice stopped me from opening the car door. I'd nearly
sideswiped a wheelbarrow in which lay a trussed goat.

Fernando, my driver and guide for the morning, asked the man
pushing the barrow to stop for my camera. He cheerfully raised a knee
and planted his foot on the barrow's rim. He leaned on one arm against
a power pole, casually, as if he didn't need it for support — you've got to
love Brazilian machismo. Surrounding the goat were four plump hens,
also bound with string. Their brown feathers rippled gently. The kid's eyes
were closed, his terrified grip on life evident only in the rapid rise and fall
of his little lungs. He was headed for the sacrificial pot of the African-
rooted, syncretic religion that is Candomblé.

Oxalá, *axé*, Orixá: the language of Candomblé is exotic. It doesn't fall
from the tongue of Brazilians much more easily than from that of this

Australian. The stress doesn't naturally fall on the second-last syllable, as it does in Portuguese, so a plethora of accents are used. *Axé*, pronounced 'ah-shay', is the creative energy that makes things happen, as I'd discovered on previous visits to Salvador. The name for the deities themselves, Orixás, is pronounced 'ohreeshas', and the god of the sky, Oxalá, is 'ohshala'. Also called Obatalá, he is the greatest of the Orixás, although there's an ultimate power beyond even him.

Some things in life seem simple. They are familiar, things you feel you have always known: that bird-song signals dawn; that blossoms indicate imminent spring; that grey clouds suggest rain. Others, you grasp little by little, each piece in the jigsaw dependent on the one before. American author Annie Dillard wrote about writing-as-process, but her sentiment also applies to how we learn: 'It grows cell to cell, bole to bough to twig to leaf.'

Some things you learn about easily, incidentally, by virtue of growing up in a specific place. Australian Rules football is like that. I have watched exasperated five-year-olds try to explain the intricate rules and scoring to bamboozled Europeans with university degrees. It's just not as straightforward as one goal equals one point. It simply doesn't make much sense for a long while, but in the meantime, by golly, there's a lot of action.

Religion is like that for me: I pick up the rules just a bit at a time, and, with Candomblé in particular, there's a lot of action. Probably because it plays to my sense of theatricality, I find Candomblé bewitching.

The city of Salvador is the Candomblé capital, boasting more than one thousand temples. Walking the streets of Salvador, you see offerings to Exú at crossroads, gifts for Oxum near streams. As Fernando and I drove around the city, I saw that he had a blue-beaded sachet on his keyring. 'It is a sign of Ogum. The god of war and iron has become god of roads,' he explained. 'It is supposed to give us his company and help us to open our ways on the roads.' Worth a try, I thought, but it didn't seem to be helping; we were still stuck in Salvador's perennially choked traffic.

For the Candomblé initiate, the African market in Salvador, to which

Fernando had driven me, provides everything you need to practise your faith. At the gate, a *curandeiro, a healer,* swept two damp, leafy branches up and down my torso. He released a handful of popcorn over my scalp; it tumbled over my clothes like a shower of sparks. Figuring a blessing never goes astray, I dropped a couple of *reais* into his hand.

Entering the first aisle of the market, Fernando and I brushed past wooden crates piled high with aromatic green herbs and taxidermied cow heads mounted on boards. We wound past tracks of orange earthen-wear pots; if one overbalanced, it would knock me out. Rainbows of candles and incense were arrayed in windows. Mounds of tiny dried shrimp blazed like bonfires.

Fernando told me that many Brazilians, including his parents, fear Candomblé. 'I bought the picture,' he said, referring to the prejudice against Candomblé he was brought up with. He was taught that Candomblé was something from the devil, 'that they were calling for the devil in a ceremony, but it was actually the opposite'. His devout Catholic parents still don't like it, he told me, but they do make use of some of the religion's medicinal herbs. 'Now, many Brazilians consult Candomblé.' Although not a *filho de santo* — a child of the saints — Fernando, as a gay Brazilian, has found acceptance among the Candomblé community, and drops in on a ceremony every now and then 'to get some *axé*'.

In the market, you can buy long masks of withered straw to cover the pox-ridden form of the Orixá Omolú. Despite animal sacrifice being a tradition reputedly less common now, there were tall stacks of caged brown hens, snow-white ducks, goats, pigeons, and pigs. Massive wooden mortars were purchased with pestles as tall as me. We dodged around life-sized statues of bare-chested black men, their legs encased in scales; they would make fine bowsprits.

Most of the market stalls are named for the gods: Palácio de Oxóssi, whose realm is the forest; House of Xangô, for the deity of thunder, the warrior spirit. Some stalls you can befriend on Facebook. Small boxes of charms promised me wealth, health, or my chosen one. Thick ropes of tobacco lay curled in crates, ready to be given to — or stolen by — the deity Exú. Long loops of beads in every colour cascaded down walls like waterfalls. It was an eclectic mix: hanging from one ceiling were clusters of brass pots, wooden ladles, and sieves; plugs of cured meat; long-locked mop heads; and aluminium crowns in red and green and gold.

~

One of the jobs of religion is to explain why the world is the way it is. The Bible focuses mostly on human stories; if you pared it down to the sections that deal with natural history, the Bible would be the size of a pamphlet.

Candomblé, however, like many religions with roots stretching into the pre-Christian days, provides a multitude of stories that explain the natural world, such as this, in the words of anthropologist Paul Christopher Johnson: the Earth and the Sky were 'locked in a smothering embrace, like two halves of a closed calabash', before Oduduá (the Earth) threw Obatalá (the Sky) from her body. The resulting separation made space for land, the air (personified as the Orixá Orungan), and the seas (as the Orixá Yemanjá).

Secrecy plays a large role in Candomblé. Before you arrive at the *terreiro* for a ceremony, private rituals will have been performed to prepare both the space and the initiates to receive the gods. The liturgy is complex: in a private courtyard an initiate will bathe with herbs that the secret lore prescribes before dressing in fresh — usually white — clothes. For the women, there are skirts the shape of flower bulbs; the men wear loose cotton pants and a muslin shirt, often embroidered. It is before the public ceremony, if the *terreiro* follows traditional practice, that the animals are sacrificed. Then they are put into the cooking pot.

The first offering is always made to Exú, mischievous god of paths, doors, and crossroads. He is the go-to guy, the messenger between Earth and the supernatural world. He is what Brazilians call a *malandro*: a trickster, a rogue. Unless properly bribed, Exú can sabotage a ceremony.

Untidy, ambitious, and greedy, he is a lovable rascal who can be placated or cajoled with items such as honey, palm oil, or money.

A Candomblé ceremony is about appeasing gods as much as celebrating them, about heading potential problems off at the pass. The gods like to party, eat, drink, and dance, and by giving them the opportunity to do so, it is hoped that they will help, rather than hinder, their followers.

Although the gods each have their favourite day of the week, the modern world is such that Friday and Saturday nights are the most convenient for the long rituals to occur. To the trained eye, the liturgical details of Candomblé ceremonies change from temple to temple, distinguishing one group from another but, to me, they seemed similar and were all enthralling. This scene is representative of the ceremonies I've seen in Salvador; it is composed of details from all of them. It is, however, unusual — but not unheard of — for an audience member to participate quite as much as my guide, Luís, did on my first experience of a ceremony; I never saw it again but include it here for interest's sake. The nights went something like this:

Crack-crack! Fireworks report that the ceremony is soon to start. I am clad in white, seated in the gender-segregated audience with similarly dressed women. In the centre of the 'stage', or against the rear wall, there is an altar. It is draped with leaves and symbols, such as snakes and cow horns, rainbows and African masks, fish, mirrors, and shells. Pots of flowers sit on the floor — white for Oxalá, if it's Friday. Three wooden, barrel-like drums of varying height stand on a raised platform off to one side. Young men sprawl around the drums, chatting. Nearby are the seats reserved for special visitors.

My eyes are drawn to the open shutters by the whiskery flutter of paper tied to the eaves. Beside me, two teenage girls with coloured beads woven into their hair are giggling, glancing at the boys across the aisle.

People — mostly in white, though a few are in jeans — come and go through the front door, greeting and gossiping. They are not nervous like me, not fearful of making some foreigner's gaff.

At some signal I don't see, the congregation stands. Rhythmic hands beat the skins of the drums, called *atabaques*. Hand bells are rattled and struck, *clack-clink-clack-clink-clink*, in a maniacal, mesmerising — and slightly irritating — call to the gods.

As if someone has popped the cork from a bottle of champagne, dancers spill like bubbles through the door. Mostly women, in various shades of skin colour, they dance to the stage and bend low to kiss the ground. Round as mushrooms, their white skirts cascade past the knee; hoops bounce high as hems hit the floor. The dancers' legs are encased in lace and cotton, their necks and bosoms draped with beads. Backsides pump from side to side; the skirts are so wide they bump together. Then the dancers form a circle. They move anti-clockwise, chanting, clapping, and winding the clock back to a mythical past when the Orixás walked the Earth.

This first part of the ceremony is for the 'horses', who will be 'mounted', to open themselves up so each one's god can come visit. I notice Luís, who brought me to the *terreiro*, rising from his chair every few moments. He gestures for me to stay seated. Bad back? I wonder.

In the front, a plump woman begins to shake. An attendant moves quickly to her side. The woman lurches, as if disoriented, and then stills before lapsing into a gently undulating sway. After a few moments, she dances with renewed vigour, pulsating towards the drummers with a movement that is half-shimmy, half-bow.

Some women continue to kneel to kiss the ground, while others have become still. Luís rather languidly bends towards the floor. He is the only person in the visitors' section to do so.

The Mãe de Santo — the 'Mother of the Saints' — chants, calling to the gods. More dancers shake, still, and then sway. It is at this point (though only on that first visit) that Luís falls to the ground, displacing his chair with a crash I hear over the drums. He lies on the floor quivering, as if in the throes of a palsy. Two male attendants run to him and help him up. Luís remains bent at the waist, and the men throw a cloth over him as if he were a table. The white material quakes and quavers as the men try to help the bent figure across the central space to the rear door. Unable to manage more than a few small steps, Luís is hoisted on the back of one of the men, cloth and all. Staggering under Luís' weight, the attendant carries him into the hidden bowels of the *terreiro*. (Luís later told me he had been taken by Oxalufá, one of the identities of Oxalá, gnarled with age. He said he'd have to give up visiting ceremonies, because being ridden by a deity without proper preparation took too great a toll on his health.)

When the human horses have been mounted, the gods begin to dance. The transformed are taken by attendants called *equedes* into the hidden sanctuary of the *terreiro*; more than one god needs to be cajoled into going. The *equedes* adorn the charges in each god's favourite colours and ornaments, and hand them their favourite props, before leading them back into the main space to party.

The gods do not restrict themselves to initiates of the same gender. Oxalá can 'have the head' of a 'daughter of the saints'. Or a 'son of the saints' can be 'ridden' by Yemanjá or by Oxum. Oxum's favourite offerings are the goat and the hen. Her realm is 'sweet' water — rivers, streams, lakes, and ponds. She is fond of honey. One of Xangô's three wives, she is responsible for fertility. Her colours are gold and blue, her day is Saturday, and — because Brazilians often prefer to syncretise their beliefs — her star sign is cancer.

The liturgical details of Candomblé are multifarious. For a ceremony celebrating the day of Oxalá, there must be white food: chicken, manioc, and rice. Omolú's food also matches his favourite colours: black beans, white manioc flour, and *dendê* oil the colour of sunset. Diseased himself, his is the realm of sickness and cure. Pockmarked, his form is covered top-to-toe with straw. Oxumaré likes beans with eggs and shrimp, Oxóssi does not eat pork, the supreme god Oxalá will only drink water, both Yemanjá and Oxum like bubbly, and Xangô is partial to stout.

After the brief interval, fireworks announce that the Orixás are ready to party. The drums begin to beat and a painter's palette of colour explodes through the door. Like confetti whirling in a tornado, the gods bounce and swirl across the stage. Scientists who suggest that colour is merely an illusion would do well to meet these gods. A golden skirt flows out as Oxum spins by like a shining ballroom dancer.

The drums encourage frenzy: *bob-bom-bob-bom-bob-bob-bom*. Hips and shoulders shimmy, bottoms wag. One of the gods dances with his face low to the ground — Luís's god Oxalufá, crippled with age?

Two teenage boys peer in from the street, through the open shutters. A woman stands at another window, a baby on one hip. The drumbeat changes, and a circle forms around one of the dancing deities. He or she wears a crown of blue, studded with cowrie shells and peacock feathers: Yemanjá? When her turn at centre stage is complete, a figure with a helmet woven from corn husks takes her place.

Next Oxum dances — at least, I think it's Oxum. The features of the goddess of rivers are hidden by streams of golden coins. Leaving the circle, she glides towards the pews and throws her arms around the teenager in front of me with bruising enthusiasm. The hug is so boisterous, I'm glad to be in the back row. The recipient looks pleased, though, and the goddess glides down the row, demanding hug after hug. Her forearms are encased in golden bands. As she passes, people raise their hands to catch the *axé*.

Another Oxum, this one in yellow, blue, and gold, dances towards the open door; an *equede* heads off what looks like a half-attempted escape.

An Orixá can manifest in more than one *filha* or *filho*, and an initiate can have multiple gods (I heard of one who had sixteen gods that took her head, sixteen! I wondered how large her psych bill was). I had learnt that which god or gods is determined by throwing the cowrie shells. The *jogo de búzios*, the divining 'game of shells', is how some Brazilians resolve a range of issues. The shells can provide suggestions such as how to cure an illness, find a job, or resolve matters of the heart.

Your personal traits might have already hinted to the diviner of the shells who your god is, or gods are, before he or she throws them. God of war Ogum's children are known to be intelligent, creative, and sensitive; they're impulsive but practical, transparent, and fearless. Likewise, daughters of Yemanjá, the goddess who gave birth to most of the Orixás, carry traits often associated with the maternal: they are authoritarian, have good taste, and are hard-working, sensitive, and competent. Sounds just like my own mother.

When the gods are spent and have returned to the heavens, the humans close the night with a party. The *terreiro* provided a feast, and as I tucked into a tasty stew I couldn't help but wonder if it was the kid-goat in the barrow at the market.

~

A psychologist called Mihaly Csíkszentmihalyi developed what he called 'flow theory'. It's when one is immersed in an activity with such total concentration that it produces a 'deep sense of exhilaration that is long cherished and becomes a landmark in memory for what life should be like'. The focus on performing the activity is so very total that its by-product is a kind of ecstasy. 'The experience itself is so enjoyable that people will do it even at a great cost, for the sheer sake of doing it,' he observed. You may well have had the experience where your immersion in something is so deep you lose all sense of self, time, and the world around you. Writing can be like that. I felt like that racing sports cars in rallies.

Artists know the feeling, and religion has been looked at through the lens of flow theory. Whirling Dervishes attain the flow state. It has been found to occur more often in public religious experiences than in meditation or private prayer. An ecstatic zone where nothing else matters. Travelling — being bathed in Robert Dessaix's 'epiphanic delight' — can sometimes be like that too. The world beyond your immediate zone matters not one jot. Certainly Candomblé initiates, when they are visited by the gods, look to be in a world of their own. Indeed, they find themselves in a place of such ecstasy that, watching them, I found myself more than slightly envious.

Chapter Seventeen

King of the Badlands

PIRANHAS, ALAGOAS

'The definition of a cangaceiro *depended on who was asked. To tenant farmers, they were heroes and protectors ... To farm girls, they were fine dancers and romantic heroes. To the mothers of those girls,* cangaceiros *were defilers and devils ... to the colonels ...* cangaceiroes *were blights that the colonels and their fathers, grandfathers, and great-grandfathers before them had had to withstand.'* Frances de Pontes Peebles

For me, this story began with a photograph.

One of the most famous photographs in Brazilian history was taken on 22nd June 1938, on the stone steps of the Piranhas Town Hall. It shows the steps carefully draped with cloth. Someone had taken pains to tuck the edges of the cloth under. The same person, or another perhaps, had smoothed the cloth to better define the ledges. In the photo, the steps look like a bookcase, a display case. Someone had made an elaborate arrangement of booty. And upon the cloth that person had rested eleven heads on their severed necks. That person, or those persons, had closed the eyelids and balanced the heads to lean slightly forward, to rest the chins on the cloth. Perhaps one or two toppled over and needed to be righted, but eventually all was ready for the camera to take its shot.

A macabre tableau.

~

Piranhas — named after the famous flesh-eating fish — is in the middle of the backlands, northeast of Canudos, south of New Jerusalem, and southwest of the *quilombo* memorial, near the point where three states meet. Whether you start from Maceió, the capital of Alagoas, or from interstate, it is a trek.

From Salvador, capital of Bahia, an overnight bus took me to Paulo Afonso, a town I've yet to find a use for (possibly because I arrived at five in the morning). Throughout the night, my fellow passengers were talking — not whispering, not murmuring — on mobile phones. Who on earth were they talking to at three a.m.? In Paulo Afonso, the ticket-seller for my next bus put aside her prayer book and told me to ask the driver to let me off at the *colectivo* stand in Delmiro Gouveia. Delmiro hadn't figured in my research.

Every nation seems to have — or perhaps requires — at least one infamous outlaw. It adds a dash of rogue to the national character. Infamous outlaws are useful for promoting rural tourism, as well. In Australia, we have Ned Kelly; in the United States, where there is more of everything, there's Jesse James, Doc Holliday, Billy the Kid. The British have Dick Turpin and Robin Hood. In Brazil, I was on the trail of Lampião, who was the most famous of the *cangaceiros*, as the Brazilians call their outlaws. Revered by some and feared by many, his band wandered, pillaged, and plundered the backlands in the 1920s and 1930s.

It seemed to me that I had been haunted by the outlaw for quite some time. Everywhere I turned, his image was there. He was featured at the first Carnaval I attended in Rio. Lampião's visage graced drink coasters I bought, and keyrings, posters, and notebooks I didn't. There was even a giant statue of him and his wife at our lunch stop on the day I visited Nova Jerusalem.

Lampião was born Virgulino Ferreira da Silva in the state of Pernambuco in 1897: the year that Canudos was finally destroyed. His nickname, 'Lantern', was bestowed because he was so fast with his trigger finger that he lit up the night.

Vengeance was a primary concern in the Brazilian backlands. It played a vital role in Antônio Conselheiro's early years, with most of the men in his family fallen in a long-running blood feud. But whereas the counsellor fashioned himself a saviour, revenge became an obsession for Lampião. His father, a hard-working mule driver and farmer, was hounded by a more-powerful family, and forced to move from village to village. When his father was shot by police while shucking corn, Lampião, certain the police were acting on orders from his father's enemy, swore vengeance against all with authority or power. Thus began his rampage of retribution; he became a *cangaceiro* — in Australia, we'd call him a bushranger.

When I told the bus driver I wanted to go to Piranhas, he motioned for me to leave my luggage near the front door: he'd look after it and let me know when to get off. Brazilians love to be helpful. They will tell you when the zip of your backpack has crept open or when your shoelace has come undone. I have even had a complete stranger advise me to get my teeth fixed. Straight white teeth are a symbol of status in Brazil, and mine are gappy and protrude because I never had the patience required to care for braces. The previous week, my pocket had been picked — the only time it ever has been in Brazil — by a woman while she was telling me that my face was getting sunburned. Still stung, I went through the turnstile and took a seat at the front so I, too, could keep an eye on my bag as it lay next to the open door.

Whether you board a bus through the front door or the rear differs depending on where you are in Brazil. Why have something as mundane as routine? Usually, buses have a conductor who sits at the turnstile — sometimes found at the front, sometimes rear — dispensing tickets. His job description also includes giving a coin two sharp raps on his metal tray, *clack-clack*, so the driver knows when to close the door. Assuming the door closes at all. You can't rely, in my experience, on conductors. There have been times when I've asked a conductor to tell me when to get off and they haven't. Did they not know? Did they forget? Did they not understand me? But drivers always know where you are going; they understand you, they remember, and they tell you where to get off.

We left the state of Bahia and entered Alagoas, and an hour later the bus pulled up next to a line of vans. Bellowing '*Tenho uma passageira,*' the driver waited patiently as I made my way through the bus' rear exit and up to the front to collect my bag, before taking off with a lurch.

I climbed into the back of the small truck: what we'd call a ute in Australia, but with a roof. It's as popular a form of transport in the Brazilian backlands as in the Australian bush. This ute was full — there must have been twenty people in the back. I ducked in under the roof to squish my backside between one that looked too big for the woman attached to it and a horizontal metal bar. The bar was all that would stop me from sliding down the open tailgate and onto the fast-flowing tarmac.

Of the many forms of transport in Latin America, *colectivos* are, perhaps, the most interesting. These shared taxis or trucks act as small private buses, moving people from town to town, stopping in the middle of nowhere to set down or take on passengers, who pay as many notes or coins as nominated by the driver (through his window) when they alight. *Colectivos* come in all shapes and sizes, the universal trait being that they only depart when they absolutely, positively cannot possibly fit one more passenger into them. Even with a shoehorn.

We picked up and set down passengers all along the hot, dry road, so it wasn't clear exactly where we were when the driver indicated to me, with a bang of his hand on the roof, that the dusty bus shelter we had stopped next to was, in fact, the end of his line. A sign said Xingó, not Piranhas. '*É longe*? Piranhas?' I asked, dropping some coins into his hand through the window. He gestured carelessly forward and then sped off, leaving me feeling somewhat bereft.

In Brazil, I had learned that a suitcase with wheels works well and is easier on my bad back than a pack. And I blended in more; or, rather, I stuck out less. But if I'd had my backpack, I would've slung it over my shoulders and hopped aboard one of the *mototáxis* that formed a short line on the hot road. It would have been a scene reminiscent of *Easy Rider*, though the bike was more likely to be a kerosene-powered Honda than a rumbling Harley.

Instead, I sat on a grimy bench under a television in a cage; there was a *telenovela* on its snowy screen. Swatting flies, I pondered my plight glumly. But soon a thin guy with a rolling gait that reminded me of the Fonz in *Happy Days* came up and asked where I was from. When I answered, he said, '*Canguru!*' He gave a little hop and asked if he could call me a taxi. My luck — saint, goddess, guardian angel, whichever you prefer — had not, after all, deserted me. The cab eventually arrived, and we followed a horse-pulled cart into the historical centre of Piranhas, passing statues of both Padre Cícero, a famous backlands priest, and the outlaw Lampião on the way.

One of nine children, Lampião's first job was to tend to sheep and goats, but before long he was promoted to cattle. As a cowboy, he became expert with horse, rifle, and rope. After his father was murdered in 1921, he took over as head of the family, despite having two older brothers. Those brothers became his lieutenants.

Turnover rates for members of the *cangaço* were high. At any one time, the group ranged in size from eight to sixty men, and usually included a few women, too. The band made the *caatinga*, the backlands scrub, their home.

Caatinga: we don't use a double 'a' in English. When I say it with my Australian accent, my tongue sinks low and the back of my throat seems to expel demons. The language of the interior of the Northeast is dry in any accent: *caatinga, sertão*, backlands. Dry and dangerous.

There were a range of attributes that could qualify you as a potential victim of the outlaw and his band. It was automatic if you were linked in any manner to anyone responsible for his father's death, or if you had slighted one of his friends. Although he had a set against anyone with power, police were his favourite targets. With his father killed by officers, I guess he had better reason than many to hate police. But he wasn't so picky about his targets: you could even be punished for being a friend of someone who had hurt or even slighted a friend of his friend.

In 1922, for instance, Lampião took 'vengeance' on one 'colonel' — the ubiquitous self-proclaimed leaders of country towns in Brazil — because that colonel was friends with a certain police commander, and that police commander had beaten up one of Lampião's friend's lieutenants and his family. The link seems confusing and tenuous to me, too.

Murder wasn't the outlaw's sole enterprise. The band made a healthy living robbing the rich, and sometimes they did give to the poor. They burned down houses and farm buildings, raped women, and kidnapped for ransom. With their highly decorated half-moon-shaped hats on their heads — and a price as well — the band was recognised wherever they roamed.

The half-moon-shaped hat is to Lampião what Ned Kelly's helmet is to the Australian bushranger: an iconic image. His wife often wore such headgear too. When depicted together, Lampião and Maria Bonita are generally holding hands. The couple met when the *cangaceiro* visited her parents' farm. And Maria Bonita's severed head is one of the eleven in the photo taken of the steps of the Piranhas Town Hall.

Frances de Pontes Peebles' novel *The Seamstress* is loosely based on the story of Maria Bonita. The author's imagination was captured by the bandit woman who sewed jewels, playing cards, bullets, and other booty onto the *cangaceiros'* leather hats, shirts, vests, and trousers. The *cangaceiros* took turns in lugging an old sewing machine through the *caatinga*; it was probably manufactured by Singer. Film footage shows Maria Bonita bent over the machine in the evenings, after dinner, while the men take turns spinning the round metal wheel for her as she sews.

My *pousada* in Piranhas was named after Maria Bonita. It had a regal view over the river and into the neighbouring state of Sergipe. I'd barely managed to catch my breath after climbing the stone steps to it — steps that were slightly too high for my legs — before Manuel, the owner, and Francisco, my taxi driver, had me organised. In forty-five minutes, a canoe would take me to walk the Rota do Cangaço, the Route of the Outlaw, a little way down the São Francisco River. The trip would include lunch. I would take a catamaran up the river at nine o'clock the next day to see the other local sight, the Xingó Canyon. After that, Francisco — who, like his father, was named for the river that is so long it's called the 'river of national unity' — would take me back to Delmiro Gouveia since, he assured me, the *colectivos* do not run on a Sunday. '*Entendeu?*' he asked. In my experience, *colectivos* worked every day, but hey, why upset such a perfectly stacked apple cart?

It doesn't seem like it would have been a romantic life, trudging up and down the hot backlands, your damp skin being pricked by the sly, silvery *caatinga*. I guess that's why the *cangaceiros* wore leather despite the heat.

One of the reasons Lampião and Maria Bonita became idolised, and why their story remains such a vibrant chapter of the national story, is that some of their life was captured on film. A charismatic Lebanese-born filmmaker called Benjamin Abrahão Botto persuaded Lampião to allow him to document a few weeks of mostly staged activities of the *cangaço* among the scrubby *caatinga*. He captured forever the lives of this Brazilian Bonnie and Clyde. Apart from sewing, footage shows Maria Bonita practising on the shooting range, laughingly twirling her long skirts after each successful shot, and Lampião directing a shootout from behind candelabras of enormous cacti. The film was confiscated by the Vargas dictatorship, badly stored, and only recently re-discovered. Not all of the footage could be saved.

As promised, forty five minutes later the canoe arrived and took me downriver. Three goats stood rock-still on the shore as the canoe skidded over a filmy patch of water. Half a dozen green butterflies were sucked along in our wake. The river is surrounded by craggy, cacti-studded hills. I could imagine the *cangaceiros* scrabbling up them on their bellies to peer over a crest.

The canoe slid onto the sand in front of a hut that boasted three shiny solar panels on its roof. The boatman led me through a small forest of stacked green plastic tables and chairs and introduced me to a woman — she was barely out of her teens, and called Kelly — who had appeared on the hut's patio. Kelly was dressed in a uniform of greying khaki with a fake ammunition belt criss-crossing her chest *cangaceiro*-style. Asking me where I was from, she greeted my response with only a nod.

The *caatinga* where the band made their home is a silvery scrub of stunted trees and thorny bushes. Lampião, it turned out, had the right qualities to be an outlaw-hero. He was skilled and clever, inspiring admiration and loyalty. Kelly told me how he taught his men to fool his pursuers by walking backwards over their own footprints, and to wear fur on their boots for the dual purpose of silence and camouflage. He enforced a regular regime for the band — men and women — to practise their skills in banditry.

As is common to such stories, there was as much misinformation as truth reported by the newspapers that followed the adventures of Lampião and Maria Bonita as they evaded capture. Brazilians followed their tale as avidly as a *telenovela*.

The site of the final shootout is a hollow surrounded by rocks and boulders. It would have made a good camp for the band. I could see why Lampião — usually one to move their campsite every few days — had grown comfortable there and stayed longer than usual. But a number of forces conspired against them that night. The camp's location had been betrayed by one of their supporters, and their wine dosed with strychnine. The Piranhas police, led by a Lieutenant João Bezerra, had constructed an elaborate ruse as they tracked the bandits to their camp. And it was a night when the dogs and the sentries had sought shelter from the pounding rain.

Just on dawn, the first shots flew across the camp.

Lampião, the main target, fell early. Maria Bonita didn't survive her husband for long. One by one, the remaining *cangaceiros* lost their lives. The camp was looted and the bandits' heads cut off. (Easier to transport, one might suggest.) Wet but triumphant, the troops turned for home. Before dispatching the heads to be exhibited in the capital of Pernambuco, to the north, Lieutenant Bezerra ordered a cloth to be laid and smoothed on the Piranhas Town Hall steps so that the heads of the most wanted men and women in the Brazilian backlands could be displayed for the world to see.

~

Something about outlaws is romantic. They conjure notions of freedom, a romance that crosses borders and generations. We are captured equally by, and grow up hearing the stories of, Jesse James and Bonnie and Clyde. We know of Butch Cassidy and the Sundance Kid, who robbed trains and fled to South America, probably ending their days in a shootout in Bolivia. When watching films about the Kelly gang, Australians barrack for the bushranger and his crew; we secretly hoped Britain wouldn't be successful when the government tried to extradite the 'Great Train Robber' Ronnie Biggs, who lived the last of his days in Brazil. It is a paradox, given how onerous the precautions outlaws had to take in order to retain their 'freedom', that this is a quality for which we admire them. Living outside society is not necessarily easy. Maria Bonita and Lampião could not live with their daughter because their life in the *caatinga* was too dangerous. Still, we admire the life of outlaws: they lived the dream of not bowing to authority, even if they were eventually beaten by it.

Chapter Eighteen

Capital of Faith

JUAZEIRO DO NORTE, CEARÁ

'If you could prove it, it wouldn't be faith.' Paul Arden

In Brazil, they don't focus their machinations on the reaping of rewards in the next life: they seek results in this one. And, judging by the symbols of thanks that Brazilians leave for their saints in 'miracle rooms' across the country, supernatural interventions are granted to them on a regular basis. Although you find miracle rooms in some churches in Europe, I hadn't really been aware of them until my time in Brazil. They are a central feature of a great many churches in the country — inescapable even, especially in the Northeast.

The most famous performer of miracles who actually lived in Brazil was Padre Cícero. The first time I came across his story was when I was driving around the backlands with my language-school group, trying to find the memorial site for Zumbi's *quilombo*.

Claudio, our language teacher, spotted a statue and, quivering with a mixture of shyness and excitement, beckoned us to follow him. After we'd settled in a half-circle around the slightly-larger-than-life statue, he explained that this was Padre Cícero, 'who is venerated' — he spoke in English to make sure we all understood — 'all over Brazil'.

Claudio's face had taken on a celestial quality, framed, as it was, by dark ringlets; his shiny round spectacles had a tendency to catch the light. Handing me his camera, he slipped an arm around the padre's waist. '*Três, dois, um*,' I said, and clicked. He had me take another, and I noticed that the statue's head was disconcertingly smaller than it should have been. Claudio had me take a third shot, not trusting this *gringa* to get it right.

'I used to pray to my padrinho as a child,' he said, 'if I wanted to win a football game or had a pain in the belly.' His palm lazily circled his stomach.

The statue depicted the padre in a black cassock that fell resolutely to his feet. Some admirers had placed two small pots of plastic flowers by his hem. Like the statue of Antônio Conselheiro on the hill at Canudos, his hand was wrapped around a long wooden staff. The expression on his face might have been the weary bemusement of the often-photographed.

~

In the northeastern state of Ceará, the city of Juazeiro do Norte is a pilgrimage site for admirers of Padre Cícero. My plane to the small city landed at midnight.

Usually, I enjoy arrivals in a new place. Such arrivals are beginnings. You can look at maps for as long as you like, but they don't give you the nuances of a place. Typically, I like to walk around immediately, making mental notes about what I see, hear, smell.

John Ruskin and Alain de Botton, among others, advocate drawing as a way to get to know a place. Walking around a new town or city, it's as if my feet are a pencil, drawing a multi-dimensional map on what was a completely blank page. The page is filled slowly with all the nuances that make the locale unique and that you don't get on a physical map, no matter how detailed it is. You can include the sound of traffic at three in the afternoon, and compare it to nine in the morning. The smell of Brazilian barbecue wafting from a nearby restaurant might be added, and, if you are me, the coordinates entered in my mental GPS so I can find my way back for dinner. In your mental field notes, you can include the vision of water fleeing before the bow of a fishing boat. Or the triumphant shout of the man in shorts that leave little to the imagination — a common sight in Brazil — as he hits the sand after a successful save of the volleyball. You might stow that away in your memory next to the whine of a blender as a beach vendor conjures a fruit cocktail.

But midnight is an inhospitable time to arrive in a new place. All you want to do is get to your bed. The plane's timing suggested it was not a popular route. Most pilgrims arrive in Juazeiro do Norte by other means: bus, truck, on foot.

Claudio's padrinho — his 'Little Father' — was born Cícero Romão Batista in a nearby town in 1844. By then, Brazil was an independent empire, the unpopular Pedro Primeiro (Pedro I) had abdicated, and Pedro II had come of age and been recently crowned. It was a time when, and a region where, the clergy was thinly spread and over-stretched. Few were prepared — or perhaps able — to endure the poverty, the heat, or the perceived ignorance of those in the Northeast. But Padre Cícero was a native of the state and, fresh from the seminary, he was posted to the parish. It was 1872 and the beginning of a decades-long drought.

Aurimar, my lift, edged his taxi past tarpaulin-cloaked stalls to drop me outside the Casa Museu do Padre Cícero. My foot was hovering over the museum's bottom step when a rush of pilgrims surged through the front door like someone had let off a pop-pack of streamers. Idly examining the wares of a nearby stall, I waited for the ebb. Had I the inclination (or enough room in my suitcase), I could have bought buckets, bags, caps, popcorn, and black-robed Padre Cícero dolls in sizes that ranged from miniature to larger than life.

Inside, after signing the museum register, I joined a small, silent group that formed a halo around a low bed, slender as a coffin. Men, young and old, and wives, sisters, and mothers slipped from the circle one by one to press mementos — a handkerchief, a prayer book, a photo — onto the bedspread. The entire bed, including a black-ink portrait of the priest stencilled on the snow-white cotton, was protected by a sheet of clear plastic.

A child slid forward to brush the bed with her rag doll. A ringleted boy, who could have been Claudio's son, set his baseball cap on the undulation that passed for a pillow and waited solemnly as his mother photographed the moment. A woman of about forty rested her gaping handbag on the bed and brushed her fingers against the padre's gentle smile. Then a thin man marched past us. He snapped prayer cards across the bed as if dealing a hand of poker. He collected them expertly and strode back to the street.

Despite, in the early years of his priesthood, being so poor that his friends had to slip a few *cruzeiros* to a local woman to sew his cassocks, Padre Cícero refuted custom and refused payment for his services. He lived in a simple house with his mother and sister, and found jobs for refugees from the drought in the comparatively lush valley around the town. He encouraged the children to attend school and advised his friends on matters of the heart.

Word of his wisdom, benevolence, and piety spread fast and far. He took in poor and single women and allowed them to don the veil and live life as if formally committed to God; these *beatas* — these 'blessed' — helped him tend his flock. Life was calm and it was good. But then during one communion, Padre Cícero bestowed the white host upon the tongue of one of the *beatas* and it turned red with blood in her mouth.

I've never quite understood the significance of those types of miracles involving the sudden appearance of blood. I mean, I understand it's about the blood of Christ, but personally I prefer miracles that grant good fortune. I'd have been ecstatic if God had found a way to cure my friend Helen as her life was sapped by breast cancer. Or if some miracle had provided relief to an especially young friend as the mischievous smile was wiped from his leukaemia-ravaged lips, and his cuddly toddler's body slowly melted away. Belief in miracles, like religion itself, is a way of making sense of life, but what sense does it make when prayers fall on deaf ears?

As is usual with biographical museums, the Casa was cluttered with memorabilia and evidence of the subject's importance and popularity. The walls of one room were plastered with photographs that Padre Cícero's fans had sent. There was a snapshot of Janeide and Luciano embracing at the beach, and a formal portrait of Maria in her black graduate's hat.

By virtue of being on the wall, stickers boast of politicians' allegiances with the priest: 'Eugênia 55 para prefeitura' and 'Silvestre 45'. Brazilian elections, regardless of tier, have so many candidates that each is allocated a number. They must also be a member of a registered party: Brazil is a collective society; there are no independents.

As I was examining the walls, a tour guide blew in like an ill wind. He spun to face his group, who trailed in with dutiful enthusiasm. I shrank against one wall as he jabbed a finger upward, barking a rapid explanation of the three bicycles that hung from the ceiling (the padre rode them across the parish, presumably not at the same time). Next, he pointed to two crosses big enough to nail me to (still used for processions and ceremonies commemorating the priest).

Escaping to the rear of the house, I found the Sala dos Milagres sealed by a wall of iron bars that would not have been out of place in a jail. Most miracle rooms, like the one at Aparecida, you can just walk into. Perhaps they thought someone might steal the model church that the padre planned to build before he was suspended from the priesthood. The pointy, gaudy, turreted affair would, in my opinion, have made a more suitable home for Shrek and Princess Fiona than a temple for God.

Hanging from the ceiling were symbols of thanks I was becoming familiar with: wooden legs, hands, and feet. You might have seen such thanks — ex-votos, in Latin, from 'out of a promise' — in European churches. I had not. In Brazil, they take an astonishingly wide range of forms. Some tokens sat in rows on shelves: a dozen motorcycle helmets in silent testimony to survival, shiny sporting trophies representing a victory, and an old-fashioned cash register that suggested newfound wealth.

Padre Cícero was prone to visitations. Not long after his arrival in the parish, he saw Christ dining with his Apostles. Christ turned to the young priest and ordered him to take charge of the poor and disorderly backlanders who would soon arrive on his doorstep, fleeing the drought. Even then, Padre Cícero probably didn't think he would be anything other than an ordinary backlands cleric until that first day of March in 1889 — the same year that Brazil became a republic — when he placed the sacrament on the tongue of the *beata* Maria.

The event had occurred, church investigators subsequently found, not once but each Wednesday and Friday of Lent that year. The miracle then manifested daily for the forty-seven days from Passion Sunday to the Feast of Ascension of Christ into Heaven. Pilgrims began to arrive almost immediately, seeing the miracle as proof that Juazeiro was a millenarian site from whence they would be delivered from sin.

Despite the miracle being confirmed by a number of his own clergy, the bishop stripped Padre Cícero of his priestly power. Perhaps the bishop didn't see the backlands clergyman as an appropriate candidate for sainthood. There is little on record to indicate his reasoning, so one can easily ascribe jealousy.

The museum is only one stop on Juazeiro do Norte's pilgrimage trail. Aurimar dropped me at the padre's church, where a busload of Brazilian pilgrims stood looking down on the marble tombstone under which the bones of the padrinho were interred. A man in grey shorts was climbing, crab-like, over the tall altarpiece, stopping every foot or so to sweep dust with a small blue brush and pan. By the huge wooden doors, a sign advised pilgrims to tune into Radio Padre Cícero.

Padim Ciço, as he was also affectionately called, continued to give counsel and comfort where he could while still abiding the bishop's orders, which had been ratified by Rome. His supporters decided the answer could be found in politics, and they set his chapeau at state parliament. The new republican government had separated church and state, so perhaps the padre's people thought the move would take him beyond the bishop's powers. But the bishop had the ear of the state governor, and urged that an armed force be sent against the pretender and his faithful growing flock. The padre's followers sensed a threat and began building a wall of stone around the town.

Parts of that wall remain standing today. I hadn't learned of the siege until I gazed at one such remnant: the padre's history-keepers, it seems, prefer a different focus. It was at the beginning of the Santo Sepulcro trail, a walking path that winds around the tops of the hills near the town.

Aurimar hadn't trusted his *gringa*'s ability to walk the well-trodden, two-and-a-half kilometre track by herself, so he'd called in a guide called Buiú (appropriately for his age, pronounced 'boyo') to accompany me. Buiú didn't want to linger in front of the piece of stone wall; I could understand why. Standing about eight feet high, it felt as though the townspeople had mixed fear and sadness into the mortar. The wall seemed to emanate an almost palpable and eerie hollowness, an echo of heavy hearts; the very trees seemed to whisper their despair. A similar sentiment hangs in the air around the lush hill at Palmares and the bare rocky ground at Canudos.

On the trail, Buiú stopped a sombre pilgrim for my camera. The woman was dressed in nothing but a black sack belted with rope. I wondered if she would climb up 'Sin Rock' and squeeze herself into the kennel-like construction on top to perform penance, or stop to trace her fingers along the 'Mark of Padre Cícero': the letters of his name had been worn into the rock over the years by the fingers of the faithful. I was trying to ask her, when she shook her head and headed off down the track. Silence for her pilgrimage or because she couldn't understand me, I wondered.

A few days after the townspeople set the final brick in the wall, a military force appeared on the other side. Then, as now, Juazeiro attracted pilgrims like pollen attracts bees. Padre Cícero's congregation had continued to grow and, despite his modesty and dogged obedience to the rulings of the Church, his people regarded him with messianic fervour. Their unbending belief in the padre's miracle, their outspoken opposition to the Church's decrees, and their utter faith in their priest were taken as evidence that this 'citadel of sectarianism and fanaticism', the 'church within a church', now posed a threat not only to the Church, as the bishop assured the governor, but to the very state itself.

The governor branded Padre Cícero subversive, accusing him of aiding *cangaceiros* — Lampião in particular — and in 1913 sent troops to wrest control of the valley. The 'Wall of Resistance', as the sign calls it today, protected the people against the force for more than a month. Then they ran out of food.

The people followed the orders of their padrinho and did not fire a shot except in self-defence. They would have been under no illusions as to how perilous their position: it had been less than two decades since the War at Canudos, where thousands of peasants had been killed as they tried to live in their New Jerusalem. But they ran out of loaves and fishes, and so the padre was forced to open the gates. Then the next miracle happened. Fuelled by fervour, singing songs of praise to their padrinho, 'the divine protector of the city', the townspeople routed the troops in just three days.

After that, they marched on Fortaleza, where they found that the federal government was as unhappy as they were with the state governor. It had sent troops against him. The governor boarded the next boat for Europe, the bishop's plans were in tatters, and the padre's people returned to their town in peace.

Aurimar nursed his car up the steep cobbled street to the top of the Serra do Horto, from where a giant statue of the priest watches over Juazeiro. Aurimar told me there's usually a penitent of two walking up the street on their knees, sounding puzzled that there was not one today. On the days that commemorate Padre Cícero's birth and death (he died at the age of eighty), a procession a couple of hundred thousand strong wends its way up to the statue, some on their knees. Did they wear pads on their knees, I wondered, like a woman I saw in Morocco once, or was that regarded as cheating?

Most weekends, Aurimar said, he drove his wife up the hill, where she helped a friend who had a souvenir stall. His wife had chosen to move to Juazeiro because of Padre Cícero, he had agreed, and the life had been good to them.

The locals boast that the twenty-three-metre figure is the third highest concrete statue in the world. And perhaps it is. Circumnavigating the hem of the padre's cassock, I read that Maria and José, Afonso and Camilia, Manuel and Flávia had all 'been here'.

There was a large wooden bull near the statue's ankles. Aurimar looked a little perplexed when I declined his offer to take a photo of me astride it. It wasn't that the bull was proudly complete in a way you wouldn't see in Australia — we're a little too prudish for that — just that I don't especially like having my photo taken. Since Brazilians find this attitude challenging, I did let him take my photo in front of the image of the priest. He stood me just so, and it appears as if the kindly looking priest has his hand resting on my head.

Near the statue is another Padre Cícero museum, and it holds, perhaps, even more *ex-votos* than the miracle room at Aparecida. It is a compelling display of hundreds of thousands of symbols of thanks. Researchers tell us that modern memory is archival, and this was an archive of thanks. It seems Padre Cícero has been very busy bestowing miracles since his death in 1934. But although only two miracles are required to qualify one for sainthood, Cícero hasn't even been canonised.

Among the *ex-votos* was a glass case of moulded, nippled breasts. A large wall was chock-full of wooden legs. I supposed there were a whole range of things that could go wrong with legs: breaks, cuts, tumours, gangrene. Perhaps the padre had made someone's varicose veins disappear. Collages featured neatly dressed men, smiling grandmothers, and whole families with bright shiny cars. A gaggle of gowned graduates inspired in me a burst of pride, so ready were they to toss their mortar-boards in the air. Their faces bellowed: *It's over! I did it! Thank you for your help and inspiration, my padrinho!*

But then a display of photographs of smiling children undid me. Some were still bald. A resentment I hadn't realised was there uncoiled inside me. Here were children spared, relieved of their cancerous cells. Their parents were so grateful, and so sure of the miracle, that they had sent photos. But why these children and not my young friend? Australians expect a level playing field, the same set of rules and rewards for all. My friend was prayed for, to lots of gods, by lots of people — even by me. Like Delfino's attempt at finding a cure for his wife by taking her to the Valley of the Dawn, in certain circumstances anything is worth a go. Delfino's God didn't help his wife when he asked, either.

And I realised that this is another reason I wouldn't make a good Brazilian: it's not just because I often travel alone and don't like noise, crowds, or photographs of myself, but because I find that randomness makes more sense to me.

~

The extent to which people will go to subjugate others is astonishing, and again I have to remind myself that it's not something unique to Brazil. The padre's people were lucky; they would say they had God on their side. The original inhabitants of Tasmania, who were also trying to live their lives in peace and harmony, were not so fortunate.

Towards the end of the Black War, a plan was hatched to gather up those who had survived it — the few men, women, and children — by sweeping them, quite literally, south. It was 1830 and the government formed a human chain three hundred kilometres long and two thousand men strong. Convicts, ex-convicts, soldiers, and free men combed the land from north to south across the island colony. 'It was planned,' as historian Henry Reynolds has pointed out, 'with the care and attention to detail of a military campaign.' The plan was devised, specifically, as a 'means … for making them prisoners'. The fact that the Black Line, as it became known, resulted in just two captures is the only amusing part of this episode in the Australian national story.

After the failure of that campaign, most of the remaining Tasmanians were gathered up by a zealous Englishman called George Augustus Robinson. Robinson's efforts were aided by some tribespeople who had, it is thought, become aware of the perilous position their people were in. The Tasmanians were transported to Flinders Island. There — here, from where I write — they were settled in a windy, barren spot on the east coast.

For more than forty thousand years, these islands to the south of mainland Australia have been inhabited. Humans lived on Flinders Island, on and off, until about four thousand years ago. They abandoned the island because, researchers believe, it was too small to sustain a 'viable hunter-gatherer population'.

The settlement the Tasmanians were brought to on Flinders was — is — called Wybalenna, meaning 'black man's houses' in the local Palawa kani language. But the brick huts were white men's houses, designed and built by white men who spread white diseases. In *The Fatal Shore*, Robert Hughes called the settlement a 'concentration camp'.

Prevailing opinion holds Robinson's motives as honourable. It suggests that by taking the Tasmanians away from the violent retaliations of the whites who had stolen their land, he hoped to prevent them from dying out. It was a desperate attempt to wrestle history into triumph rather than tragedy. If it had succeeded, Robinson would be credited as saviour.

The settlement surrounded a chapel where Robinson's charges were expected to pray. You can visit it today. It was reconstructed using bricks of about the same era. The original chapel had fallen into disrepair; for some decades of the twentieth century, it was used as a shed for shearing sheep in, rather than nurtured as an important historic site.

It is a small chapel, with a space that acted as a schoolroom for the few children — white children; reports note that there were no black kids to be seen. These days, the chapel is rarely used: we go there for the occasional funeral service, but that's about it. In the spring, the field in front of the chapel is filled with irises, like something out of a Vincent van Gogh painting. As if some god might be remembering what happened there.

Visitors to Wybalenna today see chunks of bricks from the original huts strewn across the hills. They are bricks from the doctor's surgery, the houses, the prison, and the barracks. Outbuildings from the original supervisor's house still stand.

Between the years of 1832, when the first Tasmanians arrived, and 1847, when the settlement was finally abandoned, two hundred and twenty Tasmanians were transported to Wybalenna. One hundred and thirty-two died there in just fifteen years. They were buried in unmarked graves in the cemetery. Mannalargenna, a Palawa leader from whom some of my friends are descended, was among those who died on Flinders Island. Neither Robinson nor his god could prevent the people from succumbing to foreign diseases, although some, it was observed even at the time, perished from grief.

The removal of the Tasmanians to Flinders Island was an experiment that failed. It was also, of course, an exercise in power. The British had hoped that they could apply the same removal and isolation policy to the Aborigines on the Australian mainland. Flinders was even suggested as a settlement site for mainland Aboriginal Australians. Think of it: instead of being able to move with the seasons and their stories across their vast traditional lands, as they had before British sails appeared on the horizon, Australia's Indigenous peoples could have been crammed into Flinders' mere 1,333 square kilometres. As it was, a great many were forced to live without the land that contained the spirits of their ancestors, without their communities, their dreaming tracks, or familiar terrain. They were forced to live in some other windswept parts of Australia but not, in the end, on Flinders Island.

The few Tasmanians who did survive their time on Flinders Island were moved to another settlement, south of Hobart, where they continued to die from grief and disease. Truganini passed away in 1876. She has often been erroneously called 'the last Tasmanian Aborigine' — there's even a film about her called 'The Last Tasmanian' — when at most she was the last Tasmanian Aborigine of blood undiluted by non-Aborigines.

The holocaust in Tasmania was quite well known in England. The events inspired H.G. Wells' *The War of the Worlds*, published at the end of the nineteenth century. These words appear at the beginning of the novel, words Wells spoke to his brother Frank while out walking one day: 'We must remember what ruthless and utter destruction our own species has wrought, not only upon animals … The Tasmanians … were entirely swept out of existence in a war of extermination waged by European immigrants, in the space of fifty years.'

The things we do to one another. Although I can't suggest that it would have been all that different if Australia had been settled by the Portuguese: they, too, either killed or enslaved and converted the original Brazilians. The United States has history not dissimilar, of course. Is there any country that doesn't have such shameful episodes in its past? Perhaps the trick is, at least, to keep those episodes in the past and not keep perpetuating the same injustices over and over again.

Yes, I know, that does seem like a pipe dream.

Chapter Nineteen

Hopes for a Good End

SALVADOR, BAHIA

'She believed in angels, and, because she believed, they existed.'
Clarice Lispector

In Brazil, no matter my form of transport, it seems to take me, eventually and sometimes by roundabout routes, to Salvador. The original capital has the manic air of the tropics and the constant beat of a drum. On arrival, I am always immediately entranced by its sound.

The Old City sits on a cliff like a matriarch surveying her brood. Many of the forts, built to protect the city from native, French, and Dutch incursion, remain standing, testimony to the skill of Portuguese masons.

Pelourinho, the UNESCO World Heritage–listed site, is the historic centre. It is named for the stone post to which recalcitrant slaves were chained when they were whipped. Pelourinho isn't for mornings; life in its cobbled plazas tends towards a slow start, building to a crescendo of music and movement well beyond midnight, when it teems with performers and tourists, beggars and beer hawkers, souvenir sellers and pickpockets. The plazas host *rodas*, circles of onlookers that surround *capoeira* players who move in graceful arcs, seeking to score points in this elegant syncretisation of dance, game, and martial art. Typically, the morning streets are exhausted from the night before, when the tourists, mesmerised by the twang of the *berimbau* and the looping legs of the *capoeiristas*, were hit up for coin, either in the form of a politely proffered cap or the sly hand of a thief.

Customarily in the Terreiro do Jesus, the main plaza that is surrounded by stone churches, souvenir shops, and *cachaça* saloons, the new day begins slowly. A typical morning goes like this:

Outdoor tables sparkle with last night's dew. The first of the *vendadores* wanders in and props her board of charcoal portraits against a power pole with an echoing pop that startles the cats sleeping on restaurant stoops. Like most Brazilians, she can't abide silence, so tinny music, perhaps the Brazilian music known as *forró*, plays on her cell phone. Soon, a coconut seller pulls his wagon from a side street. He clacks the lid up and snaps four poles into place. A schoolgirl with shiny skin skips along, clapping her hands. From the arterial road below, horns sound. One or more of the church bells toll. Wheelie-bins rumble over the cobbles. Then a jackhammer digs in behind the partitions that stand in front of a peach-coloured colonial building, drowning out all else.

This is the start to my day I expected, stepping through the doorway of my hotel. Instead, the blast of a brass band hit me like a 747 on touchdown. From around the corner, with the force of a storm, marched the Sons of Gandhi.

I hopped backwards onto the stone step to let the two hundred or more Filhos de Gandhy stream past me in their crisp uniforms, coloured white for Oxalá and blue for Ogum. They had turned out for the Lavagem do Bonfim, the cleaning of the steps of the Nosso Senhor do Bonfim church.

I followed their rear guard. As we marched down the hill, little puffs of smoke appeared here and there in the blue sky: their brass band was so loud, it drowned out the fireworks.

The Thursday before the second Sunday after Epiphany — which that year fell on 17th January — is the best-attended of the four-day festival in honour of Senhor do Bonfim, the Lord of the Good End. Manifesting as Christ crucified, he is the patron saint of Bahia, with two state hymns and more than a few churches to his name. It is to Bonfim you pray to provide a good end to your travail or predicament. There is an image, of course, but this one's appearance wasn't mysterious, and it doesn't come out until the final day of the festival. Then it leads a smaller, shorter, and considerably more solemn procession from another church to the Igreja do Bonfim. But this first procession is led by a group of Baianas (traditionally attired, female descendants of African slaves), who clean the steps of the Church of Nosso Senhor do Bonfim.

Following the noisy throng down the sloping cobbled streets to the lower city, I joined the thousands of people milling outside the Church of Our Lady of Immaculate Conception, just under the Lacerda. The concrete elevator joins the upper city with the lower and the port. Before it was built, slaves used to carry goods uphill from the wharves to the city on their backs.

Before me was further evidence that Brazilians don't generally feel the need to keep their religions separate. Coming out of the church were women in the snowy-hooped skirts and lacy white tops of Candomblé, and men in the dark robes of the priesthood. The women are the public face of the Lavagem do Bonfim.

A man in an expensive suit spoke into a microphone at length as I watched a couple of Baianas pose amiably with tourist after tourist dressed in white shorts, shoes, and baseball caps. Every sliver of shade had been taken by other hot souls, and by the time the fireworks wracked the air again, my blouse was soaked with sweat. Eventually the giant ball-balloons that rolled above the crowd, promoting tourism and health, began moving forward.

There seemed to be scores of bands scattered along the procession and, because they each played their own choice of music, they were not always in harmony.

My foot sent a beer can scudding across the asphalt. The streets were lined with *vendadores* selling beer, water, and food. There were hand-pulled wagons of popcorn and coconuts, and more than one man hoiking a pole of dangling fairy floss, speckling pink and yellow over the white-dressed crowd like sprinkles on ice-cream.

In Brazil, beer cans can come in some odd sizes. Stopping to buy one, mainly so I could cool off in the shade of the *vendadore*'s umbrella, I was handed a slightly smaller can than I was used to: 269 millilitres instead of 350. It's called a *piriguete*: the Portuguese word for floozy.

At the next stall, a man was making *caipirinhas* with *cachaça*, sugar, and limes, with a theatricality the world hasn't seen since the movie *Cocktail*. A skinny, greying man sambaed to the music that blared from speakers in front of the cocktail stand. His t-shirt was wrapped around his dark hand, his abdominal muscles working out right there under his neatly defined ribs.

Prejudices and habits often come into sharp focus when travelling. My formative years were accompanied by the strains of anti-littering jingles, and I was finding that every time my foot fell on an empty can or water bottle, I had to stifle the urge to pick it up. The road was strewn with cans, bottles, skewers, and more, and it would have taken me all day to clear just a fraction of the six-kilometre procession path. So, unable to bring myself to drop the *piriguete*, I stopped to look for a rubbish bin.

A group of Baianas strode towards me, preceded by a pack of backwards-scrambling men attached to paparazzi lenses. You can usually tell the difference between tourists and professional photographers by the length of their lenses, but sometimes I've been fooled by some tourist who has spent more on his camera equipment than his health fund. The women bobbed along in their bulbous skirts in the current of admirers like buoys in a harbour.

In former times, the women cleaned the entire Bonfim church, inside and out, from bell tower to vestibule, in echo of the Portuguese tradition of cleaning the church in payment for an answered prayer. But the tension between the sacred and the secular — or, rather, the not-strictly

Catholic — led church authorities to close their doors, allowing only the steps to be attended to.

Unable to spy a rubbish receptacle, I jammed the can into the pouch at my waist to free my hands for the camera. As I focused, a slim Baiana, balancing a vase on her head, dropped her own beer can to the ground, and her companion's foot sent it skidding into my ankle. Resisting the temptation to make a game of it, I responded to a nudge and stepped out of the way of a patrol of military police. Their leader, who'd nudged me, curled his hand into the thumbs-up signal that is so well used in Brazil; in this case it was a private apology as he led them past. They trudged along, eyes forward, wearing belts that held black batons and dark pistols.

I was resigning myself to having to drop the can onto the road (my hesitation was entirely ridiculous, of course; a small army of street sweepers would have it spotless by dark) when I spied a thin, ragged man stomping on cans before popping them into his hessian sack. He looked surprised when I offered him mine.

The procession ended in a shady plaza in front of the church. Two golden bell towers gleamed in the sunlight. A girl of about twelve, under one of the heavy-leaved trees — were they elms? — had attracted a crowd. I wandered over to see that she had a small furry animal in her hands, and she was smothering it — literally in danger of smothering it — with kisses. The people around me were laughing and pointing. I assumed it was a kitten. But then my attention was snagged by a figure crawling down one of the trees behind the girl, shaking as if it had a palsy.

It was a small monkey, and it was screaming.

Startled, I swung back to the girl, realising with horror that the animal in her hands was its baby. It is the classic traveller's dilemma: what to do when your values aren't shared by the people you are visiting. The ideal solution would be to become invisible, rush over, and whisk the baby from the girl in a manner she'd probably put down to the supernatural. With no-one the wiser. I couldn't very well lecture everyone here on the prevention of cruelty to animals; after all, I was the outsider.

The girl held out the baby towards its parent. The parent crawled a little further down the bark, hope sparking in its eyes. The girl snatched her prize away and the monkey scampered back up the tree. I spotted a second monkey peeking out from behind some leaves. She — for some reason I was sure that this was the mother — was keening.

A woman with the gentle face of a grandmother came up to the girl, and I exhaled with relief — although why I expected her to demand the release of the little thing I'm not sure. She patted the girl on the head, said something to her, and turned back to her food stall. The girl put the monkey on one of her bare shoulders, where it clung, eyes fixed on the tree trunk that its father — perhaps the father — was once again descending nervously.

My family and I were in Morocco a couple of decades back when we passed two boys wrestling in a schoolyard. The Texan couple travelling with us marched up to the boys and pulled them apart, lecturing them (in English) about fighting, despite our Moroccan guide's visible disapproval. The guide's expression said that he was sick of Westerners who thought they had a right to interfere in the ways of his people. I felt sympathy for the guide and for the boys, who had really just been mucking around, and was embarrassed, not wanting to be linked by association with the imperialism of the situation. But now I wished that those Texans were with me — although they, too, could well have been unconcerned by this situation. There was no doubt that these animals were far more helpless than those boys, but there were twenty or more of the girl's compatriots standing around and encouraging her. I wish I could report otherwise, but I spun on my heel and fled, abdicating responsibility, hoping the Lord of the Good End would manage to return the baby to its distraught parents.

Forcing my attention back to the church, I realised with a start that the ceremony was over. In Brazil, the climax of an event is often lost in the press of the crowd or in some distracting scene, and this was one of those times. Those in-the-know would have taken up a position at the church steps around dawn that morning so they could see the women washing them. In fact, the ceremony was over so quickly that I suspected the women had simply upended their vases and kept on walking.

People packed the steps, trying to get to the iron bars at the top, from which fluttered a rainbow of ribbons. There looked to be no room to tie even one more of the tiny wish-ribbons, but hundreds of people seemed to think they could still add theirs. So I bought a bunch for myself and joined the crush. Eventually I made it to the fence, but diverted, instead, through the gate. Perhaps my wishes for the kidnapped monkey's safe return would be more powerful if I tied my ribbons to the tall gates that covered the church's doors, protecting the sacred from the profane.

Meanwhile, the plaza in front of the church had become a party zone. Big black speakers broadcast music. I walked past the tree, nervous of what I might find. But the girl, her audience, and the monkeys had all disappeared. The grandmother was serving steaming dishes to a six-deep queue.

So I left the plaza to return to my hotel and discovered that the entire procession-route had become a street party, as is so often the case in Brazil. With no hope of getting a cab, I tossed beer down my throat and cans onto the street with some abandon the whole six kilometres back to Pelourinho. While the rest of the city celebrated, I tried to get the image of the terrified baby monkey out of my mind and hoped fervently that my wish had been granted by the Lord of the Good End.

Chapter Twenty

Gandhi of the Amazon

XAPURI, ACRE

'God is big but the forest is bigger.' Brazilian proverb

In Brazil, death can come with a price tag. Revenge and self-interest are the fertile seeds of many of Brazil's tragic tales. Take this hitman's price list circa 1990, which I found in Alex Shoumatoff's *Murder in the Rainforest*: 'A union leader costs $500 to $1200; a town councilman or lawyer, $1500; a padre $3,500–$4,000; a judge, state deputy, mayor, or bishop $25,000.'

Murders, in the name of opposing 'causes', occur in Brazil at a startling rate. There have been more than one thousand murders over land conflicts alone since 1980. That's a rate of nearly one a fortnight, just for land conflicts. In 1987, eighty-eight union leaders were killed because someone didn't like them trying to establish some form of workers' rights. Doing good in Brazil comes at a cost, as a man called Chico Mendes found out when he got in the way of 'progress'.

Acre is Brazil's western-most state. It was once all Amazon rainforest. The state capital is Rio Branco, and its main thoroughfare is called Chico

Mendes Way. Peter and I were being driven down Chico Mendes Way after hopping a *colectivo* from where they queued outside Rio Branco bus station. On my left was a bony guy in a cowboy hat who pecked the journey away on his mobile phone. To my right, Peter had one of our bags jammed under his knees. A slim, worn-out looking woman in her thirties sat in the front, staring into space.

Our *colectivo* driver was fairly typical, too, as Brazilian taxi drivers go. He took phone calls and typed text messages for the entire hour and a half, as if he was in his lounge room. I would have been pleased that it was tarmac all the way, except the seat belts didn't work. But, long ago, Brazil taught me that it can be curiously liberating travelling at such speeds that if something goes wrong, you know you won't survive.

I had learned a whole new language travelling in the Northwest. Acreano culture is encapsulated in the terminology. *Grilagem,* for example, is the system that ranchers and other entrepreneurs use to enlarge their holdings. Say they buy 50 hectares, they register those hectares as 500. Then they pay someone to add another zero and suddenly they have 5,000 hectares, not 50. Inventive, *sim*?

I had gained, too, a vocabulary for discussing death and killing that my language classes had failed to teach me. A *mandante* is one who commissions the death of another. A *pistoleiro* is a hired gun, the person who will carry out the murder. And the word I found most horrifying, *anunciado,* is quite common, apparently, on the continent. Five syllables that do a big job. It's an adjective and a noun and a most specific form of torture: you are *anunciado* when your imminent murder has been announced.

As with pretty much any town in Latin America, it is inadvisable to arrive in Xapuri on a Sunday. We finally found lunch in a dingy shack. I thought the grilled chicken was fine, but avoided the raw bits close to the bone; Peter wouldn't touch it, but he hoed into the rice and the beans, leaving me what passed for salad.

While we ate, the cook reclined in a deckchair, watching *telenovelas.* Her thighs oozed out from under her denim skirt. She had dressed that morning in a red lacy bra that poked up from her low-cut top like sunset-tinted mountain peaks. The effect was so deliberate — and so startling — that it had me wondering if cooking was her main profession.

On Monday, Xapuri was a different town: horses pulled wagons down the main street; taxi drivers gossiped in the square. The Chico Mendes Foundation and Chico Mendes' house were both open. Small and brightly painted, the shack-like building is in the centre of town; it is the site of Mendes' assassination, just before the Christmas of 1988.

Chico Mendes was born Francisco Alves Mendes Filho (that is, Junior). Chico's grandparents had joined the hundreds of thousands of backlanders from the Northeast who were forced to migrate by the droughts of the late nineteenth and early twentieth century. The government offered incentives for people to move to the interior, where labour was needed to help rich *seringalistas,* rubber barons, exploit its treasures.

Chico's people arrived from the state of Ceará, where they may have heard Padre Cícero preach. Like most *flagelados,* as the refugees were called, they came up the river system. They probably stopped at Manaus, the city that had been transformed by the rubber boom a couple of decades before. Manaus was founded in the 1600s as a Portuguese defence post, and the boom brought the Industrial Revolution not only to the city but also to the rest of Brazil.

In Brazil, the history of rubber-use is long. The Portuguese saw that the *índios* used it to make balls and pouches, for waterproofing, and for syringes to deliver herbal enemas. In the Western world, it took Charles Goodyear to vulcanise rubber before it was seen as useful. Then Dunlop invented the tyre and Ford invented the car, and suddenly the jungle was filled with the sound of society parties and automobiles. Ballgowns were sewn and yachts were raced. *Pâtè* was imported from France, and butter from Cork. The Teatro Amazonas was built. (The ornate, full-service opera house, complete with a stained-glass dome, is still one of Manaus' major sights today.) It was a time of 'firsts': Manaus was the first city in Brazil to get streetlights and a sewerage system; Brazil's first federal university educated the heirs of the rubber barons. But the rubber boom ended unexpectedly early in the twentieth century.

By then, an Englishman called Henry Wickham had sailed seventy thousand seeds of the *Hevea brasiliensis* tree from the Amazon across the Atlantic and planted them in London's Kew Gardens. The English then planted their holdings in Malaysia with rubber, Wickham was knighted, and the world went elsewhere for their erasers and tyres, for their plumbers' friends.

The rubber industry in Acre, though gutted, continued. Chico Mendes' family became *soldados da borracha,* soldiers of rubber, and were soon trapped by the *aviamento* system that makes the feudal system look quite generous. The rubber tappers were forced to sell their harvest to the one landowner, to whom they also paid rent for the trees they tapped. They were compelled to buy their goods from the shop run by the same *seringalista.* Landowners took advantage of the workers' illiteracy and paid them less than their rubber was worth and charged them more for the goods they bought, often on credit. It was a system of debt-bondage whereby the worker never managed to pay off his bill to the landowner.

Chico Mendes became a third-generation tapper when his father taught him from a young age how to cut the V into the bark of the tree, how to set a pot in which to catch the white sap, and how to spot a tree that had recovered sufficiently from its last tapping. While tapping rubber trees, Chico met a stranger in the *seringais.* Euclides Távora, a man marked by his communist sympathies, was hiding in the jungle during the Vargas era. He saw intelligence in the boy and taught him to read. Over time, Távora nurtured in Chico the desire and ability to lead his fellow rubber-tappers towards a better life.

Inoperância: a kind of apathy. It is a state enhanced by the soporific effects of the tropics, encouraged by successive generations of dictatorial governments, and perpetuated by religion. Jean-Paul Sartre might call it 'bad faith': a failure to take responsibility, to merely accept one's lot, to not try to change things. But pushing for change can be a dangerous business in Brazil.

The CIA had backed the military coup of 1964 that installed Humberto Castelo Branco as president of a Brazilian government that began sweeping reforms. They had a plan they called Operation Amazônia to clear the rainforest, to populate it with labourers in order to further exploit the land, and to rid the jungle of the subversives they suspected of hiding in it — subversives including Euclides Távora. He disappeared one day during a visit to Rio Branco when Chico Mendes was twenty-one.

By the 1970s, mining companies and cattle-ranchers from southern Brazil had begun to buy up tracts of Acre. They planned to throw the tappers off the land and clear it. The burning of the Amazon is still common today (after they log it). It occasionally makes the news: scenes show menacing black smoke spiralling to the skies. Like the bombing of Dresden.

Despite the fact that a good many of the tappers could claim some form of ownership of their plots by various means, including under squatters' laws, many — perhaps suffering from *inoperância* — simply walked away when they were told to do so. More than three hundred thousand people were evicted from their homes and deprived of their livelihoods by less than one hundred and fifty landowners. Those landowners cleared land at the rate of more than ten thousand hectares a year in the Xapuri region alone.

Although opposed to any kind of armed confrontation, Chico Mendes encouraged his fellow *soldados da borracha* to unite, to make a stand against the *seringalistas*. He formed a plan: those who had not yet left their land would stay, and they would refuse to pay rent to the *seringalistas*.

Chico wasn't working alone. He had found a new mentor in a union leader called Wilson Pinheiro. Pinheiro instigated an especially effective form of protest called the *empate*, the standoff or human barricade. Women and children would face off the *pistoleiros*, who had been hired by the landowners, but who didn't countenance violence against women and children and so would walk away. One such *pistoleiro* took out Wilson Pinheiro on the steps of the Rural Workers' Union office in 1980. The cost of the hit could have been as little as one thousand US dollars; no one was ever prosecuted for the murder.

Liberation theology was on the rise in Latin America, much to the dismay of Pope John Paul II. It preached 'the gospel of earthly salvation', actively promoting social change. Its proponents formed an alliance with the working class to promote change in this life, not just the next. This appealed to many Brazilians. Soon, eight hundred evangelist groups sprouted around the region, preaching the new theology. Chico Mendes, attracted by these ideas, became leader of one such church group.

It wasn't only liberation theology that was embraced by Acreano workers around this time; the Rural Workers' Union membership grew to twenty thousand in its first three years. Chico Mendes became one of its leading officials. The death of Pinheiro began a war between the members of the Rural Worker's Union and the *seringalistas*. It was a conflict over agrarian reform and would see more than seven hundred deaths in less than a decade.

The Church kept a list: in 1988, the year that Chico Mendes was murdered, the deaths of three hundred and fifty people had been *anunciadas* because they supported land reform and the ecological struggle of the Amazon. The list included bishops and cardinals, judges and workers. Mendes had been on the list for quite some time before they shot him.

At the museum, having left Peter to sleep in, I was trailed by a shy teenager who seemed convinced that she couldn't communicate with me. This was despite watching me not merely read but also take notes from the information boards on the museum's walls. Each time I tried to engage her, she flitted away like a skittish kitten. In shops all over Brazil, sales assistants trail you, hoping to be helpful. This different sales ethic is something that makes Australians uncomfortable. It's an attention to service that we don't have; for the most part, we prefer to be left alone in our shopping. But this was a museum — I wasn't here to buy anything. Perhaps the teenager was trailing me not to answer my questions but because she thought I might steal something from the glass cases. I wondered if she had a baby at home — almost every female I had seen of child-bearing age in Xapuri had been carrying a baby. The locals clearly didn't support the factory that manufactures condoms on the outskirts of town.

The girl just shook her head when I asked about Chico's first wife. I couldn't see any photos from Chico's first marriage, to a woman who was said to have regularly kicked him and who slept under the house. Chico's family were aghast at her behaviour: 'I kept telling him to beat her,' Chico's aunt told the author of *Murder in the Rainforest*, Alex Shoumatoff.

Eventually, Chico married again. In the museum, there were lots of photos of his second wife, Ilzamar, one of three sisters he taught to read and write, and the couple's two children. There was also ample evidence of the esteem in which he was held and fame he achieved, by way of keys to cities and other international commendations, including the United Nations Global 500 Award.

Chico transformed rubber-tappers into the heroes of the global environmental movement. He was flown to present his case at international conferences and eco-rallies. The tappers' plight was no longer merely a domestic matter. He spruiked his plan for the land to be placed in the care of the tappers, who would work the rainforest sustainably, in plots called extractive reserves. It was an idea that has since been implemented by a number of countries seeking agrarian reform.

Between his plan for extractive reserves, his ability to unite the workers, and his increasing presence on the world stage, the name Chico Mendes was never likely to be found on the invitation lists to the *seringalistas'* dinner parties.

Chico Mendes knew the landowners would get him in the end: 'In Brazil, when someone calls you up and tells you that you are going to die, it is not so much a threat as a statement of fact.' He didn't succumb to *inoperância*, though; he did all he could to survive. Spending much time in hiding, he wrote letters and sent telexes — hundreds of them — telling politicians and other influential people that he feared for his life, that he wanted to see his children grow up. That the prospect of martyrdom didn't hold much appeal. Some foreigners believed that his international fame would afford protection, but in Brazil it only made him more of a target.

The Mendes house is a tiny wooden A-frame, like a doll's house, and painted pastel-blue and -pink. It is opposite the Chico Mendes Foundation, which houses the memorial to his life and continues the struggle for agrarian reform. I can imagine Chico and his family in the small house:

Chico, a shortish man with a face becoming worn by worry, calls out to his wife that he is off to take a shower. Ilzamar answers absently, engrossed in her *telenovela*. (The television — a small rotund Blaupunkt — still sits in the lounge-room.) Chico walks out of the bedroom with a towel over one shoulder. He passes his two ill-equipped and undertrained guards, who are playing cards on the formica kitchen table. Pushing at the back door — perhaps it's a little swollen from heat — he starts as it gives with a clatter. The sound alerts the gunmen (police would find evidence of two, although only one confessed). Shots are fired. Chico looks down at his buckshot-ridden singlet in surprise. 'Damn, they got me,' he manages, before he falls down on the stoop, dead.

There is a photo of Chico Mendes lying on a gurney in the morgue. It shows a homely-looking man, his mouth held closed with a white rag that's been tucked behind his ears and disappears into his hair like a road lost to forest. His belly is testament to his good manners: Brazilian etiquette dictates one never refuses a meal when visiting. A moustache floats over his smile. His brown eyes, which, in other photographs, were deep as gems and sparked with wonderment at the world, are closed. Shots speckle his chest, and his head is surrounded by an unruly halo of dark curls.

We've a tendency, I think, to regard history as accurate and immutable. And perhaps we believe in fate rather too much. It wasn't fate that killed Chico Mendes; it was people.

I was about six or seven when my parents bought a farm on Flinders Island. A few years later Dad made the change from farming to fishing. So we lived some of our lives on the island, flying there from Melbourne every holiday and long weekend. My brother and I knocked around with the local kids, exploring the island's one hundred and twenty beaches or the other fifty-odd islands nearby. We farmed, fished, and read. It was a blessed life.

Flinders Island had been inhabited, although not by many, since the abandonment of the settlement at Wybalenna. Later, a scheme bestowing land on returned soldiers grew the population after World War II. Some of the other farms were owned by families like ours, who lived 'away'.

A lot of the kids we hung out with on Flinders Island were Aboriginal. At school in Melbourne, however, we were taught that Truganini was the last Tasmanian Aboriginal. Confusion tapped me on the shoulder, demanding argument with my teacher. Tasmanian Aboriginal people lived on Flinders Island: women I called 'Aunty', children I called friends. Heads were shaken in disbelief: both mine and the teacher's. It took a while to get to the bottom of the mystery. History books, of course, are selective and sometimes just plain wrong.

While the whites on mainland Tasmania were preoccupied with the Black War, a parallel history was unfolding in the Furneaux group of islands, the largest of which is Flinders. As the Flinders Island Aboriginal Association website now points out, in the 1810s and 1820s 'European sealers and Aboriginal women, some forcibly abducted, established an Aboriginal Islander community on the Furneaux Islands'. So, before Wybalenna, before the Black Line, Tasmanian women were making a life — some by choice, others not — on the islands that dot the southern Bass Strait. Probably unwittingly, they ensured the survival of a people. These women and the children they bore appear in Robinson's and others' records from that time.

It wasn't an easy life, but the women had families: by 1826, there were more than twenty children among the islands. The women harvested muttonbirds from rookeries on the islands, as they had done for millennia — as their descendants, some of whom are my friends, do today — and they were excellent hunters. These families survived on a traditional diet of wallaby, possum, and fish, as well as pig, goat, sheep, potato, wheat, and other introduced crops that the Straitsmen, as their men became known, grew. The Straitsmen sold the skins and meat of seals, whales, and marsupials, while the women supplied the fast-growing market with feathers from the muttonbird, also now known as the short-tailed shearwater.

In this way, as John Lort Stokes noted when he surveyed the Bass Strait islands in the HMS *Beagle* in the early 1940s, the Bass Strait community survived, even thrived, while the last of their compatriots were taken to Wybalenna, where they withered or died.

This explains why my teacher held so fixedly to the view that there were no Tasmanian Aboriginals left: that version of history didn't suit the history-keepers. And today I can watch Aunty Bernice make necklaces in the traditional way, from *maireener* shells, and I can hear Aunty Vicki practise the Palawa kani language. I can watch my friends work in the same ways their ancestors did each April during the muttonbird season, and I can join the celebrations for National Aborigines and Islanders Day in July.

There's a common debate about who has the right to tell stories or to write histories, but who, I wonder, has the right to say that you don't, or shouldn't, exist?

Chapter Twenty-one

Among the Believers

CÉU DO MAPIÁ, AMAZONAS

*'It led to good things too, eventually, / But there and then I saw
no sign of those, / And can't say even now how I had come / To be
there, stunned and following my nose / Away from the straight path.'*
Dante (*Inferno*)

First to tell me about the Santo Daime sect was Ernesto, who worked
at the hotel owned by the 'Big Basílica' at Aparecida. It is a sect in the
sense that its followers would regard it as a Christian religion, but most
branches of Christianity would regard its beliefs as heretical. Throughout
my travels in the Amazon region I had heard about the hallucinogen
ayahuasca, which the Amazonians have been taking for centuries and is
central to Santo Daime.

Ernesto hadn't told his strictly Catholic family that he sometimes
joined a local chapter of the sect to drink that hallucinogen, which is
crucial to their ceremonial activities. He offered to take me to a ceremony
down south.

Travelling in the Amazon region, I had heard constantly about ayahuasca. Backpackers in Ecuador and Peru, in particular, were rumoured to take part in bizarre jungle scenes with shamans and dancing and visions. But I never actually met anyone who'd had the experience first-hand. And in fact, I'm not sure why I thought it might be a good thing to do in Brazil. It did give me a chance to delve into another new religion, of course. But really it was one of those things that seemed a good idea, if inexplicably, at the time.

Santo Daime is a shamanic religion. Shamanism's 'basic features', according to Bruce Chatwin, who spent some time reading up on nomads and shamanic religions, are 'a Celestial Being identified with the Sky, direct communication between Heaven and Earth, and an Infernal region connected with these loci by a Cosmic Axis'.

Santo Daime is also syncretic. Its founder, Raimundo Irineu Serra, harvested aspects of every other Brazilian religion he could find: Catholic, Spiritist, Amazonian *índio*, and African. He took the ingredients — details from their liturgy, rituals, symbols, even deities — and mixed them up like ingredients for a Christmas cake. Then he infused it with ayahuasca, which he called 'daime', from the Portuguese words *'dar me'*, 'give me'. It gave him, apparently, light, love, and knowledge. Daime is made by mixing the vine *Banisteriopsis caapi* with the *Psychotria viridis* leaf, and the fact that it has been used by the natives of the Amazon for centuries suggests there might be something useful about it. But I can't tell you what that might be. Of its advertised effects, my research in the field would only confirm its tendency to induce vomiting and diarrhoea.

Instead of accepting Ernesto's offer to take me to a ceremony, I chose the hard way: spotting the opportunity to play the Adventuring Heroine, I decided to attend a ceremony in the heart of the continent, where the Mother Church lies in the bosom of the deep, dense jungle. If the vicissitudes of the journey had been plainer and, later, the nature of the ceremony and the attendant agonies known to me, I would have guessed I might become a Grumpy Expeditioner, *à la* Paul Theroux.

Getting to the Santo Daime headquarters at Céu do Mapiá was a long, uncomfortable drama. Peter and I travelled to Brazil's western-most city, Rio Branco, where we bumped into two eager Daimistas from the United States at out hotel's breakfast buffet. It seemed, at the time, sensible — even a sign from the heavens — to travel with them.

With a tan so even it screamed solarium, Patricia had an unnatural leanness and wore her hair in a taut ponytail as though wishing her cheerleading days were not so far behind her. She boasted that it was her fourth visit to Céu do Mapiá. You'd have thought as I did: surely this would make the journey easy.

Before heading off, Patricia planned to take her companion, Betti, a plump and wild-haired woman probably in her fifties, on a pilgrimage to the memorial tomb of Mestre Irineu, founder of the Santo Daime. Patricia claimed to have been there several times before and told us she had arranged for 'her' driver to collect them at noon. I'd been hoping to see the tomb myself, so I decided to tag along. Peter, sensibly, stayed at the hotel.

The afternoon went something like this:

Patricia is in the front seat, Betti and I are in the back. Patricia directs the driver imperiously and in execrable Portuguese: '*Seem, seem*, this way — there, turn right! No! Stop.' We stop outside one of Santo Daime's rival ayahuasca religions, União do Vegetal (Union of the Vegetable). 'Hmm, it must be on the other side of the city,' she mutters. 'The Highway — where's the Highway?' The driver also looks at a loss. Me — usually Ms Organised, Ms Well-planned, has left the guidebook with Peter, convinced by Patricia's confidence.

Visualising the map, I suggest that the memorial is to the west of the city, on the bus route called 'Irineu Serra', after the cult's founder. Patricia ignores me; she stops someone to ask for directions and then instructs the driver north. I suggest that going north would deliver us to Colônia Cinco Mil, the city headquarters of the Santo Daime, not the memorial. And so it does.

Off again, we circle for another hour before we find it, and Patricia discovers that her shorts are not on the list of acceptable attire to enter the memorial. Betti and I are both wearing skirts, the safest attire for the religious *turista*. The look Patricia gives me is poisonous.

And so you might have thought that the confusions of the afternoon would have warned me against travelling further with Patricia and Betti. But no, I wasn't so smart. Later that day, there being no room in the taxi for Peter and I because of Patricia's huge suitcases of heavy crystals, we rendezvoused with the pair in a river town called Boca do Acre, after five hours sliding down and across muddy roads in a *colectivo*.

The next morning, it became apparent that sticking to her own schedule wasn't one of Patricia's talents. The journey was supposed to take around eight hours. She'd ordered us, somewhat imperiously, to be ready at eight in the morning, but it was 9.30 before she hired four strapping lads to carry her suitcases to the motorised canoe she'd hired.

After that, she wanted to go shopping. We walked around the small town for an hour and a half, with Patricia repeatedly losing her bearings. There was no map for the town — not that she was likely to have consulted one, anyway. After all, she didn't ask the rest of us if we knew in which direction the river was. Peter, who expected us to be on our way hours ago, was fuming. I was trailing behind her, also annoyed, and dreamy-eyed Betti brought up the rear. Betti was a calm woman who had obviously spent her formative years as a flower-child in Haight-Ashbury. She seemed content to follow Patricia around.

Finally we arrived at the riverbank. 'Rivers must have been the guides which conducted the footsteps of the first travellers,' Henry David Thoreau observed. He probably would have arranged a more comfortable form of transport.

We had all taken our places on the hard canoe benches when Patricia had the boatman wait so she could make 'one last phone call before we lose the signal'. Her exuberant love-chatter (Peter and I suspected there was actually no 'Matt darling' on the other end) held us up another twenty-five minutes. Peter spent the time gazing longingly at the sleekly modern — and considerably faster — boats that other pilgrims were taking to Céu do Mapiá. I tried not to watch him, feeling I was to blame.

By that time, the painter was untied and thrown into the boat. Even before the canoe had slid away from the rickety pier, my butt was sore. The river was the colour of milky coffee; birds dipped into it in search of fish, and I already wished we were back on shore.

An hour and a half into the journey, we turned off the River Purus and up an overgrown tributary. The smaller waterway was like those travelled by Theodore Roosevelt in this region: 'not merely unknown but unguessed at'. It was too small even to be one of Thoreau's 'guides'. Reminding myself that I had wanted to play adventuress, I tried to stave off my growing trepidation.

After another hour or so, I was red from sunburn and welted with insect bites. Peter was getting tired and the looks he was giving me grew progressively darker. He had to jump out of the boat every time the boatman needed help pushing the canoe, heavy with Patricia's suitcases, over logs, snags, and sandbanks. I was feeling pretty weighed-down myself: with regret, with embarrassment. Why had I foisted this on Peter? Patricia seemed oblivious to our discomfort.

We had various mosquito-ridden and often superfluous stops on the way. And I think the man driving the canoe had a weak bladder. The longest stop came while we waited for Patricia to visit her 'friend', in a tiny village where she bought homemade sweets for which I suspected she was charged several times more than they were worth.

It was nearing midnight when I finally spotted the lights of the town twinkling through the jungle, and slumped, relieved: I'd been looking for those light for hours, and trying to avoid Peter's eyes. Our journey, expected to take around six hours, had taken nearly twelve. But we were here at last, and soon we would try the drug and see the ceremony that had so intrigued me I'd insisted on making this journey. And then I would get Peter out of here.

Despite Patricia's assurances that she'd get us a room at her *pousada*, when Peter and I arrived, we found — to our relief — it was a full house. The guests were foreign pilgrims: all from the United States, as far as I could tell. After struggling up the steep hill with each of Patricia's suitcases, the boatman took us to a sparsely furnished two-storey building boasting only one other guest. Tucking the bottom edge of the mosquito net under the mattress, I turned to say good night to Peter only to see that he was already asleep.

In the morning, we found the other guest, Aubrey, reading in a hammock near the river. He struggled his way to sitting as he heard us approach the gazebo (I, too, am yet to discover a technique that allows you to exit a hammock with any grace), and greeted us with a smile. Swinging on the hammock like a child, he introduced himself, asking if we had registered at the town office yet. After a shake of my head, he launched into a lecture. After breakfast we would need to register and pay our visitors' fee, he said. We were lucky: tonight was the main ceremony of the June Festival. (Lucky?! I nearly spluttered, having, of course, planned this.) We *were* going to take the Daime, weren't we? Because anyone who attended the ceremony had to take the Daime. We were to wear white. Did we know about the church? He proceeded without pause, confirming — and, to give him his due, adding to — what I already knew about the history of the sect.

Mestre Irineu was a descendant of African slaves. He came to the state of Acre to tap rubber and escape the drought-stricken Northeast. He was prone to visions. He saw the Queen of the Forest, whom he aligned with the Virgin Mother, but he called her Clara. Native rubber-tappers gave him ayahuasca to drink, and apparently he travelled to the astral plane. There, Clara bade him sing hymns she transmitted to him telepathically and which he wrote down in a book. She gave him great powers for healing, and commissioned him to start a new church to follow the Doctrine of the Santo Daime.

Clara continued to send Mestre Irineu hymns until he died in 1971. Those hymns — together with others transmitted to his successor,

Padrinho Sebastião, and Sebastião's wife, Madrinha Rita — are sung by Daimistas at ceremonies.

'You can visit his tomb when you get back to Rio Branco,' Aubrey said, bobbing his head in a kindly nod. He hopped off the hammock and wandered up to his room.

Later in the day, Aubrey took us around the town. It looked pretty similar to most other Amazonian towns. Its buildings, raised from the ground by wooden stilts, were made from snugly fitted wooden boards. Judging by the few and sparsely stocked shops, the followers mostly grew their own food.

Aubrey pointed out the low, squat school and took us across the bridge that provided access (mostly for pedestrians and cyclists; there were few motorised vehicles) to the homes of the church leaders in the posh part of town. He gestured to an attractive ranch-style house. I peered through an archway of bougainvillea vines, shoots splayed from the lattice like Medusa's snakes. 'This is the home of Padrinho Alfredo, who now heads the church,' Aubrey said. There were glass panes in the windows; these are not so common in northern Brazil, where wooden shutters, as at our *pousada*, more usually held out the elements.

Leading the way back across the bridge to the main part of town, Aubrey said that the church leaders were concerned by the growing tendency for younger generations not to take the Daime, so they started holding special events to encourage them. I was startled by the idea that parents might want to encourage their children to use a drug, so indoctrinated am I that drug use is bad.

Aubrey was excited about attending a Daime dance party in the jungle later that week. I didn't need to be a psychologist to understand that he had come to Brazil to escape working for the company his father ran — no doubt with an iron fist — and to 'find himself'. Slender and freckled, Aubrey would never have been popular with girls, and probably not comfortable with guys. He felt, I guessed, he was running out of time before he had to find a career, settle down, and start a family. So here he

was, taking drugs with a strange religious sect in the Amazonian jungle.
'The party's going to be sick!' he chortled.

It wasn't long after taking ayahuasca that evening that I was plunged into
a torrent of consequences which would, it seemed to me then, provide
me with a new beginning for this book. But first I had to survive the
night. I've noticed that if a writer doesn't begin their travel narrative
with his or her departure from home — the setting-forth upon their
quest — they often open with a near-death experience. Peter Robb does
this in the first chapter of *A Death in Brazil*: his lover takes a knife to
him in the middle of the night. Robert Dessaix does it in *A Mother's
Disgrace*: he begins with his brief kidnapping in Cairo, 'just', he admits,
'for the purposes of seduction'. But now that I was here, it was all I
could do to wonder why I had thought this might be an interesting
thing to do.

The drug took about twenty minutes to come on. Catching sight of
Betti from the corner of my eye as she made her way, woozily, from the
church to retch onto the grass, I bent over and vomited up the contents
of my almost-empty stomach. And immediately vomited again. And
again, until my very stomach lining threatened to spew forth. In agony,
I wondered if it would look like the tripe my father tried to get us to eat
when we were children.

Things crawled at the edges of my vision, refusing to come into focus.
A round woman waddled towards me as if to shoo them — or me,
perhaps — away. She sounded as if the air was swollen between us. I
squinted. She seemed to be suggesting I might be more comfortable away
from the building. To be honest, I felt like telling her I'd probably be more
comfortable in hell.

As far as I could tell, no one else who had taken the hallucinogen —
and everyone at the church had; it was required — looked quite like I felt.

Even retching, Betti had a kind of beatific look on her face. Perhaps others were just more discreet in their plight.

I directed the round woman's attention to my feet. My ankles were so swollen that my calves now ran straight from my knees to the soles of my feet, which were resting against a concrete pillar. No way was I moving further from the light of the church into the dark, where the creeping tendrils of hallucination might resolve into something even more solid and sinister.

I couldn't see Peter anywhere.

The open-sided building was more big-top than traditional church. It was too small to fit the entire dancing and singing congregation, who numbered more than one hundred. The pillar elevating my feet was part of a larger, new structure, mostly funded by donations from members of the sect living in the United States.

The drug stretched time. Several eternities after I had drunk the small glass of dark liquid — it had tasted more of tobacco than anything — my stomach settled enough for me to try to join the dancing. The musicians' beat was mesmerising. Beside the rearmost dancers in the women's section, I copied the movements of those in front of me. We shuffled four short steps to the left, four short steps to the right. I felt like a hypnotic lapping wave. Peter, I could now see, was in the men's section opposite. He was performing the steps smoothly, obviously having a better experience with the drug than me.

Brazilians are born with rhythm and grace, two ingredients God left out of the mix if He made me. Luckily, even I could perform these steps — when my body wasn't trying to evict my stomach-lining. Four short steps to the left, four short steps to the right. The rings of light from the ceiling created a stuttering effect on my vision. It was like one of those cartoon books we had as kids that, when the pages are fanned, produces the illusion of movement in staccato.

In Brazil, the drug is legal for religious purposes. But it is not in most of the fifty countries where the Santo Daime boasts chapters. It is illegal in the United States, except, as Patricia had proudly informed me, in Oregon, where the drug's devotees won a court battle to legalise it for religious purposes. When Betti referred to the Oregon chapter, she spoke in a kind of reverent whisper. Being from that chapter seemed to bolster Patricia's standing at Céu do Mapiá.

Those who were initiated — both men and women — could be identified by a gold star on their white lapels. Most of the men were dressed in fine white suits. With their black neckties and their slicked-back hair, they looked like a shuffling gaggle of Elvises. Some, I had to admit, were as handsome. Dancing opposite the men — taking four short steps left, four short steps right — the fifty or so women wore long white skirts that swayed like those at a Hawaiian luau. The skirts were overlaid with short green pleated skirts that shimmered like a heat mirage as the dancers shuffled. The green sashes that crossed at their breasts glimmered with stars. Each woman was crowned — Patricia and Betti too, as both seemed to be initiates — with a plastic tiara, each fairly glittering with diamantés.

Social scientists have suggested that the voices religious followers hear, and the spirits that possess them, are the result of hypnotism. Certainly the designers of Santo Daime had used everything at their disposal to mesmerise their congregations.

It's all very organised, the Santo Daime doctrine: prescriptive, almost military. Let's face it: it was never going to appeal to me. During ceremonies, male and female Daimistas are divided into two battalions, each battalion sectioned into senior, middle, and junior. Followers are ranked according to several criteria — age, marital status, doctrinal experience, and height. Battalions are further divided into ranks and rows. As at the Casa at Abadiana, the aim is symbiotic: by dancing and singing, every participant contributes strength and energy to the spiritual current that heals, strengthens, and protects.

After another bout of retching subsided, I tried to join in again — four short steps to the left. I didn't have a hymn book to hold, as

Patricia did; she was singing as if her life depended on it. Suddenly, I was overwhelmed by the need to squat over the porcelain-encased hole in the women's toilet block. Just making it in time, I dabbed a soggy tissue ineffectively at the sweat that trickled down my neck. My other hand tried to hold my long skirt clear. There was brackish-looking fluid streaming from my anus, and my aim wasn't all that accurate. I fervently hoped I wouldn't need to spin around and vomit in the pan too. Between blurts I wondered if, as is usual in Brazil, there was a plate by which the toilet attendant collected her salary. I would need to leave notes rather than coins.

Back in my seat beside the church, I had just noticed that my hem was spotted with blood — was I bleeding now too? — when the itching started.

It began where my bra met the skin beneath my breast. Hoping the shawl (which I had been required to buy because my top revealed too much upper arm) would provide enough cover, I slid my hand under my top to scratch.

Then it got worse. And it spread.

The prickling travelled down my belly and up my breasts. It was worst where my clothes were tight or touched my skin. How, I wondered desperately, how could armpits be itchy?! I sank lower in the chair and found myself promising God — reverting to cultural habit, it was the Christian God I prayed to — that I would return to the dancing, and with appropriate enthusiasm, if only He would stop this infernal itching.

The itching spread to the soles of my feet and to the crest of my scalp. I was itchy under my fingernails. I itched so badly and for so long that I didn't feel the need for sudden conversion.

One of the things about metaphor is that one needs to have something familiar to apply, or link it to, for it to be useful. I had never had an experience like this and, it won't surprise you, never want to again. I didn't, I confess, return for the second half of the ceremony. Perhaps I'm not as adventurous as I thought. Peter assured me it was just like the first: drug-taking and slow dancing till dawn. It was apparent by the time he woke next afternoon that he'd indeed had a better experience than me, merely been to the toilet a few times, but he had been bored. And, he reminded me — not for the first time — it hadn't been he who had wanted to come here.

It took me several days to convince the sect's leaders that we were both serious about leaving, and that they should call us a boat. I began to fear that I had checked us into Hotel California. And when the canoe finally showed up and we checked out of the Pousada São Miguel, we were charged double the agreed rate. But Peter wouldn't let me argue, lest we miss the boat.

Chapter Twenty-two

Carnaval Parade

O SAMBÓDROMO, RIO DE JANEIRO

'It was not Brazil that invented Carnaval, but on the contrary, it was Carnaval that invented Brazil.' Roberto DaMatta

As things often don't run on time in Brazil, it was fitting that I arrived late for my Big Brazilian Moment. Perhaps my subconscious had hoped to miss it entirely. It had been almost impossible to get a cab, and I couldn't walk because the shoes I'd been issued were two sizes too big for me.

In order to better understand Brazil, I thought it would be a good idea to take part in the Greatest Show on Earth. The Parade to End All Parades. Surely, it would be illuminating to be part of all the flamboyant freedom that erupts every year when Rio's best samba schools dance down the runway at the Sambódromo. You've probably seen the parade on television. It stars all the beautiful people: Brazil's finest dancers, Brazil's finest singers, Brazil's most popular *telenovela* stars. It features skimpy costumes, loud music, crowds, exuberance, and fun. Since

Carnaval is supposed to be for everyone, transformative, would I too, be 'inverted'?

To take part in Rio's Carnaval Parade is a dream shared by millions, in Brazil and elsewhere. It's an unachievable goal for most. Fulfilling none of the usual criteria, such as being a long-standing member of a samba school, or having a time-honed talent for song or dance, some months earlier I had gone online to buy my place in Rio's samba-school parade.

There had been about twenty costumes to choose from. Which school I paraded with would depend on which costume I chose. It wouldn't do to choose a costume that belonged to any school with a reasonable chance of winning, obviously, lest their chances be damaged by my ineptness. Something comfortable, with no heavy headdress, no high heels, and no skimpiness, either.

But then I'd spotted it: I could be Chico Rei, one of my favourite Brazilian heroes. I clicked 'buy', too excited to apply my earlier criteria.

Chico Rei was leader of his tribe when he was stolen by slave traders and taken to work in Ouro Preto, where he mined gold that may have been used to pay Aleijadinho to sculpt his sacred art. The slave worked hard and saved enough to buy freedom for himself and his son. His former master so admired the man's commitment that he bequeathed a gold mine to Chico Rei. 'King' Chico then worked hard to free his family, friends, and other captives, and donated some of his earnings to the Church in thanks for his good fortune. The mine still makes a mint: Peter and I had once been charged ten bucks each for a two-and-a-half-minute walk along one of its barren shafts.

Of course it's almost impossible to get a cab in Rio during Carnaval, and even when you can, it can't get through the traffic. I resigned myself to walking to the Sambódromo. The straps of my too-big shoes — at least they were flat — kept sliding down my heels, providing my gait with a kind of stalking movement more appropriate to a cat. A metal frame featuring leopard-face epaulettes covered my torso, digging into my more rounded bits. Down my back flowed a leopard-print cape, from which dangled furry tails that tickled the backs of my knees. Little crowns of straw were stuck on my shoulders, occasionally prickling my chin, and tucked under one arm was my headdress: an elaborate, heavy crown of elephant tusks, carved from dense foam. None of this was making me any less nervous. A mask would have been nice.

Eventually managing to flag down a cab, I got in and watched some of the floats being unveiled as the driver inched along Avenida Presidente Vargas. The lifting of one tarpaulin revealed an entire swimming pool, complete with waterslide. Then the driver dropped me at the wrong entrance, and I was limping along once again.

The cowries had begun to shed from my costume back in the hotel room. As soon as I removed the frame from the black garbage bag it had been issued in, shells had rolled into corners and under the bed. But that was just one of a range of my sins I could read in the eyes of our wing's director when I finally found the other Chico Reis. He stared at me with something approaching horror.

He pointed to my black exercise shorts and, in a haughty voice, ordered me to take them off. I reluctantly did so, relieved that my emergency precautions had included donning black bikini briefs and not the black g-string that had pooled around my ankles when I first put it on.

Refusing to take off the black singlet I'd donned over the miniscule bra provided, I pointed to the rash that had broken out across my chest from sweat and fear. That I was late, of course, added to his fury, and he waved imperiously to a seamstress, who led me away to be fixed.

There were, I counted — standing still so as not to get jabbed by the woman's swift needle — at least four other women in Chico Rei costumes who had been allowed to keep their black shorts on. So much for the level playing field. *Jeitinho:* different rules for different people.

A slim man hoisted my headdress into place. Then we waited. My back, never good since I fractured a vertebrae in a hockey game as a teenager, began to complain about me standing for so long, under the headdress, on concrete, in shoes that were no more than boards of plywood.

A couple of hours later, as I was wishing I'd stuck some painkillers down my bra, we were rounded up and herded to another waiting area closer to the arena. The noise made me more nervous: music, fireworks, helicopters, singing, cheering all amalgamated into a wall-of-water roar in my ears.

Each samba school can have up to five thousand (no, I didn't add a zero) parading members who have only eighty minutes in which to complete their pass through the Sambódromo. Huge Banco Bradesco–sponsored digital clocks counted the time elapsed since the first dancers set foot on the runway.

There were, I guessed, about eighty of us in our wing alone. The Chico Rei on my left was a New Yorker, who assured me I'd have a ball. 'I've *always* wanted to do this,' he gushed. 'Haven't you?' He was buff — had he shaved that shining torso? Finely crafted muscles emerged from the leopard faces that covered his bulging biceps; his calves were long and toned. The golden sheathes that decorated *his* shins weren't going to knock on his knees as he danced. He wasn't sweaty, or short, or fearful … Then suddenly my thoughts were halted by an unseen force moving us forward. We turned the corner and we were there.

Light blasted its way from the heavens. It was as if the gods were shining mag lights from the clouds. My ears roared; my blood surged. Seventy thousand people were singing and cheering. Terror forced every word of Salgueiro's theme song — words I had tried to learn, as instructed — out of my head.

Adrenalin spiked through me. The lights, which seemed many times more powerful that those that flooded the Melbourne Cricket Ground, were blinding. Cued by my friend from the Big Apple, I shuffled and stepped, trying for something like samba. Back-forward-forward, we angled first to the left and then to the right. Though my steps were small, I bumped into the Chico Rei in front of me. Stopping, I readied my retreat. Then the instructions sounded in my head: never go backwards! I felt like the blow-up clown I had as a child, lurching forwards and back but going nowhere; being pushed from all directions, but never falling over. Then we were abreast of the first of the judges' boxes. Surely you get points for trying.

The judges score across ten categories, including on how well the school's song is sung by all participants. My head turned away from the judges' box. Smile plastered on my face, moving with the rhythm a little better, I was still trying to remember the words to the song. The floats and props form one judging category, as does the performance of the flag bearer and of the vanguard group. And, of course, the costumes are scored, too.

Then a man of about seventy stumbled in from my left. It took me a moment to realise that the director had physically pushed him — with some force — back into his place in the line. In the Sambódromo, it seemed, Carnaval was neither rule-free nor master-less.

Dancing down the runway, you don't see anything of the rest of the parade; you are just one word of an entire novel. I had no idea that there was a wing of Che Guevaras not far in front. Not that it mattered — nothing mattered at that moment but song. Back-forward-forward. I had caught the rhythm, was energised by the beat. Was this what it felt like to be Brazilian? It wasn't until I saw the replay later on YouTube that I realised our parade included a troop of acrobatic Lampiões tumbling about in half-moon hats. Or that a Michael Jackson (they love Michael Jackson in Brazil) in calf-hugging black pants had moonwalked along, with a tightly choreographed circle of 'paparazzi' swirling around him.

The float we followed had an African theme. Wild animal masks peered out from behind leaves. Women, made thick-thighed by samba, strutted and preened in slinky cat suits.

Swing-step-step, swing-step-step: it was beginning to be second nature. There was just me and the crowd. No time to overthink everything here.

Perhaps not a master-less, rule-less event where anything goes, Carnaval at the Sambódromo does have the power to transform. You may know the story of Renato Sorriso. Dressed in his orange street-sweeping uniform, Renato's job was to sweep up glitter along the edge of the runway. During the 1997 parade he was so infected by the music and the joy that, with a larrikin smile, he started dancing. To the astonishment of the seventy-thousand-strong audience, he performed a fast and flawless samba without letting go of his broom. The crowd, as they say, went wild, and he threw aside the broom and danced like a Carnaval queen. His spinning feet were a blur: *chat-ta-chat-ta-chat-ta-chat*. Officials moved to stop the impromptu performance, but his audience roared their disapproval and they backed away. Renato Sorriso continued his rapid-fire samba the length of the runway and made it into the history books.

Until then, the street-sweeper barely made enough to feed his family. After his Carnaval experience, he became a professional dancer, and in 2013 the Samba School Acadêmicos do Grande Rio featured a wing of sambaing street-sweepers led by the man himself. In Brazil, Renato Sorriso is a household name, and his fame is spreading: you may have seen him dance at the closing ceremony of the London Olympics.

Back-forward-forward, back-forward-forward: eventually I could see the end of the runway. I felt a pang of something — surely not disappointment? The large clock said sixty-two minutes. My shoes hadn't fallen off, my headdress was still in place; it even felt lighter. Our director was standing just past the gate, conducting as if he held a baton: don't stop yet, keep on dancing, the judges can see. He looked elated and relieved.

Then the gait of my companions became a walk and the Chico Reis around me pulled off their crowns. Gratefully, I accepted a bottle of water from a woman wheeling an esky.

The New Yorker had already bounded off. Off to one side, a pair of Che Guevaras were embracing. I looked around, feeling a little hollow, and, lifting the costume over my head, made a mental note to buy a suitcase big enough to keep it safe on the long trip home.

Paraders continued to flood through the gates behind me, relentlessly, like a river running down its bed. I signalled to a beer-seller at the gate, pulled a note from my bra, and cracked open the ice-cold can. And then, with my headdress under one arm and the rest of my costume under the other, I began traipsing through the busy streets of Rio de Janeiro, totally unconcerned that I was clad only in my underwear.

Epilogue

'The world is like that — incomprehensible and full of surprises.'
Jorge Amado

This is a false ending, like the sun that fades on today. It'll rise again tomorrow, as we know, we trust, or we hope. It is beginnings that are imbued with promise and wonder. Here's another:

When the travel bug sinks its teeth in, I am lying on a hospital bed in Papua New Guinea. Perhaps it flew in through the air-conditioning. It is just before my ninth birthday.

My appendix had burst in Madang, a resort town on the north coast, and threatened to kill me. My parents managed to get me to the capital, but the airline refused to fly me, not wanting to be responsible if I died in the air. Yet there was a glistening new training hospital in Port Moresby, and surgeons on hand to cut a nine-year-old appendix out of a very sick kid.

I wake, groggy, in a bed next to an Australian woman, her usually milky skin blue-black from a car crash. She is crying over her golden wedding band that the surgeons had sawn off her swollen ring finger. My father is under my bed, asleep on a mattress the nurses have kindly provided.

The post-operation hours drag until dawn, when Dad rises from the floor and spreads open the curtains, one in each hand. The window is like a miracle. It becomes my own private cinema screen. Through it I watch the families of the Papuan patients. They have set up camps in a designated area between the staff and visitors' car parks, which I can see through the window. They cook meals on campfires and then disappear from view, carrying the carefully prepared food to their loved ones. Kids help, run errands, play games, and sleep on grass mats.

Is it that we remember tragedy better than happier times? Because I can remember the woman crying over her ring — I was amazed that she could feel such sentiment over a ring when she obviously had so much physical hurt to cry over. Or is it that the familiar takes precedence over the unfamiliar? Perhaps there was just too much movement, too many details, for my drowsy mind to remember. I do know that it wasn't only these strange people's nakedness, or the darkness of their skin compared to my own, that I found entrancing. It was the whole notion of difference. The city I lived in was, then, mostly white and middle-class. It was in that hospital room that it first dawned on me that there were other ways to live.

My parents learned to be my tribe. It took a few days of hinting from the hospital staff for them to work it out. Mum washed me, Dad changed my bedlinen and hospital gown, and they brushed my long blonde hair. The hospital did feed me, probably figuring my parents had nowhere to light a campfire, even if they knew how.

The appendix scar was smaller and straighter than any of my friends'. Like the travel bug, it's become a part of me. Two souvenirs from my first 'other' country that I still have today.

~

Brazil is another beginning. The beginning of a personal conversation about who we are — or who we are not. It is about who we, as people, might have been and who, perhaps, we should be. 'Perhaps' because it sounds like a utopian plan. If it's too lofty or supercilious, just substitute 'I' for 'we'.

Travelling, they say, we can better 'find ourselves'. But this self I know pretty well, I think; a better reason for travel is to escape the self. I am interested in other selves. Travel is good for pleasure, for leisure, and to learn about new cultures, but it is also through travelling — and this was one big revelation for me — that we can better see who we are not, who we might have been. How people treat each other, I've found, also comes into sharper focus. This is where Mark Twain's observation that 'travel is fatal to prejudice, bigotry, and narrow-mindedness' is relevant. Walking in someone else's Havaianas, flip-flops, or thongs, I can see how I might have lived, or even what I would have called such footwear. But for a quirk of fate (or, if you like, because your god had a different design) — well, it puts a whole new slant on 'love thy neighbour as thyself', doesn't it, if you realise that is the self you might have been?

Who might I have been, born in Brazil? Most likely I'd be a member of a religious community, and thus could explain the world according to the lore of one or more gods. Possibly descended from African slaves, I'd almost certainly live in the eastern half of the country in an urban environment. I would follow the fortunes of my local football team and our national team, and, each evening, my favourite *telenovela* characters in the company of family and friends. I would watch for signs in my daily life that might suggest the winning numbers or animal in the Jogo do Bicho that I would bet on each week, though it's not strictly legal. In my wardrobe, you would find few clothes that are black, probably an outfit or two in white, perhaps a work uniform, maybe some fine costumes and masks. I would paddle in the water with my family or friends at the beach, never having been taught to swim. I would wear a bikini but not *fio dental*, the 'dental floss' that the younger women wear.

I would have been born under the military dictatorship that ruled Brazil from 1964 to 1985. One or more of my family members or friends might have been killed or tortured by its agents.

If I had been born in Brazil, I'd most likely have adult children, probably three, but only five grandchildren due to the falling birth rate. If I had paid work, I would earn maybe seventy per cent of the male wage. I'd no doubt be better with a needle (it would, after all, be almost impossible for any version of myself to be worse at sewing than I currently am). I would make *fantasias* for my family to wear at festivals and during Carnaval.

But these speculations are relevant only if I'd been born in Brazil around the same time as I was in Australia, and into the middling classes. In Brazil, I might have been born into a whole range of communities. Communities are central to Brazilian life in a way that is less common now in the 'West'. The modern Western world emphasises the individual. We are encouraged to work long hours that don't nurture community, family, or, in truth, one's self. Individual rights trump those collective. That most famous of lists by *Forbes* lauds individual rather than collective wealth. We compete with each other: faster, higher, stronger.

Brazilians (of course, this is to generalise horribly) are members of groups. They are members of samba schools and Carnaval *blocos*. They are members of church groups, *terreiros*, or other faithful clans. They have neighbourhoods — something I remember being more common in Australia when I was a child. On holidays, they might go on pilgrimage or join a tour. They might travel with family and friends, but seldom alone. The company one keeps is as fundamental to a Brazilian's identity as their communities are vibrant and varied. And they determine, it seems to me, who you are — or at least who you are perceived to be.

Which is, of course, why Brazilians find me strange. They can't fit me into their worldview. I am unexpected, solitary, a bit like the wolf that so struck me on a night long ago. Brazilians are never at the edges; they have a swirl of people around them. They are communal, they fit in. Even the street kids at Candelária. They may have been regarded — and treated — as rubbish to be removed; they may have been on the fringes of society. But they had their 'family': they were Brazilians, and as such, members of a community, however else you may regard them.

Here, then, is an ending:

The morning after parading at the Sambódromo, I went searching again for the memorial to the children at Candelária. There was indeed one: I'd found it on Google Earth.

I had also found grainy film footage, shot the night before the Candelária Massacre, probably on a Super 8 camera. It shows the street-kid community celebrating a birthday on the church steps. Thin, lithe bodies expertly dance the samba. Some of the teenagers play musical instruments, and children of all ages clap out the beat. 'Without music, a Brazilian is dead,' Wagner dos Santos told his biographer, Julia Rochester. He had survived being shot in the face by the same men on the same night as the Candelária victims.

My original assumption about that night of 23rd July 1993 was that all eight victims had been gunned down in the church plaza. That was how many of the reports had read. In fact, I had since learned that two of the older boys were murdered earlier that night, after being hustled into a car with Wagner dos Santos.

The effects of the killings reached far beyond those who died, of course. Witnesses were threatened; some were even killed. Wagner dos Santos moved to Switzerland, fearing for his life. Another boy, sleeping in the plaza at the time of the massacre, woke to gunshots and found four of his friends already dead. He was Sandro do Nascimento. A few years later, out of his right mind, Sandro hijacked a bus outside the botanical gardens in Rio. The media broadcast the entire siege live-to-air as he held his hostages for four hours. Towards the end, a young woman was killed, hit accidentally by shots fired from a policeman's gun and then by Sandro's when he retaliated, seemingly without thinking. There are at least two films about the siege. Sandro do Nascimento surrendered, and was smothered to death in the back of a police car.

Of those shot that night at Candelária, Come-Gato was the last to go. He died the day after the first of the funerals; he had not woken from his coma. One by one, the dead were farewelled and interred, 'pushed into simple vaults in the walls of the Caju cemetery'. No marble monoliths for them, but no mass grave, either. One teenager, who went by the nickname 'Little Skunk', has never been formally identified.

It took three years of investigation to bring three of the military policemen who shot these children to trial. A fourth died before enough evidence was gathered to justify his arrest. It is thought that there were more men involved, and that there were two cars, not one, but this has not been proved. Eventually the three men confessed, two performing these about-faces at trial, much to the discomfort of their lawyers. No big crises of conscience, though: they were seeking lesser sentences.

Marcos Vinícius Borges Emmanuel's final sentence was three hundred years, and Marco Aurélio Dias Alcântara's, two hundred and four. In this age of information, where 'facts' are so unstable, reports vary as to which of these men served eighteen years of his sentence and which just nine, before being released. Nelson Oliveira dos Santos Cunha was acquitted at retrial of all counts of murder, but was sentenced for the shooting of Wagner dos Santos. He served less than half of his eighteen-year term. I wonder how the men feel about being remembered for committing such appalling acts against fellow humans. Not all share my view: some callers to a police hotline suggested the men be congratulated for ridding the streets of 'vermin'.

The Candelária church was built in thanks for lives saved. Men aboard a storm-caught vessel survived to build the monument to Our Lady of Candelária. I walked to the church through smelly streets that were relatively quiet in the early morning of Carnaval Monday.

When I first looked for a memorial, on Independence Day, I hadn't looked down, not expecting to find it under my feet. But, apart from its position beneath us all, it is a fitting tribute to the children whose deaths should be printed in indelible ink in the minds not only of Brazilians but of us all. I crossed the small service road in front of the church steps, and there it was. There they were.

Eight silhouettes had been painted in crimson on the black and white tiles. The figures are watched over by angels, which decorate the church's ornate facade. The images are small, their arms are raised, elbows bent, hands level with their small heads. The artist may have meant the figures' arms to be resting above their heads like sleeping babies. That was what

I first thought on seeing pictures of the memorial. But some things don't become apparent until you're actually there, seeing them in person. Standing there looking down at them, I realised that the shadows of the children could equally be raising their hands in silent surrender.

The memorial doesn't name the victims of the Candelária Massacre, but I will:

Marcos Antônio Alves da Silva, 'Cat-Eater', aged twenty
Paulo José da Silva, eighteen
'Little Skunk', whose birth name will never be known, seventeen
Leandro Santos da Conceição, fifteen
Valdevino Miguel de Almeida, fourteen
Marcelo Cândido de Jesus, 'Baldy', fourteen
Anderson Thomé Pereira, 'One-eyed', thirteen
Paulo Roberto de Oliveira, named 'Little Man', eleven.

References

Prologue

Mark Twain, *Innocents Abroad*, Project Gutenburg, 2006 (orig. published 1869), Chapter 4, www.gutenberg.org/files/3176/3176-h/3176-h.htm; Robert Dessaix, *As I Was Saying: a collection of musings*, North Sydney, Random House Australia, 2012, p. 110; Patrick Holland and Graham Huggan, *Tourists with Typewriters: critical reflections on contemporary travel writing*, Ann Arbor, University of Michigan Press, 1998, p. 19.

1: The Sound of Commitment

John Updike, *Brazil*, London, Penguin, 1995, p. 68; James McQueen, *The Candelária Massacre*, Melbourne, Addison Wesley Longman, 1998; Bruce Chatwin, *In Patagonia*, New York, Penguin Books, 1988, p. 1.

2: Rebellion in the Rainforest

Peter Robb, *A Death in Brazil*, Potts Point, Duffy & Snellgrove, 2003, p. 16; Boris Fausto, *A Concise History of Brazil*, Cambridge, Cambridge University Press, 1999, p. 16; Peter Russell, *Prince Henry 'The Navigator': a life*, London, Yale University Press, 2000, pp. 3, 15, 23, 243; Ernesto Ennes, 'The Palmares "Republic" of Pernambuco: its final destruction, 1697', *The Americas* 5, no. 2, 1948, p. 206; John Hemming, *Red Gold: the conquest of the Brazilian Indians*, London, Papermac/Macmillan, 1987, p. 245.

3: The Sisterhood of Good Death

Frances de Pontes Peebles, *The Seamstress*, London, Bloomsbury, 2009, p. 437; Gilberto Freyre, *The Masters and the Slaves*, New York, Knopf,

1966, p. 532; Ludwig Wittgenstein, *Philosophical Investigations*, Oxford, Basil Blackwell, 1958 (third edition, 1986, trans. G.E.M. Anscombe), Part 1: no. 129; Martin Thomas, 'Because It's Your Country', *Australian Book Review* 350, April 2013.

4: Goddess of the Sea

John Updike, *Brazil*, op. cit., p. 4; 'MPF recorre de decisão da Justiça que não reconhece umbanda e candomblé como religiões', *O Globo*, 16 May 2014, www.oglobo.globo.com/sociedade/mpf-recorre-de-decisao-da-justica-que-nao-reconhece-umbanda-candomble-como-religioes-12507234; Bruce Chatwin, *Anatomy of Restlessness*, New York, Penguin Books, 1997, p. 76; Michael Crichton, *Travels*, New York, Harper Perennial, 2002, p. xii.

5: War on a New Jerusalem

Roberto DaMatta, 'Brazil: an overview', *XIII* (paper presented at 'Managing in a Global Economy: management challenges for a new world' at The Eastern Academy of Management, Brazil, 21–25 June 2009), p. 12, www.eaom.org/_i_/Rio/arch/ManagingInA_GlobalEconomyXIII.pdf; Frances de Pontes Peebles, *The Seamstress*, op. cit., p. 319; Peter Fleming, *Brazilian Adventure: a quest into the heart of the Amazon*, London and New York, Tauris Park Paperbacks, 2011 (orig. published 1933), p. 59; Euclides da Cunha, *Rebellion in the Backlands (Os Sertões)*, Chicago and London, University of Chicago Press, 1944, pp. 89, 212, 407, 424–5; Mario Vargas Llosa, *The War of the End of the World*, New York, Farrar, Straus, and Giroux, 1981, p. 17; Lissa Johnson, 'What Makes Them Tick: inside the mind of the Abbott government', *New Matilda*, 26 October 2014, www.newmatilda. com/2014/10/26S/what-makes-them-tick-inside-mind-abbott-government; Bertold Brecht, *Life of Galileo*, New York, Grove Press, 1966, scene 7, p. 83; *Guerra de Canudos* (The War at Canudos), directed by Sérgio Rezend, Columbia Pictures/Sony, 1997.

6: Passion in the Backlands

Hermann Hesse, *Steppenwolf,* Penguin Classics, Kindle Edition, 2012, p. 175; Antonio C. La Pastina, 'Product Placement in Brazilian Prime Time Television: the case of the reception of a telenovela', *Journal of Broadcasting and Electronic Media* 45, no. 4, 2001, pp. 547, 548.

Interlude: Folk Carnaval

John Updike, *Brazil,* op. cit., p. 65.

7: City of Hope

Juscelino Kubitschek (in Portuguese), in James Holston, *The Modernist City: an anthropological critique of Brasília,* Chicago, University of Chicago Press, 1989, p. 16; 'Washington, D.C.', *City Data,* 2009, www.city-data.com/us-cities/The-South/Washington-D-C-History.html; Alex Shoumatoff, *Capital of Hope: Brasília and its people,* New York, Vintage Books, 1990, p. 39; Roland Barthes, *Empire of Signs,* New York, Hill and Wang, 1982, p. 30.

8: Valley of the Dawn

Pai Seta Branca, plaque on site; James Holston, 'Alternative Modernities: statecraft and religious imagination in the Valley of the Dawn', *American Ethnologist* 26, no. 3, pp. 607, 618; Sophie Cunningham, *Warning: the story of Cyclone Tracy,* Melbourne, Text Publishing, 2014, p. 41.

9: Replaying the Reconquista

Ida Pfeiffer, *A Woman's Journey Round the World from Vienna to Brazil, Chile, Tahiti, China, Hindostan, Persia, and Asia Minor,* Alexandria, Library of Alexandria, 2012, Chapter 2; Roland Barthes, *Empire of Signs,* op. cit., p. 11; Peter Fleming, *Brazilian Adventure,* op. cit., p. 54; Anthony Bourdain, *Kitchen Confidential: adventures in the culinary underbelly,* New York, Harper Perennial, 1987, p. 83; *Black Man's Houses,* directed by Steve Thomas, Ronin Films, 1993.

10: Peddling Hope

Roger Bastide, *The African Religions of Brazil: toward a sociology of the interpenetration of civilizations*, Baltimore, John Hopkins University Press, 1978, p. 9; Marjoe Gortner, *Marjoe*, directed by Howard Smith and Sarah Kernochan, RCA/Columbia Pictures, United States, 1972.

Interlude: True Virgins

Alan Hansen, 'World Cup 2002', *BBC*, www.news.bbc.co.uk/sport3/worldcup2002/hi/sports_talk/newsid_1939000/1939683.stm; Roberto DaMatta, 'Carnaval as a Cultural Problem: towards a theory of formal events and their magic', Working Paper #79, Kellog Institute for International Studies, September 1986, p. 14; Lewis Carroll, *Alice's Adventures in Wonderland*, Project Gutenberg, Chapter 1, 2008.

11: The Virgin Who Appeared

Frances de Pontes Peebles, *The Seamstress*, op. cit., p. 11; Don Watson, *American Journeys*, North Sydney, Vintage Books, 2009, p. 28; in Eri W. Kramer, 'Law and the Image of a Nation: religious conflict and religious freedom in a Brazilian', *Law and Social Inquiry* 1, p. 53; James Holston, 'Alternative Modernities', op. cit., p. 607; Bishop Edir Macedo, www.bispomacedo.com.br/en/2010/07/25/the-uckg-temple-project; Ida Pfeiffer, *A Woman's Journey Round the World*, op. cit, Chapter 2.

12: The Little Cripple

Alain de Botton, *The Art of Travel*, New York, Vintage Books, 2004, p. 54; Stefan Zweig, *Brazil: land of the future*, New York, Viking, 1941, pp. 236, 244; Milan Kundera, *Testaments Betrayed: an essay in nine parts*, translated by Linda Asher, New York, Harper Collins, 1996, part four.

13: Father of Flight

Paul Hoffman, *Wings of Madness: Alberto Santos-Dumont and the invention of flight*, London and New York, Fourth Estate, 2003, p. 312; Mark

Twain, *Innocents Abroad*, op. cit., Chapter 2 and Conclusion; 'Alberto Santos-Dumont', *Encyclopaedia Britannica*, 2015, www.britannica.com/biography/Alberto-Santos-Dumont.

14: Dictated by the Dead
Emmanuel in *Nosso Lar* by André Luiz/Chico Xavier, Conselho Espirita Internacional, 2010, Preface; *Chico Xavier*, directed by Daniel Filho, Globo Films & Lereby Productions, Brazil, 2010; Robert M. Levine, *Vale of Tears: revisiting the Canudos massacre in northeastern Brazil, 1893–1897*, Berkeley, University of California Press, 1992, p. 126; Guy Lyon Playfair, *Chico Xavier: medium of the century*, London, International Spiritist Council and Roundtable Publishing, 2010, p. 45; Alexandre Caroli Rocha et al., 'Investigating the Fit and Accuracy of Alleged Mediumistic Writings: a case study of Chico Xavier's letters', *Explore: the journal of science and healing* 10, no. 5, Sep–Oct 2014; Guy Lyon Playfair, *Chico Xavier: medium of the century*, op. cit., pp. 92, 93; Brian Foster, 'Allan Kardec — the Great Codifier', www.nwspiritism.com/spiritist-knowledge/allan-kardec-the-great-consoler; Martin Thomas, 'Because It's Your Country,' op. cit.

15: Candelária Massacre
Alex Shoumatoff, *Murder in the Rain Forest: the Chico Mendes story*, London, Fourth Estate, 1991, p. 287; Julia Rochester, *The Candelária Massacre: how Wagner dos Santos survived the street children's killing that shook Brazil*, London, Vision, 2008, pp. 28, 54, 70; 'National Strategy of Defense', Ministry of Defense, Brazil, 2008, p. 38, www.defesa.gov.br/projetosweb/estrategia/arquivos/estrategia_defesa_nacional_ingles.pdf; Lissa Johnson, 'Everything You Ever Wanted to Know About Why We Torture Asylum Seekers, But Were Too Afraid to Ask,' *New Matilda*, 28 May 2015, www.newmatilda.com/2015/05/27/everything-you-ever-wanted-know-about-why-we-torture-asylum-seekers-were-too-afraid-ask.

Interlude: Street Carnaval

Jorge Amado, *O País do Carnaval*, quoted in Roberto DaMatta, *Carnivals, Rogues, and Heroes: an interpretation of the Brazilian dilemma*, Notre Dame, University of Notre Dame Press, 1991, p. 63; 'Best of the Blocos for 2012 Carnival', *Rio Times*, 14 February 2012, www.riotimesonline.com/brazil-news/rio-entertainment/best-of-the-blocos-for-2012-carnival; 'History of Carnival in Rio', *Ipanema.com*, www.ipanema.com/carnival/history.htm.

16: Dancing with the Gods

Jorge Amado, *Captains of the Sands*, New York, Avon, 1988, p. 18; Annie Dillard, *The Writing Life*, New York, Harper Perennial, 1990, p. 15; Paul Christopher Johnson, *Secrets, Gossip, and Gods: the transformation of Brazilian Candomblé*, Oxford and New York, Oxford University Press, 2002, p. 43; Larry E. Frase, 'Flow Theory' in *Encyclopedia of Educational Leadership and Administration*, Thousand Oaks, SAGE Publications.

17: King of the Badlands

Frances de Pontes Peebles, *The Seamstress*, op. cit., p. 11.

18: Capital of Faith

Paul Arden, *God Explained in a Taxi Ride*, London, Penguin, 2007, p. 36; Ralph Della Cava, *Miracle at Joaseiro*, New York and London, Columbia University Press, 1970, pp. 82, 44, 154; Henry Reynolds, *A History of Tasmania*, Cambridge and Melbourne, Cambridge University Press, 2012, pp. 61, 62; Flinders Island Aboriginal Association Inc., www.fiaai.org.au/timeline; *Black Man's Houses*, op. cit.; Robert Hughes, *The Fatal Shore: a history of the transportation of convicts to Australia, 1787–1868*, London, Collins Harvill, 1987, p. 423; H.G. Wells, *The War of the Worlds*, London, Penguin Classics, 2005 (orig. published 1898), p. 9.

19: Hopes for a Good End

Clarice Lispector, *The Hour of the Star*, New York, New Directions, 2011, p. 31; Michael D. Jackson interviewed in 'The Dreaming Tracks', *New Philosopher* 8, May–July 2015, p. 105.

20: Gandhi of the Amazon

Alex Shoumatoff, *Murder in the Rain Forest*, op. cit., pp. 3, 43, 65, 70, 287; Flinders Island Aboriginal Association Inc., www.fiaai.org.au/timeline.

21: Among the Believers

Dante Alighieri (trans. Clive James), *The Divine Comedy*, London, Picador, 2013, p. 3; Bruce Chatwin, *Anatomy of Restlessness*, op. cit., p. 95; Henry David Thoreau, *A Week on the Concord and Merrimack Rivers*, New York, Library of America, p. 12; Theordore Roosevelt, *Through the Brazilian Wilderness*, United Kingdom, Ægypan Press, 2006 (orig. published 1914), p. 176; Robert Dessaix, *A Mother's Disgrace*, Sydney, Harper Perennial, 2007, p. 194.

22: Carnaval Parade

Roberto DaMatta, 'Carnaval as a Cultural Problem', op. cit., p. 33.

Epilogue

Jorge Amado, *Gabriela, Clove and Cinnamon*, New York, Vintage International, 2006, p. 227; from Julia Rochester, *The Candelária Massacre*, op. cit., pp. 5, 80; *Ônibus 174* (Bus 194), directed by José Padilha and Felipe Lacerda, Zazen Produções, 2002; *Última Parada 174* (Last Stop 174), directed by Bruno Barreto, Moonshot Pictures et al., 2008; Julia Rochester, *The Candelária Massacre*, op. cit., p. 239.

Further Reading

Almeida, Bira, *Capoeira, a Brazilian Art Form: history, philosophy, and practice* (2nd ed.), Berkeley, North Atlantic Books, 1986.

Amado, Jorge, *Captains of the Sands*, New York, Avon, 1988.

——, *Dona Flor and Her Two Husbands*, London, Serpent's Tail, 1986.

——, *Gabriela, Clove and Cinnamon*, London, Abacus, 1984.

——, *The War of the Saints*, London, Serpent's Tail, 1994.

Bastide, Roger, *The African Religions of Brazil: toward a sociology of the interpenetration of civilizations*, Baltimore, Johns Hopkins University Press, 1978.

Bergad, Laird W., *The Comparative Histories of Slavery in Brazil, Cuba, and the United States*, Cambridge and New York, Cambridge University Press, 2007.

Bourne, Richard, *Lula of Brazil: the story so far*, Berkeley, University of California Press, 2008.

Brazil Archdiocese of São Paulo and Dassin, Joan (trans. Wright, Jaime), *Torture in Brazil: a shocking report on the pervasive use of torture by Brazilian military governments, 1964–1979*, New York, Vintage Books, 1986.

Burns, Bradford E. (ed.), *A Documentary History of Brazil*, New York, Knopf, 1966.

Callcott, Maria; Hayward, Jennifer; Caballero, M. Soledad, *Maria Graham's Journal of a Voyage to Brazil*, Anderson, Parlor Press, 2010.

Cardoso, Fernando Henrique and Winter, Brian, *The Accidental President of Brazil: a memoir*, New York, PublicAffairs, 2006.

Chandler, Billy Jaynes, *The Bandit King: Lampião of Brazil*, College Station, Texas A&M University Press, 1978.

Cumming, Heather and Leffler, Karen, *John of God: the Brazilian healer who's touched the lives of millions*, Atria Books/Beyond Words, New York and Hillsboro, 2007.

DaMatta, Roberto, *Carnivals, Rogues, and Heroes: an interpretation of the Brazilian dilemma*, Notre Dame, University of Notre Dame Press, 1991.

Dávila, Jerry; Morgan, Zachary R.; Skidmore, Thomas E., 'Since Black into White: Thomas Skidmore on Brazilian race relations', *The Americas* 64, no. 3 (2008), pp. 409–23.

Dawson, Andrew, *Santo Daime: a new world religion*, London, Continuum, 2013.

Dean, Warren, *With Broadax and Firebrand: the destruction of the Brazilian Atlantic forest*, Berkeley and London, University of California Press, 1995.

Della Cava, Ralph, *Miracle at Joaseiro*, New York and London, Columbia University Press, 1970.

Dos Passos, John, *Brazil on the Move*, London, Sidgwick and Jackson, 1963.

Esteves, Acúrsio Pereira, *The "Capoeira" of the Entertainment Industry: body, acrobatics and spectacle for "tourists"*, Salvador, Bureau, 2012.

Fausto, Boris, *A Concise History of Brazil*, Cambridge, Cambridge University Press, 1999.

Fawcett, Percy Harrison and Fawcett, Brian, *Exploration Fawcett: by Lt.-Col. P. H. Fawcett ... arranged from his manuscripts, letters, log-books, and records by Brian Fawcett*, London, Hutchinson Phoenix Press, 1953.

Fleming, Peter, *Brazilian Adventure: a quest into the heart of the Amazon*, London, Tauris Park Paperbacks, 2011.

Freyre, Gilberto; Putnam, Samuel; Kislak, Jay I., *The Masters and the Slaves (Casa-Grande & Senzala): a study in the development of Brazilian civilization*, New York, Knopf, 1946.

Guillermoprieto, Alma, *Samba*, New York, Vintage Books, 1991.

Haddad, Annette and Doggett, Scott (eds), *Travelers' Tales Brazil: true stories*, San Francisco, Travelers' Tales, 2004.

Harding, Bertita, *Amazon Throne: the story of the Braganzas of Brazil*, London and Sydney, Harrap, 1944.

Hemming, John, *Red Gold: the conquest of the Brazilian Indians, 1500–1760*, London, Papermac, 1978.

Hess, David J., and DaMatta, Roberto, *The Brazilian Puzzle: culture on the borderlands of the Western world*, New York, Columbia University Press, 1995.

Hoffman, Paul, *Wings of Madness: Alberto Santos-Dumont and the invention of flight*, London and New York, Fourth Estate, 2003.

Holston, James, *The Modernist City: an anthropological critique of Brasilia*, Chicago, University of Chicago Press, 1989.

Jesus, Carolina Maria de, *Child of the Dark: the diary of Carolina Maria De Jesus*, New York, Dutton, 1962.

Johnson, Paul C., *Secrets, Gossip, and Gods: the transformation of Brazilian candomble*, Oxford and New York, Oxford University Press, 2002.

Levine, Robert M., *The History of Brazil*, Westport, Greenwood Press, 1999.

———, *Vale of Tears: revisiting the Canudos massacre in Northeastern Brazil, 1893–1897*, Berkeley, University of California Press, 1992.

Levine, Robert M., and John J. Crocitti, *The Brazil Reader: history, culture, politics*, Durham, Duke University Press, 1999.

Lévi-Strauss, Claude, *Triste Tropiques*, Paris, Plon, 1973.

Malathronas, John, *Brazil: life, blood, soul*, Chichester, Summersdale, 2003.

Mattelart, Michèle and Mattelart, Armand, *The Carnival of Images: Brazilian television fiction*, New York, Bergin & Garvey, 1990.

Moreira, Susan Casement (trans.), *Understanding Brazil: a reader's guide*, Brasília, Alexandre de Gusmão Foundation, 2009.

Niemeyer, Oscar, *The Curves of Time: the memoirs of Oscar Niemeyer*, London, Phaidon, 2000.

Niemeyer, Oscar and Matthieu Salvaing, *Oscar Niemeyer: mémoire du style*, Paris, Assouline, 2001.

Page, Joseph A., *The Brazilians*, Reading, Addison-Wesley, 1995.

————, *The Revolution That Never Was: Northeast Brazil, 1955–1964*, New York, Grossman, 1972.

Palin, Michael and Pao, Basil, *Brazil*, London, Weidenfeld & Nicolson, 2012.

Peebles, Frances de Pontes, *The Seamstress*, London, Bloomsbury, 2009.

Pfeiffer, Ida, *A Woman's Journey Round the World from Vienna to Brazil, Chile, Tahiti, China, Hindostan, Persia and Asia Minor*, Alexandria, Library of Alexandria, 2012.

Playfair, Guy Lyon, *Chico Xavier, Medium of the Century*, London, Roundtable Publishing, 2010.

Raffles, Hugh, *In Amazonia: a natural history*, Princeton and Oxford, Princeton University Press, 2002.

Robb, Peter, *A Death in Brazil: a book of omissions*, Potts Point, Duffy & Snellgrove, 2003.

Rochester, Julia, *The Candelária Massacre: how Wagner Dos Santos survived the street children's killing that shook Brazil*, London, Vision, 2008.

Roosevelt, Theodore, *Through the Brazilian Wilderness*, London, Aegypan Press, 2006 (orig. 1914).

Shoumatoff, Alex, *The Capital of Hope: Brasília and its people*, New York, Vintage Books, 1990.

————, *Murder in the Rain Forest: the Chico Mendes story* (also known as *The World is Burning: murder in the rain forest*), London, Fourth Estate, 1991.

Skidmore, Thomas E., *Brazil: five centuries of change*, New York, Oxford University Press, 1999.

————, *Politics in Brazil, 1930–1964: an experiment in democracy*, New York, Oxford University Press, 2007 (orig. 1967).

————, *The Politics of Military Rule in Brazil, 1964–1985*, New York, Oxford University Press, 1988.

Slater, Candace, *Trail of Miracles: stories from a pilgrimage in Northeast Brazil*, Berkeley, University of California Press, 1986.

Slesser, Malcolm, *Brazil: land without limit*, London, Allen & Unwin, 1969.

Staden, Hans and Letts, Malcolm, *Hans Staden, the True History of His Captivity, 1557*, London, G. Routledge & Sons, 1928.

Updike, John, *Brazil*, London, Penguin, 1995.

Vargas Llosa, Mario, *The War of the End of the World*, New York, Farrar Straus and Giroux, 1984.

Voeks, Robert A., *Sacred Leaves of Candomblé: African magic, medicine, and religion in Brazil*, Austin, University of Texas Press, 1997.

Guide to
Sites and Events

Please note: as the guidebooks all remind, the type of information that follows is notoriously subject to change. More information can be found at www.franbryson.com

Festivals

~ Carnaval, Brazil-wide: officially begins the Friday before Lent and finishes on Shrove Tuesday. Programs are generally available for listings of street parties and *blocos*.

~ Festa da Boa Morte, Cachoeira, Bahia: held annually on 13th to 15th August, with the profane celebration on the following two days.

~ Festa de Yemanjá (also known as Festa de Iemanjá), Salvador, Bahia: held annually on 2nd February.

~ Lavagem do Bonfim, Salvador, Bahia: the Thursday before the second Sunday after January 6th (Epiphany/Three Kings Day), with the Festa do Bonfim on the following Sunday.

~ Procissão do Círio de Nazaré, Belém, Pará: held annually on the second Sunday in October.

Museums and memorials

~ Casa de Chico Mendes and Fundação Chico Mendes Rua Dr. Batista de Moraes, Xapuri, Acre.

~ Casa da Memória Chico Xavier, Rua Dom Pedro I, 165, Parque das Americas, Uberaba, Minas Gerais and the tomb at Cemiterio Sao Joao Batista, Avenida Dona Maria Santana Borges, 01, Quadra O, numero 623.

~ Casa Museu de Padre Cícero, Rua São José, 242 Juazeiro do Norte, Ceará (generally open Monday to Saturday) and the tomb at Capela de Nossa Senhora do Perpetuo Socorro, Juazeiro do Norte, Ceará.

~ Memorial at Igreja da Candelária, Avenida Presidente Vargas, Rio de Janeiro, Rio de Janeiro.

~ Museu Aleijadinho, R. Prof. Antonio de P. Ribas, 9, Ouro Preto, Minas Gerais: www.museualeijadinho.com.br

~ Museu Casa de Santos-Dumont, Rua do Encanto, 22, Jacintinho, Petrópolis, Rio de Janeiro.

~ Museu do Vivo do Padre Cícero, Estátua do Padre Cícero and Santo Sepulcro Trail, Colina do Horto, Juazeiro do Norte, Ceará.

~ Parque Memorial Quilombo dos Palmares, União dos Palmares, Alagoas: http://serradabarriga.palmares.gov.br (in Portuguese). Black Consciousness Day is held on 20th November each year.

~ Parque Estadual de Canudos and Museu Histórico de Canudos, Canudos, Bahia: www.uneb.br/canudos/parque-estadual-de-canudos-pec (in Portugese).

Parades and performances

~ Cavalhadas de Pirenópolis, Goiás: www.pirenopolis.tur.br/cultura/folclore/festa-do-divino/cavalhadas (in Portuguese). Each year, celebrations begin on the Sunday fifty days after Easter until the Tuesday following.

~ Rio Samba Parade, O Sambódromo, Avenida Presidente Vargas, Rio de Janeiro: held annually in February or March. Half of the schools parade on the Sunday night and the rest on the Monday night of Carnaval.

~ Teatro Nova Jerusalém, Pernambuco: www.novajerusalem.com.br (in English and Portuguese). The performances occur on Easter each year. The nearest town is Fazenda Nova, and tours are conducted out of Recife and the coast all year round.

Religious sites and spiritual communities

~ Casa de Dom Inácio de Loyola, Abadiânia, Goiás: www.johnofgod.com (in English). Medium in residence (generally) from Wednesdays to Fridays.

~ Santo Daime, Céu do Mapiá, Amazonas: www.santodaime.org (in Portugese). The nearest town is Boca do Acre.

~ Santuário Nacional de Aparecida, Aparecida do Norte, São Paulo: www.a12.com/santuario-nacional (in Portuguese). The Mass is said daily; the feast day is 12th October.

~ Vale do Amanhecer, Planaltina, Distrito Federal: www.valedoamanhecer.com (in Portuguese).

Acknowledgements

During the course of writing *In Brazil*, I've become indebted to a number of people and organisations.

In Adelaide: Nick Jose (with special gratitude), Jill Jones, Phil Butterss, Sue Hosking, the Discipline of English and Creative Writing, and the University of Adelaide. I am grateful also to Margaret Galbraith and the staff at the Barr Smith Library, and to Anne Edwards for her friendship, advice, and spare room.

In Melbourne: Trudi Canavan, Lindy Cameron, Jodi Gallagher, Alison Goodman, Jane Novak, and agent John Timlin.

From elsewhere: Carmel Bird, Delia Falconer, and Paul Kenny.

At Scribe: Henry and Margot Rosenbloom, Julia Carlomagno, Bridie Riordan, Art Rowlands, Lesley Halm, and David Golding.

My 'panel of experts', friends in or from Brazil: Inna Cymlich and Ben Janse, André, Andrea, Cecilia, Lucas, Fabio, and Fernando. I am hugely grateful to Pedro Julio Costa da Mota for proofreading my Portuguese and being always ready to answer my queries.

Also in academia: Roberto DaMatta, whose writings were my major anthropological source; Scott Barton of New York University for his advice and company; Stephen Selka, Indiana University; Andrew Dawson, Lancaster University; and Martin Thomas (author of 'Because It's Your Country'), Australian National University.

And lastly: my travelling companions Judy and Lesley, who let me include them in *In Brazil*; my community on Flinders Island; my family; and, most especially and always, Peter.